Treasury
of
Literature
for Children

Treasury
of
Literature
for Children

Exeter Books

NEW YORK

First published in the USA 1984
Third U.S. impression 1985
Published by Exeter Books
Distributed by Bookthrift
Exeter is a trademark of Simon and Schuster Inc.
Bookthrift is a registered trademark of Simon and Schuster Inc. NEW YORK, New York

© Copyright this compilation The Hamlyn Publishing Group Limited 1983

ISBN 0-671-07049-5

Printed in Italy

ACKNOWLEDGEMENTS

The Publishers would like to thank the following for their co-operation, and
their permission to use extracts from their copyright material:

Methuen & Co. Ltd., and The Canadian Publishers, McClelland and Stewart
Limited, Toronto, for 'A House for Eeyore' from *The House at Pooh Corner* by
A. A. Milne.

From *The House at Pooh Corner* by A. A. Milne, illustrated by Ernest H.
Shepard, copyright 1928 by E. P. Dutton & Co., Inc.
Renewed 1956 by A. A. Milne. Reprinted by permission of the Publisher (U.S.
Publisher).

The National Trust and Macmillan London Limited for 'Rikki-Tikki-Tavi'
from *The Jungle Book* and 'A Smuggler's Song' from *'Puck of Pook's Hill* by
Rudyard Kipling.

Lord Tweedsmuir, William Blackwood and Sons Limited and Houghton
Mifflin for the chapter 'The Adventures of the Spectacled Roadman' from *The
Thirty-Nine Steps* by John Buchan.

Illustrations

Line illustrations by E. H. Shepard accompanying 'A House for Eeyore' from
The House at Pooh Corner, copyright under the Berne Convention, reproduced
by permission of Curtis Brown Limited, London.

Jacket: Line illustrations by E. H. Shepard copyright under the Berne
Convention. Copyright in the United States 1928 by E. P. Dutton & Co., Inc.
Copyright renewal © 1956 by A. A. Milne. Colouring of illustration Copyright
© 1970 by E. H. Shepard and Methuen & Co. Ltd., reproduced by permission
of Curtis Brown Limited, London.

The Publishers have made every attempt to trace copyright holders. If we have
inadvertently omitted to acknowledge anyone we should be most grateful if this
could be brought to our attention for correction at the first opportunity.

Contents

Introduction

This anthology provides a delightful introduction to over sixty well-loved stories, poems, fairytales and fables, making a collection which will tempt the most reluctant reader and enthrall the bookworm!

Some entries are complete stories, while others are in extract form to encourage the reader to go on and tackle full-length novels. Classic tales from which excerpts have been taken include *The Settlers in Canada*, *Gulliver's Travels*, *Lorna Doone*, *The Adventures of Huckleberry Finn* and *Swiss Family Robinson*. There are also extracts from such well-known authors as John Buchan, Rudyard Kipling and A. A. Milne.

Famous narrative poems like *Lochinvar*, *John Gilpin* and *Widdecombe Fair* introduce children to our rich heritage of verse, both comic and serious.

Readers of all ages will enjoy the traditional fairytales from the Brothers Grimm, Hans Andersen and Carlo Collodi; these include *Hansel and Gretel*, *Pinocchio*, *Rapunzel*, *Snow-White* and *The Wild Swans*. *The Enchanted Horse*, *The Seven Voyages of Sindbad*, and *Aladdin and his Wonderful Lamp* serve as an introduction to the magical world of the Arabian Nights; and a selection of Aesop's Fables provides a leavening of traditional wit and wisdom.

Whether readers are meeting the stories for the first time, or are returning to old favourites, these tales of adventure, mystery, humour and magic will combine to make this a favourite treasury for children of all ages.

Rumpelstiltskin

IN a certain kingdom once lived a poor miller who had a very beautiful daughter. She was, moreover, exceedingly shrewd and clever, and the miller was so vain and proud of her that he one day told the king of the land that his daughter could spin gold out of straw. Now this king was very fond of money, and when he heard of the miller's boast his greed was excited and he ordered the girl to be brought before him. Then he led her to a chamber where there was a great quantity of straw, gave her a spinning-wheel and said, 'All this must be spun into gold before morning, if you value your life.'

She began to cry over her hard fate, when suddenly the door opened, and a funny-looking little man hobbled in and said, 'Good day to you my sweet lass, what are you weeping for?' 'Alas!' answered she, 'I must spin this straw into gold, and I don't know how.' 'What will you give me,' said the little man, 'to do it for you?' 'My necklace,' replied the maiden. He took her at her word and sat himself down to the wheel; round about it went merrily and, presently, the work was done and the gold spun.

When the king came and saw this he was greatly astonished and pleased, but his heart grew still more greedy and he shut up the poor miller's daughter again with a fresh task. Then she did not know what to do, and sat down once more to weep, but the little man presently opened the door and said, 'What will you give me to do your task?' 'The ring on my finger,' she replied. So her little

friend took the ring and began to work at the wheel, till, by the morning, all was finished.

The king was again delighted to see all this glittering treasure, but still he was not satisfied and took the miller's daughter into a yet larger room, and said, 'All this must be spun tonight, and if you succeed, you shall be my queen.' As soon as she was alone the dwarf came in and said, 'What will you give me to spin gold for you this third time?' 'I have nothing left,' said she. 'Then promise me,' said the little man, 'your first little child when you are queen.' 'That may never be,' thought the miller's daughter, but as she knew no other way to get her task done she promised him what he asked, and he once more spun the whole heap of gold. The king came in the morning and, finding all he wanted, married her, and so the miller's daughter really became queen.

At the birth of her first little child the queen rejoiced very much and forgot the little man and her promise, but one day he came into her chamber and reminded her of it, and he said, 'I will give you three days' grace, and if, during that time, you tell me my name, you shall keep your child.'

Now the queen lay awake all night, thinking of all the odd names that she had ever heard, and dispatched messengers all over the land to inquire after new ones. The next day the little man came, and she began with Timothy, Benjamin, Jeremiah and all the names she could remember; but to all of them he said: 'That's not my name.'

The second day she began with all the comical names she could hear of, Bandy-legs, Hunch-back, Crookshanks and so on, but the little gentleman still said to every one of them, 'That's not my name.'

The third day one of the messengers came back and said, 'I can hear of no other name, but yesterday, as I was climbing a high hill among the trees of the forest where the fox and the hare bid each other good night, I saw a little hut, and before the hut burnt a fire, and round the fire danced a funny little man upon one leg and sang:

> 'Merrily the feast I'll make,
> Today I'll brew, tomorrow bake;
> Merrily I'll dance and sing,
> Rumpelstiltskin is my name!'
> My lady cannot play this game;
> For next day will a stranger bring.

When the queen heard this she jumped for joy, and as soon as her little visitor came and said, 'Now, lady, what is my name?'

'Is it John?' asked she.

'No!'

'Is it Tom?'

'No!'

'Can your name be Rumpelstiltskin?'

'Some witch told you that! Some witch told you that!' cried the little man, and in a rage dashed his right foot so deep into the floor that he was forced to lay hold of it with both hands to pull it out. Then he made off as fast as possible, while everybody laughed at him for having had all his trouble for nothing and for being called such a funny name.

Widdecombe Fair

'TOM Pearse, Tom Pearse, lend me your gray
   mare,'
   All along, down along, out along, lee.
'For I want for to go to Widdecombe Fair,
   Wi' Bill Brewer, Jan Stewer, Peter Gurney, Peter
   Davy, Dan'l Whiddon, Harry Hawk,
   Old Uncle Tom Cobley and all.'
      Old Uncle Tom Cobley and all.

'And when shall I see again my gray mare?'
   All along, down along, out along, lee.
'By Friday soon, or Saturday noon,
   Wi' Bill Brewer, Jan Stewer, Peter Gurney, Peter
   Davy, Dan'l Whiddon, Harry Hawk,
   Old Uncle Tom Cobley and all.'
      Old Uncle Tom Cobley and all.

Then Friday came and Saturday noon,
   All along, down along, out along, lee.
But Tom Pearse's old mare hath not trotted home,
   Wi' Bill Brewer, Jan Stewer, Peter Gurney,
   Peter Davy, Dan'l Whiddon, Harry Hawk,
   Old Uncle Tom Cobley and all.
      Old Uncle Tom Cobley and all.

So Tom Pearse he got up to the top o' the hill,
   All along, down along, out along, lee.
And he seed his old mare down a-making her will,
   Wi' Bill Brewer, Jan Stewer, Peter Gurney, Peter
   Davy, Dan'l Whiddon, Harry Hawk,
   Old Uncle Tom Cobley and all.
      Old Uncle Tom Cobley and all.

So Tom Pearse's old mare her took sick and her died,
    All along, down along, out along, lee.
And Tom he sat down on a stone, and he cried
    Wi' Bill Brewer, Jan Stewer, Peter Gurney, Peter
        Davy, Dan'l Whiddon, Harry Hawk,
    Old Uncle Tom Cobley and all.
        Old Uncle Tom Cobley and all.

But this isn't the end o' this shocking affair,
    All along, down along, out along, lee.
Nor, though they be dead, of the horrid career
    Of Bill Brewer, Jan Stewer, Peter Gurney, Peter
        Davy, Dan'l Whiddon, Harry Hawk,
    Old Uncle Tom Cobley and all.
        Old Uncle Tom Cobley and all.

When the wind whistles cold on the moor of a night,
    All along, down along, out along, lee.
Tom Pearse's old mare doth appear, gashly white,
    Wi' Bill Brewer, Jan Stewer, Peter Gurney, Peter
        Davy, Dan'l Whiddon, Harry Hawk,
    Old Uncle Tom Cobley and all.
        Old Uncle Tom Cobley and all.

And all the long night be heard skirling and groans,
    All along, down along, out along, lee.
From Tom Pearse's old mare in her rattling bones,
    And from Bill Brewer, Jan Stewer, Peter Gurney,
        Peter Davy, Dan'l Whiddon, Harry Hawk,
    Old Uncle Tom Cobley and all.
        Old Uncle Tom Cobley and all.

A House for Eeyore

A. A. Milne

Illustrated by Ernest Shepard

Few authors are better known to children than Alan Alexander Milne (1882–1956). After leaving Cambridge, he first became known as a journalist and writer of humorous pieces for "Punch". During the First World War, he began to write plays and soon after the end of the war he achieved considerable success with his light and amusing comedies. In 1923, Rose Fyleman, a fellow contributor on "Punch", invited him to write some verses for a new magazine she was starting for children. These verses grew into "When We Were Very Young" and was followed by "Now We Are Six", two of the most popular books of verse ever written for young children. Soon afterwards "Winnie-the-Pooh" and "The House at Pooh Corner" appeared. These stories were based on bedtime stories told to his son, Christopher Robin, about his own toy animals. Today, the original Pooh, Piglet, Eeyore, Tigger and Kanga live in a glass case in an American publishing company in New York. Our story comes, not from "Winnie-the-Pooh", but from its equally delightful successor, "The House at Pooh Corner".

ONE DAY when Pooh Bear had nothing else to do, he thought he would do something, so he went round to Piglet's house to see what Piglet was doing. It was still snowing as he stumped over the white forest track, and he expected to find Piglet warming his toes in front of his fire, but to his surprise he saw that the door was open, and the more he looked inside the more Piglet wasn't there.

"He's out," said Pooh sadly. "That's what it is. He's not in. I shall have to go a fast Thinking Walk by myself. Bother!"

But first he thought that he would knock very loudly just to make *quite* sure . . . and while he waited for Piglet not to answer, he jumped up and down to keep warm, and a hum came suddenly into his head, which seemed to him a Good Hum, such as is Hummed Hopefully to Others.

> *The more it snows*
> > *(Tiddely pom),*
> *The more it goes*
> > *(Tiddely pom),*
> *The more it goes*
> > *(Tiddely pom)*
> > *On snowing.*
> *And nobody knows*
> > *(Tiddely pom),*
> *How cold my toes*
> > *(Tiddely pom),*
> *How cold my toes*
> > *(Tiddely pom),*
> > *Are growing.*

"So what I'll do," said Pooh, "is I'll do this. I'll just go home first and see what the time is, and perhaps I'll put a muffler round my neck, and then I'll go and see Eeyore and sing it to him."

He hurried back to his own house; and his mind was so busy on the way with the hum that he was getting ready for Eeyore that, when he suddenly saw Piglet sitting in his best armchair, he could only stand there rubbing his head and wondering whose house he was in.

"Hallo, Piglet," he said. "I thought you were out."

"No," said Piglet, "it's you who were out, Pooh."

"So it was," said Pooh. "I knew one of us was."

He looked up at his clock, which had stopped at five minutes to eleven some weeks ago.

"Nearly eleven o'clock," said Pooh happily. "You're just in time for a little snackerel of something," and he put his head into the cupboard. "And then we'll go out, Piglet, and sing my song to Eeyore."

"Which song, Pooh?"

"The one we're going to sing to Eeyore," explained Pooh.

The clock was still saying five minutes to eleven when Pooh and Piglet set out on their way half an hour later. The wind had stopped, and the snow, tired of rushing round in circles trying to catch itself up,

now fluttered gently down until it found a place on which to rest, and sometimes the place was Pooh's nose and sometimes it wasn't, and in a little while Piglet was wearing a white muffler round his neck and feeling more snowy behind the ears than he had ever felt before.

"Pooh," he said at last, and a little timidly, because he didn't want Pooh to think he was Giving In, "I was just wondering. How would it be if we went home now and *practised* your song, and then sang it to Eeyore tomorrow—or—or the next day, when we happen to see him?"

"That's a very good idea, Piglet," said Pooh. "We'll practise it now as we go along. But it's no good going home to practise it, because it's a special Outdoor Song which Has To Be Sung In The Snow."

"Are you sure?" asked Piglet anxiously.

"Well, you'll see, Piglet, when you listen. Because this is how it begins. *The more it snows, tiddely pom—*"

"Tiddely what?" said Piglet.

"Pom," said Pooh. "I put that in to make it more hummy. *The more it goes, tiddely pom, the more—*"

"Didn't you say snows?"

"Yes, but that was *before*."

"Before the tiddely pom?"

"It was a *different* tiddely pom," said Pooh, feeling rather muddled now. "I'll sing it to you properly and then you'll see."

So he sang it again.

The more it
SNOWS—*tiddely-pom,*
The more it
GOES—*tiddely-pom*
The more it
GOES—*tiddely-pom*
On
Snowing.

And nobody
KNOWS—*tiddely-pom,*
How cold my
TOES—*tiddely-pom*
How cold my
TOES—*tiddely-pom*
Are
Growing.

He sang it like that, which is much the best way of singing it, and when he had finished, he waited for Piglet to say that, of all the Outdoor Hums for Snowy Weather he had ever heard, this was the best. And, after thinking the matter out carefully, Piglet said:

"Pooh," he said solemnly, "it isn't the *toes* so much as the *ears.*"

By the time they were getting near Eeyore's Gloomy Place, which was where he lived, and as it was still very snowy behind Piglet's ears, and he was getting tired of it, they turned into a little pinewood, and sat down on the gate which led into it. They were out of the snow now, but it was very cold, and to keep themselves warm they sang Pooh's song right through six times, Piglet doing the tiddely-poms and Pooh doing the rest of it, and

both of them thumping on the top of the gate with pieces of stick at the proper places.

And in a little while they felt much warmer, and were able to talk again.

"I've been thinking," said Pooh, "and what I've been thinking is this. I've been thinking about Eeyore."

"What about Eeyore?"

"Well, poor Eeyore has nowhere to live."

"Nor he has," said Piglet.

"*You* have a house, Piglet, and I have a house, and they are very good houses. And Christopher Robin has a house, and Owl and Kanga and Rabbit have houses, and even Rabbit's friends and relations have houses or somethings, but poor Eeyore has nothing. So what I've been thinking is: Let's build him a house."

"That," said Piglet, "is a Grand Idea. Where shall we build it?"

"We will build it here," said Pooh, "just by this wood, out of the wind, because this is where I thought of it. And we will call this Pooh Corner. And we will build an Eeyore House with sticks at Pooh Corner for Eeyore."

"There was a heap of sticks on the other side of the wood," said Piglet. "I saw them. Lots and lots. All piled up."

"Thank you, Piglet," said Pooh. "What you have just said will be a Great Help to us, and because of it I could call this place Poohanpiglet Corner if Pooh Corner didn't sound better, which it does, being smaller and more like a corner. Come along."

So they got down off the gate and went round to the other side of the wood to fetch sticks.

Christopher Robin had spent the morning indoors going to Africa and back, and he had just got off the boat and was wondering what it was like outside, when who should come knocking at the door but Eeyore.

"Hallo, Eeyore," said Christopher Robin, as he opened the door and came out. "How are *you*?"

"It's snowing still," said Eeyore gloomily.

"So it is."

"*And* freezing."

"Is it?"

"Yes," said Eeyore. "However," he said, brightening up a little, "we haven't had an earthquake lately."

"What's the matter, Eeyore?"

"Nothing, Christopher Robin. Nothing important. I suppose you haven't seen a house or what-not anywhere about?"

"What sort of a house?"

"Just a house."

"Who lives there?"

"I do. At least I thought I did. But I suppose I don't. After all, we can't all have houses."

"But, Eeyore, I didn't know—I always thought—"

"I don't know how it is, Christopher Robin, but what with all this snow and one thing and another, not to mention icicles and such-like, it isn't so Hot in my field about three o'clock in the morning as some people think it is.

"It isn't Close, if you know what I mean —not so as to be uncomfortable. It isn't Stuffy. In fact, Christopher Robin," he went on in a loud whisper, "quite-between-ourselves-and-don't-tell-anybody, it's Cold."

"Oh, Eeyore!"

"And I said to myself: The others will be sorry if I'm getting myself all cold. They haven't got Brains, any of them, only grey fluff that's blown into their heads by mistake, and they don't Think, but if it goes on snowing for another six weeks or so, one of them will begin to say to himself: 'Eeyore can't be so very much too Hot about three o'clock in the morning.' And then it will Get About. And they'll be Sorry."

"Oh, Eeyore!" said Christopher Robin, feeling very sorry already.

"I don't mean you, Christopher Robin. You're different. So what it all comes to is that I built myself a house down by my little wood."

"Did you really? How exciting!"

"The really exciting part," said Eeyore in his most melancholy voice, "is that when I left it this morning it was there, and when I came back it wasn't. Not at all, very natural, and it was only Eeyore's house. But still I just wondered."

Christopher Robin didn't stop to

wonder. He was already back in *his* house, putting on his waterproof hat, his waterproof boots and his waterproof macintosh as fast as he could. "We'll go and look for it at once," he called out to Eeyore.

They came round the corner and there was Eeyore's house.

"Sometimes," said Eeyore, "when people have quite finished taking a person's house, there are one or two bits which they don't want and are rather glad for the person to take back, if you know what I mean. So I thought if we just went—"

"Come on," said Christopher Robin, and off they hurried, and in a very little time they got to the corner of the field by the side of the pine-wood, where Eeyore's house wasn't any longer.

"There!" said Eeyore. "Not a stick of it left! Of course, I've still got all this snow to do what I like with. One mustn't complain."

But Christopher Robin wasn't listening to Eeyore, he was listening to something else.

"Can you hear it?" he asked.

"What is it? Somebody laughing?"

"Listen."

They both listened . . . and they heard a deep gruff voice saying in a singing voice that the more it snowed the more it went on snowing, and a small high voice tiddely-pomming in between.

"It's Pooh," said Christopher Robin excitedly. . . .

"Possibly," said Eeyore.

"*And* Piglet!" said Christopher Robin excitedly.

"Probably," said Eeyore. "What we *want* is a Trained Bloodhound."

The words of the song changed suddenly: "*We've finished our* HOUSE!" sang the gruff voice.

"*Tiddely pom!*" sang the squeaky one.

"*It's a beautiful* HOUSE . . ."

"*Tiddely pom . . .*"

"*I wish it were* MINE . . ."

"*Tiddely pom . . .*"

"Pooh!" shouted Christopher Robin. . . .

The singers on the gate stopped suddenly.

"It's Christopher Robin!" said Pooh eagerly.

"He's round by the place where we got all those sticks from," said Piglet.

"Come on," said Pooh.

They climbed down their gate and hurried round the corner of the wood, Pooh making welcoming noises all the way.

"Why, here *is* Eeyore," said Pooh, when he had finished hugging Christopher Robin, and he nudged Piglet, and Piglet nudged him, and they thought to themselves what a lovely surprise they had got ready. "Hallo, Eeyore."

"Same to you, Pooh Bear, and twice on Thursdays," said Eeyore gloomily.

Before Pooh could say: "Why Thursdays?" Christopher Robin began to explain the sad story of Eeyore's Lost House. And Pooh and Piglet listened, and their eyes seemed to get bigger and bigger.

"*Where* do you say it was?" asked Pooh.

"Just here," said Eeyore.

"Made of sticks?"

"Yes."

"Oh!" said Piglet.

"What?" said Eeyore.

"I just said 'Oh!'" said Piglet nervously. And so as to seem quite at ease he hummed Tiddley-pom once or twice in a what-shall-we-do-now kind of way.

"You're sure it *was* a house?" said Pooh. "I mean, you're sure the house was just here?"

"Of course I am," said Eeyore. And he murmured to himself, "No brain at all, some of them."

"Why, what's the matter, Pooh?" asked Christopher Robin.

"Well," said Pooh. . . . "The fact *is*," said Pooh. . . . "Well, the fact *is*," said Pooh. . . . "You see," said Pooh. . . . "It's like this," said Pooh, and something seemed to tell him that he wasn't explaining very well, and he nudged Piglet again.

"It's like this," said Piglet quickly. . . . "Only warmer," he added after deep thought.

"What's warmer?"

"The other side of the wood, where Eeyore's house is."

"*My* house?" said Eeyore. "My house was here."

"No," said Piglet firmly. "The other side of the wood."

"Because of being warmer," said Pooh.

"But I ought to *know*—"

"Come and look," said Piglet simply, and he led the way.

"There wouldn't be *two* houses," said Pooh. "Not so close together."

They came round the corner, and there was Eeyore's house, looking as comfy as anything.

"There you are," said Piglet.

"Inside as well as outside," said Pooh proudly.

Eeyore went inside . . . and came out again.

"It's a remarkable thing," he said. "It *is* my house, and I built it where I said I did, so the wind must have blown it here. And the wind blew it right over the wood, and blew it down here, and here it is as good as ever. In fact, better in places."

"Much better," said Pooh and Piglet together.

"It just shows what can be done by taking a little trouble," said Eeyore. "Do you see, Pooh? Do you see, Piglet? Brains first and then Hard Work. Look at it! *That's* the way to build a house," said Eeyore proudly.

So they left him in it; and Christopher Robin went back to lunch with his friends Pooh and Piglet, and on the way they told him of the Awful Mistake they had made. And when he had finished laughing, they all sang the Outdoor Song for Snowy Weather the rest of the way home, Piglet, who was still not quite sure of his voice, putting in the tiddely-poms again.

"And I know it *seems* easy," said Piglet to himself, "but it isn't *every one* who could do it."

The Fox & the Rook

THE cawing of rooks filled the air as they swept across the pink sky in a black cloud towards their untidy homes in the treetops.

They were led by an old and greying bird whose word was law, and behind him came the older members of the family followed by the younger rooks who had been hatched in the spring. These were impatient young birds, proud of their strong young wings and throaty voices. Lagging far behind them was the most conceited young rook of all.

She had no need to hurry because she was confident that she could easily catch up whenever she wanted. As her wings flapped lazily her bright eyes spotted the open window of a house and she decided to investigate.

Swooping past the window she was delighted to see a table in the room beyond laden with delicious food. Turning awkwardly she looped backwards, flew through the open window and snatched up a large piece of beef. Her heart beating, with excitement she flew with her prize to a small clump of fir trees. The meat was heavy, and breathlessly she settled on a comfortable branch, her bright eyes sparkling with satisfaction and greed.

A dying sunbeam glanced through the branches and settled on something brown and furry among the pine needles and bracken at the foot of the tree. The brown patch moved silently forward and there, in the rose of the setting sun, was a fox.

It was rather early for him to be setting out for his night's hunting, but he was very hungry and when he looked up and saw the rook with the juicy piece of meat in her mouth his mouth watered with envy.

The rook glanced down at him with scorn. She thought the fox a rather common form of life. Why, he could not even fly!

DAVID FRANKLAND.

22

The fox concentrated his gaze upon the meat, his brain working quickly, his amber eyes alive and bright. At all costs, he decided, he must have the meat. His beautiful brush swayed gently and he licked his chops. Then he smiled up at the rook and said in a soft voice. 'What vision of beauty is this that I see?'

The rook cocked her head on one side and stared downwards, still holding the piece of meat firmly in her beak.

Then she heard the fox say, 'Surely, those beautiful wings must have come from a fairy nest! And those eyes, so soft and liquid to behold, so star-like and so gentle.'

The rook fidgeted a little and thought, 'Perhaps I was mistaken. The fox appears to be a most elegant and sensible fellow.'

The fox took a breath and went on, 'Never in all my travels have I seen such exquisite poise, such dignity. And her breast! surely the swans on the lake would be green with envy if they should see such soft and fairy-like lightness!'

The rook preened herself but still held tightly to her prize. She was longing to hear more and waited expectantly. The fox continued, 'That smooth beak, those dainty feet. This must be the wonderful rook that I have heard about.'

The rook took a step to right and left upon her perch but still held on to the meat. Then the fox muttered, 'Now, if only she could sing like the nightingales! But of course, with such outward beauty she probably cannot sing at all. What a pity! If only she could sing she would be the queen of them all.'

The conceited young rook could contain herself no longer. The fox, she decided, was a gentleman of taste and quality. She must show him that her voice was every bit as beautiful as her figure and colouring. She simply could not remain silent and she opened her beak as wide as possible. 'CAW! CAW! CAW!' she croaked, making the most ugly sound that ever was heard.

There was a sudden bark of excitement from the foot of the tree as the slice of juicy meat fell on to the ground. The fox pounced upon it instantly and gripped it between his strong jaws. As he ran off the rook screamed in fury, 'CAW! CAW! CAW! You wicked thief! Give me back my meat, CAW! CAW! You wicked thief!'

Men who flatter often have an ulterior motive.

The Enchanted Horse

N the fair land of Persia, long, long ago, the first day of each year was kept as a time of great rejoicing, when people of all countries brought before the sultan any new or wonderful things they had. On one of these feast days a poor Indian came, and he claimed to have the most wonderful horse that had ever been made by man.

'I praise my horse,' said he, 'not for his looks, but for what he is able to do. He will carry me to any place I wish to visit, and if your majesty chooses, I will show you his power.'

'Go then,' replied the sultan, 'to yonder mountain and bring back to me a branch of the palm that grows at its foot.'

Mounting the horse, the Indian turned a peg in the creature's neck, and the next moment was carried into the air and out of sight. In less than a quarter of an hour he came back, bearing the palm branch in his hand.

Upon this, the sultan offered to buy the horse, but the Indian would not take money for it.

'I will take only your daughter in exchange for the horse,' he said, at which the officers standing round laughed aloud; but the prince, the son of the sultan, fearing his father might make the bargain, drew near and said, 'Sir, you surely will not insult the princess, my sister, by giving her in marriage to this vain fellow!'

'Son!' replied the sultan, 'it may be the man will take some other reward for the animal, which is so truly wonderful, that I do not

wish any other prince to become the owner of it. But, before I bargain with him, I should like to see you try the animal.'

To this the Indian agreed, and the prince mounted; but, before the Indian had told him what to do, he turned the peg, and was carried high into the air.

'Sir,' cried the Indian, turning to the sultan in alarm, 'I pray you will not blame me should any harm come to the prince, your son. I would have told him all he should know of the working of the horse had he given me the chance. Unless he finds the second peg, he cannot return to the earth again.'

On hearing this, the sultan became greatly troubled, and the Indian, in order to calm him, continued, 'Have no fear, your majesty. The horse will carry him safely over sea and land, and should he fail to see the second peg, he has but to wish to be in a certain place, and the horse will even carry him there.'

'I hope that what you say is true,' the sultan answered, 'but, in case it is not, I shall keep you in prison until my son returns.'

Now, the prince, on finding the horse travel on and on, rising higher and higher all the time, tried his best to stop it. At last, after some searching, he found the second peg, which he turned. No sooner had he done this than the horse began to descend, and the prince at length found himself on the roof of a great palace. It was now quite dark, for the night had come, but after a time he found a small staircase, which led him to a small room, where lay several enormous servants fast asleep.

Passing these with great care, he entered another room, where, on a raised bed, lay a beautiful princess, and around her several women all sound asleep. Feeling that his only safety lay in begging the princess to protect him, he wakened her.

'Princess,' he said when her eyes were open, 'you see before you the son of the King of Persia, who finds himself in your palace, and at the mercy of your servants, unless you will have the goodness to help him.'

'Prince,' replied the lady, who was the daughter of the King of Bengal, 'have no fear. In this country you will find nothing but welcome. As you must be in need of food and rest, I will send some of my women to see to your comfort, and in the morning I will hear your strange story.'

Upon this the women led the prince to a large room filled with much beautiful furniture, and, while some got food for him, others made ready a bed, on which, after he had eaten, he lay down.

In the morning the princess dressed herself with more than usual care, for she already loved the handsome prince who had come to her in so strange a manner. As soon as she was ready, she said to a servant, 'go to the Prince of Persia, and ask if he is ready to receive a visit from me.' The prince, having heard the message, awaited her coming with great joy.

'Prince,' she said, as soon as the greetings were over, 'I came here because no one will come into this room. I pray you tell me to what I owe the pleasure of seeing you in my palace.'

The prince told her of the coming of the poor Indian to the feast of the New Year, of his wonderful horse, and of his wish to exchange it for the hand of the Princess of Persia. He told her, too, of his own fear lest his father should consent, and also of his rashness in leaving the ground without first having learned the working of the animal.

'At last,' he said, 'I found a second peg, and turning it, was soon brought down to the terrace on the roof of your palace. Creeping softly down the stairs and past your servants, I reached your room and wakened you. The rest of the story is known to you, and all that is now left for me to do is to thank you for your goodness, and to declare that you have already won my heart by your beauty and your kindness.'

On this, the princess, blushing with pleasure, answered, 'Prince, I have listened to your story with great interest, but I can hardly help shaking with fear when I think of your danger. It is well that the enchanted horse brought you to my palace. I do not, however, find myself able to believe that I have won your heart, for it is far more likely that you have given it to some fair lady of Persia.'

It was now time for dinner, and the princess, leading the way to a beautiful hall, sat down with the prince to a delicious meal.

'Prince,' said the princess, when dinner was over, 'you may now be thinking of returning to your own country; but you should not leave the kingdom of Bengal without first seeing the palace of the king my father.'

Now, though the Prince of Persia would gladly have done this, he felt he could not visit the father of the princess in the clothing he then wore. When he told the princess this, she replied that she would supply him with all he needed, feeling sure that if her father saw the Prince of Persia, he would allow her to marry him.

The prince, however, would not agree. 'If you will permit me,' he said, 'I will first return to Persia and let my father know of my safety; then I will come back, not as a stranger, but as a prince, and ask for your hand in marriage.'

Yet, as the princess seemed so little pleased to let him go, he stayed on and on until he had been two whole months in the kingdom of Bengal. Banquets and balls were given in his honour; but at last he resolved to set out for Persia and to take the princess with him.

Placing her on the enchanted horse, therefore, he mounted behind, turned the peg, and was quickly carried to the chief city of his father's kingdom. Here he left the princess in the care of the housekeeper, at one of his father's smaller residences on the outskirts of the town, and hurried off to the sultan, who had long thought him dead.

When the sultan had heard the prince's story, he ordered that all signs of mourning in the court should be put away, and declared that he would not only consent to the marriage, but that he would himself go and meet the princess whom his son so dearly loved.

Before setting out, however, he sent for the Indian, to whom he said, 'I kept you in prison in order to put you to death unless my

son returned in safety. I thank God he has so returned. Go, therefore, take your horse, and never enter my kingdom again.'

Now the Indian, having learned on his way from the prison about the princess whom the king's son had brought home, resolved, on leaving the palace, to carry her off. And this he did with little trouble, for the princess, thinking he had been sent to fetch her, mounted the horse with him, and was carried away over the heads of the sultan and the prince, who, though they saw her, could not help her.

The king returned in sorrow to the palace, but the prince, dressing himself as a priest, set out to find where she had been carried. and to save her from the wicked Indian, who meant to make her his wife.

But the princess, on learning what the Indian wished, would not listen to him; so he treated her with great violence, and one day, when he was more cruel than usual, she screamed so loudly that some horsemen passing by came to her aid.

One of these horsemen proved to be the Sultan of Cashmere, and he, hearing the princess's story, slew the Indian, and took her to his own palace, meaning to marry her himself, for he was much struck by her wonderful beauty.

Though he had not yet asked her consent, he ordered the rejoicings to begin at once; but the princess, having given her word to the Prince of Persia, would not marry the Sultan of Cashmere, and, in order to stop him from forcing her to do so, she pretended to go mad.

So wildly did she behave that the sultan sent for many doctors, none of whom, however, could cure her.

At last the sultan offered a reward to any doctor of any country who should restore the Princess of Bengal to health again.

Now it chanced that the Prince of Persia heard of this, and feeling sure the sick person must be his own lost princess, went to Cashmere. By the sultan's leave he entered the room in which she was sitting, and singing softly to herself of the prince to whom she had given her heart.

On seeing him she took him for another doctor, for his beard had grown very long, so she flew into a great rage. But the prince, speaking so that none but she could hear, told her who he was, and that he had come to save her. On this she grew quiet, and the prince, returning to the sultan, said he thought he could cure her if he were allowed to do it in his own way. 'But, sir,' he said,

'it would be of great help to me if I knew how the princess came to be in Cashmere, which is very far from her own country.'

To this the sultan replied that she had been carried there by an Indian on an enchanted horse, which he had put in his treasury because it was such a wonderful animal.

'That horse,' said the prince, 'is the cause of all the trouble. The princess has been enchanted by riding on it, and I am now sure I can cure her by the aid of the animal, if your majesty will order it to be brought out into the great square before the palace.'

The very next day the enchanted horse was placed in the square, and all the people and the nobles of the court stood around, to watch the new doctor cure the Princess of Bengal of her madness.

Dressed in rich garments, with jewels sparkling on her neck and wrists, the princess came from the castle, with a great many ladies, who helped her to mount the enchanted horse. In full view of the sultan and all his people she sat, while the pretended doctor walked three times round the horse, his hands crossed on his breast, and strange words coming from his lips.

Then, placing round the horse a great many vessels of fire he had ordered to be brought, he mounted behind the princess, who was quite hidden by the thick smoke, turned the peg, and, before any one knew what was happening, both of them were carried high into the air.

'Sultan of Cashmere,' cried the Prince of Persia, as they passed over his head, 'the next time you wish to marry a lady, you had better first ask her consent.'

The enchanted horse soon carried them back to Persia, where, as soon as possible, the prince and princess were married. The Sultan of Persia was quite willing, and the King of Bengal thought his daughter greatly honoured in being chosen by so brave a man as the prince had proved himself to be.

The Kite, the Frog & the Mouse

THERE was once much argument between a frog and a mouse as to which should be master of the fen, and many pitched battles resulted.

The crafty mouse, hiding under the grass, would make sudden attacks upon his enemy, often surprising him at a disadvantage.

The frog was stronger than his rival, however, and, hoping to end the dispute, challenged the mouse to single combat.

The mouse accepted the challenge, and on the appointed day the champions entered the field, each armed with the point of a bulrush, and both confident of success.

A kite chanced to be hovering overhead at the time, and seeing the silly creatures so intent upon their quarrel, she swooped suddenly down, seized them in her talons, and carried them off to her young.

United we stand divided we fall.

33

Hansel & Gretel

ONCE upon a time there lived near a large wood a poor woodcutter, with his wife and two children by his former marriage – a little boy called Hansel, and a girl named Gretel. He had little enough to eat or drink and once, when there was a great famine in the land, he could not procure even his daily bread; and as he was sitting by the fire one evening, restless and very troubled, he sighed, and said to his wife, 'What will become of us? How can we feed our children when we have not sufficient to eat ourselves?'

'Know then, my husband,' she answered, 'we will lead them away quite early in the morning into the thickest part of the wood, and there make them a fire, and give them each a little piece of bread. Then we will go to our work and leave them alone so they will not find their way home again, and we shall be freed from them.'

'No wife,' replied he, 'that I can never do. How can you bring yourself to leave my children all alone in the wood – for the wild beasts will soon come and tear them to pieces.'

'Oh, you simpleton!' said she, 'then we must all four die of hunger; you had better plane the coffins for us.' But she left him no peace till he consented, saying, 'Ah, but I shall miss the poor children.'

The two children, however, had not gone to sleep for hunger, and so they overheard what the step-mother said to their father.

34

Gretel wept bitterly, and said to Hansel, 'what will become of us?' 'Be quiet, Gretel,' said he; 'do not cry – I will soon help you.' And as soon as their parents had fallen asleep, he got up, put on his coat, and, unbarring the back door, slipped out.

The moon shone brightly, and the white pebbles which lay before the door seemed like silver pieces, they glittered so brightly. Hansel stooped down and put as many into his pocket as it would hold; and then going back, he said to Gretel, 'Be comforted, dear sister, and sleep in peace; God will not forsake us'; and so saying, he went to bed again.

The next morning, before the sun arose, the wife went and awoke the two children. 'Get up, you lazy things; we are going into the forest to chop wood.' Then she gave them each a piece of bread, saying, 'there is something for your dinner; do not eat it before the time, for you will get nothing else.'

Gretel took the bread in her apron, for Hansel's pocket was full of pebbles, and so they all set out upon their way. When they had gone a little distance, Hansel stood still, and peeped back at the house; and this he repeated several times, till his father said, 'Hansel, what are you peeping at, and why do you lag behind? Take care, and watch your feet.'

'Ah, father,' said Hansel, 'I am looking at my white cat sitting upon the roof of the house, and trying to say goodbye.' 'You simpleton!' said the wife, 'that is not a cat; it is only the sun shining on the white chimney.' But in reality Hansel was not looking at a cat; but every time he stopped he dropped a pebble out of his pocket upon the path.

When they came to the middle of the wood, the father told the children to collect some sticks and he would make them a fire, so that they should not be cold; so Hansel and Gretel gathered together quite a little mountain of twigs. Then they set fire to them, and as the flame burned up high, the wife said, 'Now you children, lie down near the fire and rest yourselves, whilst we go into the forest and chop wood; when we are ready, I will come and call you.'

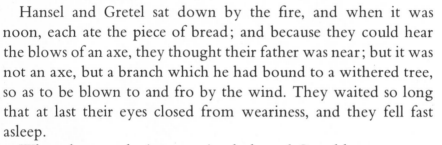

Hansel and Gretel sat down by the fire, and when it was noon, each ate the piece of bread; and because they could hear the blows of an axe, they thought their father was near; but it was not an axe, but a branch which he had bound to a withered tree, so as to be blown to and fro by the wind. They waited so long that at last their eyes closed from weariness, and they fell fast asleep.

When they awoke it was quite dark, and Gretel began to cry. 'How shall we get out of the wood?' But Hansel tried to comfort her by saying, 'wait a little while till the moon rises, and then we will quickly find the way.'

The moon shone forth, and Hansel, taking his sister's hand, followed the pebbles, which glittered like new-minted silver pieces, and showed them the path. All night long they walked on, and as day broke they came to their father's house. They knocked at the door, and when the wife opened it, and saw Hansel and Gretel, she exclaimed, 'You wicked children! why did you sleep so long in the wood? We thought you were never coming home again.' But their father was very glad, for it had made him bitterly sad to leave them all alone.

Not long afterwards there was again great scarcity in every corner of the land; and one night the children overheard their mother saying to their father, 'Everything is again eaten; we have only half a loaf left, and then everything is over; the children must be sent away. We will take them deeper into the wood, so that they may not find the way out again; it is the only means of escape for us.'

But her husband felt heavy at heart, and thought, 'it would be better to share the last crust with the children.' His wife, however, would listen to nothing that he said, and scolded and reproached him without stopping.

He who says A must say B too; and he who consents the first time must also the second.

The children, however, had again heard the conversation as they lay awake, and as soon as the old people went to sleep Hansel got up, intending to pick up some pebbles as before; but the wife had locked the door, so that he could not get out. Nevertheless he comforted Gretel, saying, 'Do not cry; sleep in peace; God will not forsake us.'

Early in the morning the step-mother came and pulled them out of bed, and gave them each a slice of bread, which was still smaller than the former piece. On the way, Hansel broke his in his pocket, and, stooping every now and then, dropped a crumb upon the path.

'Hansel, why do you stop and look about?' said the father; 'keep to the path.' 'I am looking at my little dove,' answered Hansel, 'nodding a good-bye to me.' 'Simpleton!' said the wife, 'that is no dove, but only the sun shining on the chimney.' But Hansel still kept dropping crumbs as he went along.

The mother led the children deep into the wood, where they had never been before, and there making an immense fire, she said to them, 'Sit down here and rest, and when you feel tired you can sleep for a little while. We are going into the forest to chop wood, and in the evening, when we are ready, we will come and fetch you.'

When noon came, Gretel shared her bread with Hansel, who had scattered his on the path. Then they went to sleep; but the evening arrived, and no one came to visit the poor children. In the dark night they awoke, and Hansel comforted his sister by saying, 'Only wait, Gretel, till the moon comes out, then we shall see the crumbs of bread which I have dropped, and they will show us the way home.'

The moon shone, and they got up, but they could not see any crumbs, for the thousands of birds which had been flying about in the woods and fields had picked them all up. Hansel kept saying to Gretel, 'we will soon find the way.' But they did not, and they walked the whole night long and the next day, but still they did not come out of the wood; and they got so hungry, for they had nothing to eat but some of the berries which they found upon the bushes. Soon they got so tired that they could not drag themselves along, so they lay down under a tree and went to sleep on a soft bed of ferns.

It was now the third morning since they had left their father's house, and they still walked on; but they only got deeper and deeper into the wood, and Hansel saw that if help did not come very soon they would die of hunger. As soon as it was noon they saw a beautiful snow-white bird sitting upon a bough, which sang so sweetly that they stood still and listened to it. It soon stopped and, spreading its wings, flew away; and they followed it until it arrived at a cottage, upon the roof of which it perched;

and when they went close up to it they saw that the cottage was made of bread and cakes, and the window-panes were made of clear sugar.

'We will go in there,' said Hansel, 'and have a glorious feast. I will eat a piece of the roof, and you can eat the window. Won't they be sweet?'

So Hansel reached up and broke a piece off the roof, in order to see how it tasted; while Gretel stepped up to the window and began to bite it.

Then a sweet voice called out in the room. 'Tip-tap, tip-tap, who raps at my door?' And the children answered: 'The wind, the wind, the child of heaven.' And they went on eating without interruption.

Hansel thought the roof tasted very nice, and so he tore off a great piece, while Gretel broke a large round pane out of the window, and sat down quite contentedly. Just then the door opened, and a very old woman, walking upon crutches, came out. Hansel and Gretel were so frightened that they let fall what they had in their hands, but the old woman, nodding her head,

said, 'Ah, you dear children, what has brought you here? Come
in and stay with me, and no harm shall befall you.' And so saying,
she took them both by the hand and led them into her cottage.

A good meal of milk and pancakes, with sugar, apples and nuts,
was spread on the table, and in the back room were two nice little
beds, covered with white, where Hansel and Gretel laid themselves down, and thought themselves in heaven. The old woman
behaved very kindly to them, but in reality she was a wicked
witch who waylaid children, and built the breadhouse in order

to entice them in, and as soon as they were in her power she killed, cooked and ate them, and made a great festival of the day.

Witches have red eyes, and cannot see very far, but they have a fine sense of smell, like wild beasts, so that they know when children approach them. When Hansel and Gretel came near the witch's house she laughed wickedly, saying, 'here come two who shall not escape me.' And early in the morning, before they awoke, she went up to them, and saw how sweetly they lay sleeping, with their chubby red cheeks, and she mumbled to herself, 'that will be a good bite.'

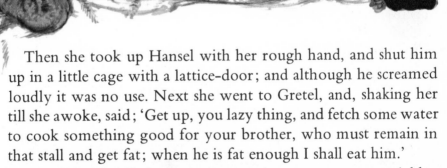

Then she took up Hansel with her rough hand, and shut him up in a little cage with a lattice-door; and although he screamed loudly it was no use. Next she went to Gretel, and, shaking her till she awoke, said; 'Get up, you lazy thing, and fetch some water to cook something good for your brother, who must remain in that stall and get fat; when he is fat enough I shall eat him.'

'Gretel,' she called out in a rage, 'get some water quickly: made her do as she wished. So a nice meal was cooked for Hansel, but Gretel got nothing else but a crab's claw.

Every morning the old witch came to the cage, and said, 'Hansel, stretch out your finger that I may feel whether you are getting fat.' But Hansel used to stretch out a bone, and the old woman, having very bad sight, thought it was his finger, and wondered very much that he did not get fatter. When four weeks had passed, and Hansel still remained thin, she lost all her patience and would not wait any longer.

'Gretel,' she called out in a rage, 'get some water quickly: whether Hansel is fat or thin, today I will kill and cook him.'

Oh! how the poor little sister grieved; but she was forced to fetch the water, and the tears ran fast down her cheeks! 'Dear good God, help us now!' she exclaimed. 'Had we only been eaten by the wild beasts in the wood, then we should have died together.' But the old witch called out, 'leave off that noise; it will not help you a bit.'

So early in the morning Gretel was forced to go out and fill the kettle and make a fire. 'First we will bake, however,' said the old woman; 'I have already heated the oven and kneaded the dough;' and so saying, she pushed poor Gretel up to the oven, out of which flames were burning fiercely.

'Creep in,' said the witch, 'and see if it is hot enough, and then we will put in the bread.' But she intended, when Gretel got in, to shut up the oven and let her bake, so that she might eat her as well as Hansel. Gretel could tell what her thoughts were, and said, 'I do not know how to do it; how shall I get in?'

'You stupid goose,' said she, 'the opening is big enough. See, I could even get in myself!' and she got up and put her head into the oven. Then Gretel gave her a push, so that she fell right in, and then shutting the iron door, she bolted it. Oh! how horribly she howled; but Gretel ran away, and left the wicked witch to burn to ashes.

Now she ran to Hansel, and, opening his door, called out, 'Hansel, we are saved, the old witch is dead!' So he sprang out, like a bird out of his cage when the door is opened; and they were so glad that they fell into each other's arms, and kissed each other over and over again. And now, as there was nothing to fear, they went into the witch's house, where in every corner there were caskets full of pearls and precious stones.

'These are better than pebbles,' said Hansel, putting as many into his pocket as it would hold; while Gretel thought, 'I will take some home too,' and filled her apron full. 'We must be off now,' said Hansel, 'and get out of this enchanted forest;' but when they had walked for two hours they came to a large piece of water. 'We cannot cross,' said Hansel; 'I can see no bridge.

'And there is no boat either,' said Gretel, 'but there swims a white duck. I will ask her to help us over;' and she sang:

> 'Little duck, good little duck,
>   Gretel and Hansel, here we stand;
> There is neither stile nor bridge –
>   Take us on your back to land.'

So the duck came to them, and Hansel sat himself on, and bade his sister sit behind him. 'No,' answered Gretel, 'that will be too much for the duck; she shall take us over one at a time.' This the good little bird did, and when they had reached the other side safely, and had gone a little way, they came to a well-known wood, which they knew better every step they walked, and at last they perceived their father's house. Then they began to run, and, bursting into the house, they fell into their father's arms. He had not had one happy hour since he had left the children in the forest; and his wife was dead. Gretel shook her apron, and the pearls and precious stones rolled out upon the floor, and Hansel threw down one handful after the other out of his pocket. Then all their sorrows were ended for ever and ever.

The Crow & the Mussel

ONCE a hungry crow discovered a mussel and tried hard to break it open with his beak so that he could get at the fish. He was struggling without success when a carrion-crow came along and said, 'I advise you to use a little strategy, my friend. Carry the mussel into the air as high as you can fly, and then let it drop down on this rock and you will find it will break open.'

The crow thanked him heartily and, thinking it a good plan, flew off, but while he was on the wing the carrion-crow remained on the ground, and ate the mussel himself when it dropped down.

Some people are kind to their neighbours for their own sakes.

The Farmer & the Stork

FINDING that cranes were destroying his newly-sown corn, a farmer one evening set a net in his field to catch the destructive birds. When he went to examine the net next morning he found a number of cranes and also a stork.

'Release me, I beseech you,' cried the stork, 'for I have eaten none of your corn, nor have I done you any harm. I am a poor innocent stork, as you may see – a most dutiful bird. I honour my father and mother. I—'

But the farmer cut him short. 'All this may be true enough, I dare say, but I have caught you with those who were destroying my crops, and you must suffer with the company in which you are found.'

People are judged by the company they keep.

DAVID
FRANKLAND.

The Dog & the Cock

A DOG and a cock decided to go on a journey together. They were travelling through a wood when night fell. The dog went to sleep in a hollow at the foot of a tree, and the cock roosted in the branches above.

It crowed at its usual hour to welcome the dawn, and its cry awoke a fox who lived nearby and who hurried to the wood, thinking he would find a meal. When he saw the cock he began to praise its voice and begged the bird to come down from the tree so that he could congratulate it properly.

'I will come down,' said the cock, who saw through the fox's plan, 'if you will first speak to the porter below to open the door.'

The fox, not suspecting the trick, did as he was told. When the dog awoke he soon put an end to the fox, and he and the cock continued their journey in safety.

Meet cunning with cunning.

D.F.

The Tortoise & the Eagle

A TORTOISE became dissatisfied with his lowly life when he saw so many birds enjoying themselves in the air.

'If I could only get up into the air, I could soar with the best of them,' he thought.

One day an eagle came to rest on a rock beside him, and, seizing such a favourable opportunity, the tortoise offered all the treasures of the sea if only the monarch of the air would teach him to fly.

The eagle at first declined the task, for he considered it not only absurd but impossible, but, being further pressed by the entreaties and promises of the tortoise, he finally agreed to try.

Taking him to a great height in the air, he loosed his hold, bidding the stupid creature to fly if he could.

Before the tortoise could express a word of thanks he fell upon a huge rock and was dashed to pieces.

DAVID FRANKLAND.

The over-ambitious often destroy themselves.

The Travellers & the Bear

TWO friends were travelling on the same road together when they came face to face with a bear.

One in great fear, and without a thought of his companion, climbed into a tree and hid.

The other, seeing that, single-handed, he was no match for Bruin the bear, threw himself on the ground and pretended to be dead for he had heard that a bear will not touch a dead body.

The bear approached him, sniffing at his nose and ears, but the man, with great courage, held his breath and kept still, and at length the bear, thinking him dead, walked slowly away.

When Bruin was well out of sight the first traveller came down from his tree and asked his companion what it was that the bear had said to him. 'For,' said he, 'I observed that he put his mouth very close to your ear.'

'Why,' replied the other, 'it was no great secret. He only advised me not to keep company with those who, when they get into difficulty, leave their friends in the lurch.'

Misfortune tests the sincerity of friends.

The Fox & the Monkey

A MONKEY once danced in an assembly of the beasts, and so greatly pleased all by his performance that they elected him their king.

A fox who envied him the honour, having discovered a piece of meat lying in a trap, led the monkey to the tit-bit and said:

'Look! I have found this store, but have not used it. It is not for the subject to lay claim to a treasure trove; the king himself should take it.'

The monkey approached carelessly and was caught in the trap, whereupon he accused the fox of leading him into the snare.

The fox replied, 'O monkey, can it be that you, with so simple a mind, could rule as king over all the beasts?'

The simple are easily deceived.

DAVID
FRANKLAND.

The Jackdaw of Rheims

THE Jackdaw sat on the Cardinal's chair!
    Bishop and abbot, and prior were there;
    Many a monk, and many a friar,
  Many a knight, and many a squire,
With a great many more of lesser degree, –
In sooth a goodly company;
And they served the Lord Primate on bended knee.
    Never, I ween, Was a prouder seen,
Read of in books, or dreamt of in dreams,
Than the Cardinal Lord Archbishop of Rheims!

    In and out through the motley rout,
That little Jackdaw kept hopping about;
    Here and there, Like a dog in a fair,
    Over comfits and cakes, And dishes and plates,
Cowl and cope, and rochet and hall,
Mitre and crosier! he hopp'd upon all!
    With saucy air, He perch'd on the chair
Where, in state, the great Lord Cardinal sat
In the great Lord Cardinal's great red hat;
And he peèr'd in the face Of his Lordship's Grace,
With a satisfied look, as if he would say,
'We two are the greatest folks here today!'
    And the priests, with awe, As such freaks they saw,
Said, 'The Devil must be in that little Jackdaw!'

The feast was over, the board was clear'd,
The flawns and the custards had all disappear'd
And six little Singing-boys, – dear little souls!
In nice clean faces, and nice white stoles,
    Came, in order due, Two by two,

50

Marching that grand refectory through!
A nice little boy held a golden ewer,
Emboss'd and fill'd with water, as pure
As any that flows between Rheims and Namur,
Which a nice little boy stood ready to catch
In a fine golden hand-basin made to match.
Two nice little boys, rather more grown,
Carried lavender-water, and eau de Cologne;
And a nice little boy had a nice cake of soap,
Worthy of washing the hands of the Pope.
    One little boy more A napkin bore,
Of the best white diaper, fringed with pink,
And a Cardinal's Hat mark'd in 'permanent ink.'

The great Lord Cardinal turns at the sight
Of these nice little boys dress'd all in white:
    From his finger he draws His costly turquoise;
And, not thinking at all about little Jackdaws,
    Deposits it straight By the side of his plate,
While the nice little boys on his Eminence wait;
Till, when nobody's dreaming of any such thing,
That little Jackdaw hops off with the ring!

    There's a cry and a shout, And a deuce of a rout,
And nobody seems to know what they're about,
But the monks have their pockets all turn'd inside out;
    The friars are kneeling, And hunting, and feeling
The carpet, the floor, and the walls, and the ceiling.

    The Cardinal drew Off each plum-colour'd shoe,
And left his red stockings exposed to the view:
    He peeps, and he feels In the toes and the heels;
They turn up the dishes, – they turn up the plates, –
They take up the poker and poke out the grates,
    They turn up the rugs, They examine the mugs –
    But, no! – no such thing; – They can't find THE RING!
And the Abbot declared that, 'when nobody twigg'd it,
Some rascal or other had popp'd in, and prigg'd it!'

The Cardinal rose with a dignified look,
He call'd for his candle, his bell, and his book!
   In holy anger, and pious grief,
   He solemnly cursed that rascally thief!
   He cursed him at board, he cursed him in bed;
   From the sole of his foot to the crown of his head;
   He cursed him in sleeping, that every night
   He should dream of the devil, and wake in a fright;
   He cursed him in eating, he cursed him in drinking,
   He cursed him in coughing, in sneezing, in winking:
   He cursed him in sitting, in standing, in lying;
   He cursed him in walking, in riding, in flying,
   He cursed him in living, he cursed him dying! –
Never was heard such a terrible curse!
   But what gave rise To no little surprise,
Nobody seem'd one penny the worse!

   The day was gone, The night came on,
The Monks and the Friars they search'd till dawn;
   When the Sacristan saw, On crumpled claw,
Come limping a poor little lame Jackdaw!
   No longer gay, As on yesterday;
His feathers all seem'd to be turn'd the wrong way; –
His pinions droop'd – he could hardly stand, –
His head was as bald as the palm of your hand;
   His eye so dim, So wasted each limb,
That, heedless of grammar, they all cried, 'THAT'S HIM! –

That's the scamp that has done this scandalous thing!
That's the thief that has got my Lord Cardinal's Ring!'
   The poor little Jackdaw, When the monks he saw,
Feebly gave vent to the ghost of a caw;
And turn'd his bald head, as much as to say;
'Pray, be so good as to walk this way!'
   Slower and slower He limp'd on before,
Till they came to the back of the belfry door,
   Where the first thing they saw, Midst the sticks and the straw
Was the RING in the nest of that little Jackdaw!

Then the great Lord Cardinal call'd for his book,
And off that terrible curse he took;
    The mute expression Served in lieu of confession,
And, being thus coupled with full restitution,
The Jackdaw got plenary absolution!
    – When those words were heard, That poor little bird
Was so changed in a moment, 'twas really absurd,
    He grew sleek, and fat; In addition to that,
A fresh crop of feathers came thick as a mat!

    His tail waggled more Even than before;
But no longer it wagged with an impudent air,
No longer he perch'd on the Cardinal's chair
    He hopp'd now about With a gait devout;
At Matins, at Vespers, he never was out;
And, so far from any more pilfering deeds,
He always seem'd telling the Confessor's beads.
    If any one lied, – or if any one swore, –
Or slumber'd in prayer-time and happen'd to snore,
    That good Jackdaw Would give a great 'Caw!'
As much as to say, 'Don't do so any more!'
While many remark'd, as his manners they saw,
That they 'never had known such a pious Jackdaw!'
    He long lived the pride Of that country-side,
And at last in the odour of sanctity died;
    When, as words were too faint His merits to paint,
The Conclave determined to make him a Saint;
And on newly-made Saints and Popes, as you know,
It's the custom, at Rome, new names to bestow,
So they canonised him by the name of Jim Crow!

What Katy Did

Susan Coolidge was the pen-name of Sarah Chauncey Woolsey (1835–1905). Her most famous book is 'What Katy Did', which proved so popular that she followed it with four others about members of the Carr family. Mrs Carr had died when the youngest of her six children was still very young and now Katy, the eldest, though crippled following an accident, helps her father with the running of the household.

IT was a pleasant morning in early June. A warm wind was rustling the trees, which were covered thickly with half-opened leaves, and looked like fountains of green spray thrown high into the air. Dr. Carr's front door stood wide open. Through the parlour window came the sound of piano practice, and on the steps, under the budding roses, sat a small figure busily sewing.

This was Clover, and she was now over fourteen. Clover was never intended to be tall. Her eyes were blue and sweet, and her apple-blossom cheeks pink. Her brown pig-tails were pinned into a round knot, and the childish face had gained almost a womanly look. Old Mary declared that Miss Clover was getting quite youngladyfied, and 'Miss Clover' was quite aware of the fact, and mightily pleased with it. It delighted her to turn up her hair; and she was very particular about having her dresses made to come below the tops of her boots. She had also left off ruffles, and wore narrow collars instead, and little cuffs with sleeve-buttons to fasten them. These sleeve-buttons, which were a present from Cousin Helen, Clover liked best of all her things. Papa said that he was sure she took them to bed with her, but of course that was only a joke, though she certainly was never seen without them in the day-time. She glanced frequently at these beloved buttons as she sat sewing, and every now and then laid down her work to twist them into a better position, or give an affectionate pat with her forefinger.

Very soon the side-gate swung open, and Philly came round the corner of the house. He had grown into a big boy. All his pretty baby curls were cut off, and his frocks had given place to jacket and trousers. In his hand he held something. What, Clover could not see.

'What's that?' she said, as he reached the steps.

'I'm going upstairs to ask Katy if these are ripe,' replied Phil, exhibiting some currants faintly streaked with red.

'Why, of course, they're not ripe!' said Clover, putting one into her mouth. 'Can't you tell by the taste? They're as green as can be.'

'I don't care, if Katy says they're ripe I shall eat 'em,' answered Phil defiantly, marching into the house.

'What did Philly want?' asked Elsie, opening the parlour door as Phil went upstairs.

'Only to know if the currants are ripe enough to eat.'

'How particular he always is about asking now!' said Elsie. 'He's afraid of another dose of salts.'

'I should think he would be,' replied Clover, laughing. 'Johnnie says she never was so scared in her life as when Papa called them, and they looked up, and saw him standing there with the bottle in one hand and a spoon in the other!'

'Yes,' went on Elsie, 'and you know Dorry held his in his mouth for ever so long, and then went round the corner of the house and spat it out! Papa said he had a good mind to make him take another spoonful, but he remembered that after all Dorry had the bad taste a great deal longer than the others, so he didn't. I think it was an *awful* punishment, don't you?'

'Yes, but it was a good one, for none of them have ever touched the green gooseberries since. Have you got through practising? It doesn't seem like an hour yet.'

'Oh, it isn't; it's only twenty-five minutes. But Katy told me not to sit more than half an hour at a time without getting up and running round to rest. I'm going to walk twice down to the gate, and twice back. I promised her I would.' And Elsie set off, clapping her hands briskly before and behind her as she walked.

'Why – what is Bridget doing in Papa's room?' she asked, as she came back the second time. 'She's flapping things out of the window. Are the girls up there? I thought they were cleaning the dining-room.'

'They're doing both. Katy said it was such a good chance, having Papa away, that she would have both the carpets taken up at once. There isn't going to be any dinner today, only just bread and butter, and milk, and cold ham, up in Katy's room because Debby is helping too, so as to get through and save Papa all the fuss. And see,' exhibiting her sewing, 'Katy's making a new cover for Papa's pincushion, and I'm hemming the ruffle to go round it.'

'How nicely you hem!' said Elsie. 'I wish I had something for Papa's room, too. There's my washstand mats – but the one for the soap-dish isn't finished. Do you suppose, if Katy would excuse me from the rest of my practising, I could get it done? I've a great mind to go and ask her.'

'There's her bell!' said Clover, as a little tinkle sounded upstairs. 'I'll ask her if you like.'

'No, let me go. I'll see what she wants.' But Clover was already halfway across the hall, and the two girls ran up side by side. There was often a little strife between them as to which should answer Katy's bell. Both liked to wait on her so much.

Katy came to meet them as they entered. Not on her feet; that alas! was still only a far-off possibility; but in a chair with large wheels, with which she was rolling herself across the room. This chair was a great comfort to her. Sitting in it she could get to her closet and her bureau drawers, and help herself to what she wanted without troubling anybody. It was only lately that she had been able to use it. Dr. Carr considered her doing so as a hopeful sign, but he had never told Katy this. She had grown accustomed to her invalid's life at last, and was cheerful in it, and he thought it unwise to make her restless by exciting hopes which might after all end in fresh disappointment.

She met the girls with a bright smile as they came in, and said:

'Oh, Clovy, it was you I rang for! I am troubled for fear Bridget will meddle with the things on Papa's table. You know he likes them to be left just so. Will you please go and remind her that she is not to touch them at all? After the carpet is put down, I want you to dust the table, so as to be sure that everything is put back in the same place. Will you?'

'Of course I will,' said Clover, who was a born housewife, and dearly loved to act as Katy's prime minister.

'Shan't I fetch you the pincushion, too, while I'm there?'

'Oh, yes, please do! I want to measure.'

'Katy,' said Elsie, 'those mats of mine are almost done, and I would like to finish them and put them on Papa's washstand before he comes back. Mayn't I stop practising now and bring my crochet up here instead?'

'Will there be plenty of time to learn the new exercise before Miss Phillips comes, if you do?'

'I think so, plenty. She doesn't come till Friday, you know.'

'Well, then, it seems to me that you might just as well as not. And Elsie, dear, run into Papa's room first and bring me the drawer out of his table. I want to put that in order myself.'

Elsie went cheerfully. She laid the drawer across Katy's lap, and Katy began to dust and arrange the contents. Pretty soon Clover joined them.

'Here's the cushion,' she said. 'Now we'll have a nice quiet time all by ourselves, won't we? I like this sort of day, when nobody comes in to interrupt us.'

Somebody tapped at the door as she spoke. Katy called out, 'Come in,' and in marched a tall, broad-shouldered lad, with a solemn, sensible face, and a little clock carried carefully in both his hands. This was Dorry.

'Here's your clock, Katy,' he said. 'I've got it fixed so that it strikes all right. Only you must be careful not to hit the striker when you start the pendulum.'

'Have you really?' said Katy. 'Why, Dorry, you're a genius! I'm ever so much obliged.'

'It's four minutes to eleven now,' went on Dorry, 'so it'll strike pretty soon. I guess I'd better stay and hear it, so as to be sure that it is right. That is,' he added politely, 'unless you're busy and would rather not.'

'I'm never too busy to want you, old fellow,' said Katy, stroking his arm. 'Here, this drawer is arranged now. Don't you want to carry it into Papa's room and put it back into the table? Your hands are stronger than Elsie's.'

Dorry looked gratified. When he came back the clock was just beginning to strike.

'There!' he exclaimed; 'that's splendid, isn't it?'

But alas! the clock did not stop at eleven. It went on – twelve, thirteen, fourteen, fifteen, sixteen!

'Dear me!' said Clover, 'what does all this mean? It must be the day after tomorrow, at least!'

Dorry stared with open mouth at the clock, which was still striking as though it would split its sides. Elsie, screaming with laughter, kept count.

'Thirty, thirty-one – Oh, Dorry! Thirty-two! thirty-three! thirty-four!'

'You've bewitched it, Dorry!' said Katy, as much entertained as the rest.

Then they all began counting. Dorry seized the clock, shook it, slapped it, turned it upside down. But still the sharp, vibrating sounds continued, as if the clock, having got its own way for once, meant to go on till it was tired out. At last, at the one-hundred-and-thirtieth stroke, it suddenly ceased, and Dorry, with a red, amazed countenance, faced the laughing company.

'It's very queer,' he said, 'but I'm sure it's not because of anything I did. I can fix it, though, if you'll let me try again. May I, Katy? I'll promise not to hurt it.'

For a moment Katy hesitated. Clover pulled her sleeve, and whispered, 'Don't!' Then, seeing the mortification on Dorry's face, she made up her mind.

'Yes, take it, Dorry. I'm sure you'll be careful. But if I were you, I'd carry it down to Wetherell's first of all, and talk it over with him. Together you could hit on just the right thing. Don't you think so?'

'Perhaps,' said Dorry; 'yes, I think I will.' Then he departed with the clock under his arm, while Clover called after him teasingly: 'Lunch at 132 o'clock; don't forget.'

'No, I won't,' said Dorry. Two years before he would not have borne to be laughed at so good-naturedly.

'How could you let him take your clock again?' said Clover, as soon as the door was shut. 'He'll spoil it. And you think so much of it.'

'I thought he would feel mortified if I didn't let him try,' replied Katy quietly; 'I don't believe he'll hurt it. Wetherell's man likes Dorry, and he'll show him what to do.'

'You were real good to do it,' responded Clover; 'but if it had been mine, I don't think I could.'

Just then the door flew open and Johnnie rushed in.

'Oh, Katy!' she gasped, 'won't you please tell Philly not to wash the chickens in the rainwater tub? He's put in every one of Speckle's, and is just beginning on Dame Durden's. I'm afraid one little yellow one is dead already –'

'Why, he mustn't, of course he mustn't!' said Katy. 'What made him think of such a thing?'

'He says they're dirty, because they've just come out of egg-shells! And he insists that the yellow on them is yoke of egg. I told him it wasn't, but he wouldn't listen to me.' And Johnnie wrung her hands.

'Clover!' cried Katy, 'won't you run down and ask Philly to come up to me? Speak pleasantly, you know.'

'I spoke pleasantly – real pleasantly, but it wasn't any use,' said Johnnie, on whom the wrongs of the chicks had evidently made a deep impression.

'What a mischief Phil is getting to be!' said Elsie. 'Papa says his name ought to be Pickle.'

'Pickles turn out very nice sometimes, you know,' replied Katy, laughing.

Pretty soon Philly came up, escorted by Clover. He looked a little defiant, but Katy understood how to manage him. She lifted him into her lap, which, big boy as he was, he liked extremely; and talked to him so affectionately about the poor little shivering chicks that his heart was quite melted.

'I didn't mean to hurt 'em, really and truly,' he said; 'but they were all dirty and yellow – with egg, you know, and I thought you'd like me to clean them up.'

'But that wasn't egg, Philly – it was dear little clean feathers, like a canary-bird's wings.'

'Was it?'

'Yes, and now the chickies are as cold and forlorn as you would feel if you tumbled into a pond and nobody gave you any dry clothes. Don't you think you ought to go and warm them?'

'How?'

'Well, in your hands, very gently. And then I would let them run round in the sun.'

'I will,' said Philly, getting down from her lap. 'Only kiss me first, because I didn't mean to, you know!' – Philly was very fond of Katy. Miss Pettingill said it was wonderful to see how that child let himself be managed. But I think the secret was that Katy didn't 'manage', but tried to be always kind and loving and considerate of Phil's feelings.

Before the echo of Phil's boots had died away on the stairs, old Mary put her head into the door. There was a distressed expression on her face.

61

'Miss Katy,' she said, 'I wish *you'd* speak to Alexander about putting the wood-shed in order. I don't think you know how bad it looks.'

'I don't suppose I do,' said Katy, smiling and then sighing. She had never seen the wood-shed since the day of her fall from the swing which had crippled her. 'Never mind, Mary; I'll talk to Alexander about it, and he shall make it nice.'

Mary trotted downstairs satisfied. But in the course of a few minutes she was up again.

'There's a man come with a box of soap, Miss Katy, and here's the bill. He says it's resated.'

It took Katy a little time to find her purse, and then she wanted her pencil and account-book, and Elsie had to move from her seat at the table.

'Oh dear!' she said. 'I wish people wouldn't keep coming and interrupting us. Who'll be the next, I wonder?'

She was not left to wonder long. Almost as she spoke there was another knock at the door.

'Come in!' said Katy, rather wearily. The door opened.

'Shall I?' said a voice. There was a rustle of skirts, a clatter of boot-heels, and Imogen Clark swept into the room. Katy could not think who it was at first. She had not seen Imogen for almost two years.

'I found the front door open,' explained Imogen, in her high-pitched voice, 'and as nobody seemed to hear when I rang the bell, I ventured to come right upstairs. I hope I am not interrupting anything private?'

'Not at all,' said Katy politely. 'Elsie, dear, move up that low chair, please. Do sit down, Imogen. I'm sorry nobody answered your ring, but the servants are cleaning house today, and I suppose they didn't hear.'

So Imogen sat down and began to rattle on in her usual manner, while Elsie, from behind Katy's chair, took a wide-awake survey of her dress. It was of cheap material, but very gorgeously made and trimmed with flounces and puffs; and Imogen wore a jet necklace and long black earrings, which jingled and clicked when she waved her head about. She had little round curls stuck on to her cheeks, and Elsie wondered what kept them in their places.

By and by the object of Imogen's visit came out. She had called to say goodbye. The Clark family were all going back to Jacksonville to live.

'Did you ever see the Brigand again?' asked Clover, who had never forgotten that eventful tale told in the parlour.

'Yes,' replied Imogen, 'several times. And I get letters from him quite often. He writes *beautiful* letters. I wish I had one with me, so that I could read you a little bit. You would enjoy it, I know. Let me see – perhaps I have.' And she put her hand into her pocket. Sure enough there *was* a letter.

Clover couldn't help suspecting that Imogen knew it all the time.

The Brigand seemed to write a bold, black hand, and his note-paper and envelope was just like anybody else's. But perhaps his band had surprised a pedlar with a box of stationery.

'Let me see,' said Imogen, running her eye down the page. ' "Adored Imogen" – *that* wouldn't interest you – hm, hm, hm – ah, here's something! "I took dinner at the Rock House on Christmas. It was lonesome without you. I had roast turkey, roast goose, roast beef, mince pie, plum pudding and nuts and raisins. A pretty good dinner, was it not? But nothing tastes first-rate when friends are away." '

Katy and Clover stared, as well they might. Such language from a Brigand!

' "John Billings has bought a new horse," ' continued Imogen; 'hm, hm, hm – "him." I don't think there is anything else you'd care about. Oh, yes! just here, at the end, is some poetry:–

> ' "Come, little dove, with azure wing,
> And brood upon my breast."

'That's sweet, ain't it?'

'Hasn't he reformed?' said Clover. 'He writes as if he had.'

'Reformed!' cried Imogen, with a toss of the jingling earrings. 'He was always just as good as he could be!'

There was nothing to be said in reply to this. Katy felt her lips twitch, and for fear she should be rude, and laugh out, she began to talk as fast as she could about something else. All the time she found herself taking measure of Imogen, and thinking: 'Did I ever really like her? How queer! Oh, what a wise man Papa is!'

Imogen stayed half an hour. Then she took her leave.

'She never asked how you were!' cried Elsie indignantly. 'I noticed, and she didn't – not once!'

'Oh, well – I suppose she forgot. We were talking about her, not about me,' replied Katy.

The little group settled down again to their work. This time half an hour went by without any more interruptions. Then the doorbell rang, and Bridget with a disturbed face came upstairs.

'Miss Katy,' she said, 'it's old Mrs. Worrett, and I reckon she's come to spend the day, for she's brought her bag. Whatever shall I tell her?'

Katy looked dismayed. 'Oh dear!' she said, 'how unlucky. What can we do?'

Mrs. Worrett was an old friend of Aunt Izzie's, who lived in the country, about six miles from Burnet, and was in the habit of coming to Dr. Carr's for lunch on days when shopping or other business brought her into town. This did not occur often; and, as it happened, Katy had never had to entertain her before.

'Tell her ye're busy, and can't see her,' suggested Bridget. 'There's no dinner nor nothing, you know.'

The Katy of two years ago would probably have jumped at this idea. But the Katy of today was more considerate.

'N—o,' she said; 'I don't like to do that. We must just make the best of it, Bridget. Run down, Clover dear, that's a good girl, and tell Mrs. Worrett that the dining-room is all in confusion, but that we're going to have lunch here, and, after she's rested, I should be glad to have her come up. And, oh, Clovy! give her a fan the first thing. She'll be *so* hot. Bridget, you can bring up the luncheon just the same, only take out some canned peaches, by way of a dessert, and make Mrs. Worrett a cup of tea. She drinks tea always, I believe.'

'I can't bear to send the poor old lady away when she has come so far,' she explained to Elsie, after the others were gone. 'Pull the rocking-chair a little this way, Elsie. And, oh! push all those little chairs back against the wall. Mrs. Worrett broke down in one the last time she was here – don't you recollect?'

It took some time to cool Mrs. Worrett off, so nearly twenty minutes passed before a heavy, creaking step on the stairs announced that the guest was on her way up. Elsie began to giggle. Mrs. Worrett always made her giggle. Katy had just time to give her a warning glance before the door opened.

Mrs. Worrett was the most enormously fat person ever seen. Nobody dared to guess how much she weighed, but she *looked* as

if it might be a thousand pounds. Her face was extremely red. In the coldest weather she appeared hot, and on a mild day she seemed absolutely ready to melt. Her bonnet-strings were flying loose as she came in, and she fanned herself all the way across the room, which shook as she walked.

'Well, my dear,' she said, as she plumped herself into the rocking-chair, 'and how do you do?'

'Very well, thank you,' replied Katy, thinking that she never saw Mrs. Worrett look half so fat before, and wondering how she *was* to entertain her.

'And how's your Pa?' inquired Mrs. Worrett. Katy answered politely, and then asked after Mrs. Worrett's own health.

'Well, I'm so's to be round,' was the reply, which had the effect of sending Elsie off into a fit of convulsive laughter behind Katy's chair.

'I had business at the bank,' continued the visitor; 'and I thought, while I was about it, I'd step up to Miss Pettingill's and see if I couldn't get her to come and let out my black silk. It was made a long while ago, and I seem to have grown stouter since then, for I can't make the hooks and eyes meet at all. But when I got there she was out, so I'd my walk for nothing. Do you know where she's sewing now?'

'No,' said Katy, feeling her chair shake, and keeping her own countenance with difficulty. 'She was here for three days last week to make Johnnie a school dress. But I haven't heard anything about her since. Elsie, you might run downstairs and ask Bridget to bring a—a—a glass of iced water for Mrs. Worrett. She looks warm after her walk.'

Elsie, dreadfully ashamed, made a bolt from the room, and hid herself in the hall closet to have her laugh out. She came back after a while, with a perfectly straight face. Luncheon was brought up. Mrs. Worrett made a good meal, and seemed to enjoy everything. She was so comfortable that she never stirred till four o'clock! Oh, how long that afternoon did seem to the poor girls, sitting there and trying to think of something to say to their vast visitor!

At last Mrs. Worrett got out of her chair and prepared to depart.

'Well,' she said, tying her bonnet strings, 'I've had a good rest, and feel all the better for it. Aren't some of you young folks coming out to see me one of these days? I'd like to have you first-rate if you will. 'Tain't every girl would know how to take care of

67

a fat old woman, and make her feel at home, as you have me, Katy. I wish your aunt could see you all as you are now. She'd be right pleased; I know that.'

Somehow this sentence rang pleasantly in Katy's ears.

'Ah! don't laugh at her,' she said later in the evening, when the children, after their tea in the clean, fresh-smelling dining-room, were come up to sit with her, and Cecy, in her pretty pink lawn and white shawl, had dropped in to spend an hour or two; 'she's a real kind old woman, and I don't like to have you laugh at her. It isn't her fault that she's fat. And Aunt Izzie was fond of her, you know. It is doing something for her, when we can show a little attention to one of her friends. I was sorry when she came; but now it's over I'm glad.'

'It feels so nice when it stops aching,' quoted Elsie mischievously, while Cecy whispered to Clover:

'Isn't Katy sweet?'

'Isn't she?' replied Clover. 'I wish I was half as good. Sometimes I think I shall really be sorry if she ever gets well. She's such a dear old darling to us all, sitting there in her chair, that it wouldn't seem so nice to have her anywhere else. But, then, I know it's horrid in me. And I don't believe she'd be different, or grow rough and horrid, like some of the girls, even if she were well.'

'Of course she wouldn't!' replied Cecy.

It was six weeks after this that, one day, Clover and Elsie were busy downstairs, they were startled by the sound of Katy's bell ringing in a sudden and agitated manner. Both ran up two steps at a time, to see what was wanted.

Katy sat in her chair, looking very much flushed and excited. 'Oh, girls,' she exclaimed, 'what do you think? I stood up!'

'What?' cried Clover and Elsie.

'I really did! I stood up on my feet! by myself!'

The others were too much astonished to speak, so Katy went on explaining.

'It was all at once, you see. Suddenly, I had the feeling that if I tried I could, and almost before I thought, I *did* try, and there I was, up and out of the chair. Only I kept hold of the arm all the time! I don't know how I got back, I was so frightened. Oh, girls!' – and Katy buried her face in her hands.

'Do you think I shall ever be able to do it again?' she asked, looking up with wet eyes.

'Why, of course you will,' said Clover; while Elsie danced about, crying out anxiously: 'Be careful! Do be careful!'

Katy tried, but the spring was gone. She could not move out of the chair at all. She began to wonder if she had dreamed the whole thing.

But next day, when Clover happened to be in the room, she heard a sudden exclamation, and, turning, there stood Katy absolutely on her feet.

'Papa! Papa!' shrieked Clover, rushing downstairs. 'Dorry, John, Elsie – come! Come and see!'

Papa was out, but all the rest crowded up at once. This time Katy found no trouble in 'doing it again.' It seemed as if her will had been asleep; and now that it had waked up, the limbs recognised its orders and obeyed them. When Papa came in he was as much excited as any of the children. He walked round and round the chair, questioning Katy and making her stand up and sit down.

'Am I really going to get well?' she asked, almost in a whisper.

'Yes, my love, I think you are,' said Dr. Carr, seizing Phil and giving him a toss into the air. None of the children had ever before seen Papa behave so like a boy. But pretty soon, noticing Katy's burning cheeks and excited eyes, he calmed himself, sent the others all away, and sat down to soothe and quiet her with gentle words.

'I think it is coming, my darling,' he said, 'but it will take time, and you must have a great deal of patience. After being such a good child all these years, I'm sure you won't fail now. Remember, any imprudence will put you back. You must be content to gain a very little at a time. There is no royal road to walking any more than there is to learning. Every baby finds that out.'

'Oh, Papa!' said Katy, 'it's no matter if it takes a year – if only I got well at last.'

How happy she was that night – too happy to sleep. Papa noticed the dark circles under her eyes in the morning and shook his head.

'You *must* be careful,' he told her, 'or you'll be laid up again. A course of fever would put you back for years.'

Katy knew Papa was right, and she *was* careful, though it was by no means easy to be so with that new life tingling in every limb. Her progress was slow, as Dr. Carr had predicted. At first she only stood on her feet a few seconds, then a minute, then five minutes, holding tightly all the while by the chair. Next she ventured to let go the chair and stand alone. After that she began to walk a step at a time, pushing a chair before her as children do when they are learning the use of their feet. Clover and Elsie hovered about her as she moved, like anxious mammas. It was droll, and a little pitiful, to see tall Katy with her feeble, unsteady progress, and the active figures of the little sisters following her protectingly. But Katy did not consider it either droll or pitiful; to her it was simply delightful – the most delightful thing possible. No baby of a year old was ever prouder of his first steps than she.

Gradually she grew adventurous, and ventured on a bolder flight. Clover, running upstairs one day to her own room, stood transfixed at the sight of Katy sitting there, flushed, panting, but enjoying the surprise she caused.

'You see,' she explained, in an apologising tone, 'I was seized with a desire to explore. It is such a time since I saw any room but my own! But oh dear, how long that hall is! I had forgotten it could be so long. I shall have to take a good rest before I go back.'

Katy did take a good rest, but she was very tired next day. The experiment, however, did no harm. In the course of two or three weeks she was able to walk all over the second story.

This was a great enjoyment. It was like reading an interesting book to see all the new things and the little changes. She was for ever wondering over something.

'Why, Dorry,' she would say, 'what a pretty book-shelf! When did you get it?'

'That old thing! Why, I've had it two years. Didn't I ever tell you about it?'

'Perhaps you did,' Katy would reply, 'but, you see, I never *saw* it before, so it made no impression.'

By the end of August she was grown so strong that she began to talk about going downstairs. But Papa said, 'Wait.'

'It will tire you much more than walking about on a level,' he explained, 'you had better put it off a little while – till you are quite sure of your feet.'

'I think so too,' said Clover; 'and besides, I want to have the house all put in order and made nice before your sharp eyes see it, Mrs. Housekeeper. Oh, I'll tell you! Such a beautiful idea has come into my head! You shall fix a day to come down, Katy, and we'll be all ready for you, and have a "celebration" among ourselves. That would be just lovely! How soon may she, Papa?'

'Well, in ten days, I should say, it might be safe.'

'Ten days! that will bring it to the seventh of September, won't it?' said Katy. 'Then, Papa, if I may, I'll come down for the first time on the eighth. It was Mamma's birthday, you know,' she added in a lower voice.

So it was settled. 'How delicious!' cried Clover, skipping about and clapping her hands; 'I never, never, never *did* hear anything so perfectly lovely. Papa, when are you coming downstairs? I want to speak to you *dreadfully*.'

'Right away – rather than have my coat-tails pulled off,' answered Dr. Carr, laughing, and they went away together. Katy sat looking out of the window in a peaceful, happy mood.

'Oh!' she thought, 'can it really be? Is school going to "let out," just as Cousin Helen's hymn said? Am I going to

'"Bid a sweet goodbye to Pain?"'

'But there was Love in the Pain. I see it now. How good the dear Teacher has been to me!'

Clover seemed to be very busy all the rest of that week. She was 'having windows washed,' she said, but this explanation hardly accounted for her long absences, and the mysterious exultation on her face, not to mention certain sounds of hammering and sawing which came from downstairs. The other children had evidently been warned to say nothing; for once or twice Philly broke out with, 'O Katy!' and then hushed himself up, saying, 'I most forgot!' Katy grew very curious. But she saw that the secret, whatever it was, gave immense satisfaction to everybody except herself; so, though she longed to know, she concluded not to spoil the fun by asking any questions.

At last it wanted but one day of the important occasion.

'See,' said Katy, as Clover came into the room a little before tea-time. 'Miss Pettingill has brought home my new dress. I'm going to wear it for the first time to go downstairs in.'

'How pretty!' said Clover, examining the dress, which was a soft, dove-coloured cashmere, trimmed with ribbon of the same shade. 'But, Katy, I came up to shut your door. Bridget's going to sweep the hall, and I don't want the dust to fly in, because your room was brushed this morning, you know.'

'What a queer time to sweep the hall!' said Katy wondering. 'Why don't you make her wait till morning?'

'Oh, she can't! There are – she has – I mean there will be other things for her to do tomorrow. It's a great deal more convenient that she should do it now. Don't worry, Katy darling, but just keep your door shut. You will, won't you? Promise me!'

'Very well,' said Katy, more and more amazed, but yielding to Clover's eagerness, 'I'll keep it shut.' Her curiosity was excited. She took a book and tried to read, but the letters danced up and down before her eyes, and she couldn't help listening. Bridget was making a most ostentatious noise with her broom, but through it all Katy seemed to hear other sounds – feet on the stairs, doors opening and shutting – once, a stifled giggle. How queer it all was!

'Never mind,' she said, resolutely stopping her ears, 'I shall know all about it tomorrow.'

Tomorrow dawned fresh and fair – the very ideal of a September day.

'Katy!' said Clover, as she came in from the garden with her hands full of flowers, 'that dress of yours is sweet. You never

looked so nice before in your life!' And she stuck a beautiful carnation pink under Katy's breast-pin, and fastened another in her hair.

'There!' she said, 'now you're adorned. Papa is coming up in a few minutes to take you down.'

Just then Elsie and Johnnie came in. They had on their best frocks. So had Clover. It was evidently a festival-day to all the house. Cecy followed, invited over for the special purpose of seeing Katy walk downstairs. She, too, had on a new frock.

'How fine we are!' said Clover, as she remarked this magnificence. 'Turn round, Cecy – a pannier, I do declare – and a sash! You are getting awfully grown up, Miss Hall.'

'None of us will ever be so "grown up" as Katy,' said Cecy, laughing.

And now Papa appeared. Very slowly they all went downstairs, Katy leaning on Papa, with Dorry on her other side, and the girls behind, while Philly clattered ahead. And there were Debby and Bridget and Alexander peeping out of the kitchen door to watch her, and dear old Mary with her apron at her eyes, crying for joy.

'Oh, the front door is open!' said Katy, in a delighted tone. 'How nice! And what a pretty oil-cloth. That's new since I was here.'

'Don't stop to look at *that*!' cried Philly, who seemed in a great hurry about something. 'It isn't new. It's been there ever and ever so long! Come into the parlour instead.'

'Yes!' said Papa, 'dinner isn't quite ready yet, you'll have time to rest a little after your walk downstairs. Are you very tired?'

'Not a bit!' replied Katy cheerfully. 'I could do it alone, I think. Oh! the bookcase door has been mended! How nice it looks.'

'Don't wait, oh, don't wait!' repeated Phil, in an agony of impatience.

So they moved on. Papa opened the parlour door. Katy took one step into the room – then stopped. What was it that she saw?

Not merely the room itself, with its fresh muslin curtains and vases of flowers. Not even the wide, beautiful window which had been cut toward the sun, or the inviting little couch and table which stood there evidently for her. No, there was something else! The sofa was pulled out, and there upon it, her bright eyes turned to the door, lay – Cousin Helen!

Clover and Cecy agreed afterwards that they never were so frightened in their lives as at this moment; for Katy, forgetting her weakness, let go of Papa's arm, and absolutely *ran* towards the sofa. 'Oh, Cousin Helen! dear, dear Cousin Helen!' she cried. Then she tumbled down by the sofa somehow, the two pairs of arms and the two faces met, and for a moment or two not a word more was heard from anybody.

'Isn't it a nice 'prise!' shouted Philly, turning a somersault by way of relieving his feelings, while John and Dorry executed a sort of war-dance.

It appeared that this happy thought of getting Cousin Helen to the 'celebration', was Clover's. She it was who had proposed it to Papa, and made all the arrangements. And, artful puss! she had set Bridget to sweep the hall on purpose that Katy might not hear the noise of the arrival.

'Cousin Helen's going to stay three weeks this time – isn't that nice?' asked Elsie, while Clover anxiously questioned: 'Are you sure that you didn't suspect? Not one bit? Not the least tiny, weeny mite?'

'No, indeed, not the least. How could I suspect anything so perfectly delightful?' and Katy gave Cousin Helen another rapturous kiss.

Such a short day as that seemed! There was so much to see, to ask about, to talk over, that the hours flew, and evening dropped upon them all like another great surprise.

Cousin Helen was perhaps the happiest of the party. Besides the pleasure of knowing Katy to be almost well again, she had the additional enjoyment of seeing for herself how many changes for the better had taken place during the four years among the little cousins she loved so much.

It was very interesting to watch them all. Elsie had quite lost her plaintive look and little injured tone, and was as bright and beaming a maiden of twelve as any one could wish to see. Dorry's moody face had grown open and sensible, and his manners were good-humoured and obliging. And to him, as to all the other children, Katy was evidently the centre and the sun.

Cousin Helen looked on as Phil came in crying, after a hard tumble, and was consoled; as Johnnie whispered an important secret, and Elsie begged for help in her work. She saw Katy meet them all pleasantly and sweetly, without a bit of the dictatorial elder-sister in her manner, and with none of her old impetuous tone. And, best of all, she saw the change in Katy's own face; the gentle expression of her eyes, the womanly look, the pleasant voice, the politeness, the tact in advising the others without seeming to advise.

'Dear Katy,' she said, a day or two after her arrival, 'this visit is a great pleasure to me – you can't think how great. It is such a contrast to the last I made, when you were so sick, and everybody so sad. Do you remember?'

'Indeed I do! And how good you were, and how you helped me! I shall never forget that.'

'I'm glad! But what I could do was very little. You have been learning by yourself all this time. And Katy, darling, I want to tell you how pleased I am to see how bravely you have worked your way up. I can perceive it in everything – in Papa, in the children, in yourself. You have won the place which, you recollect, I once told you an invalid should try to gain, of being to everybody "the heart of the House".'

'Oh, Cousin Helen, don't!' said Katy, her eyes filling with sudden tears. 'I haven't been brave. You can't think how badly I sometimes have behaved; how cross and ungrateful I am, how stupid and slow. Every day I see things which ought to be done, and I don't do them. It's too delightful to have you praise me – but you mustn't. I don't deserve it.'

But although she said she didn't deserve it, I think that Katy did.

A Smuggler's Song

IF you wake at midnight, and hear a horse's feet,
Don't go drawing back the blind, or looking in the
street,
     Them that asks no questions isn't told a lie.
Watch the wall, my darling, while the Gentlemen go by!
         Five and twenty ponies
         Trotting through the dark –
         Brandy for the Parson,
         'Baccy for the Clerk;
         Laces for a lady, letters for a spy,
And watch the wall, my darling, while the Gentlemen go by!

Running round the woodlump if you chance to find
Little barrels, roped and tarred, all full of brandy-wine,
Don't you shout to come and look, nor use 'em for your play.
Put the brushwood back again – and they'll be gone next day!

If you see the stable-door standing open wide;
If you see a tired horse lying down inside;
If your mother mends a coat cut about and tore;
If the lining's wet and warm – don't you ask no more!

If you meet King George's men, dressed in blue and red,
You be careful what you say, and mindful what is said.
If they call you 'pretty maid', and chuck you 'neath the chin,
Don't you tell where no one is, nor yet where no one's been.

Knocks and footsteps round the house – whistles after dark –
You've no call for running out till the house-dogs bark.
Trusty's here, and *Pincher's* here, and see how dumb they lie –
They don't fret to follow when the Gentlemen go by!

If you do as you've been told, 'likely there's a chance,
You'll be give a dainty doll, all the way from France,
With a cap of Valenciennes, and a velvet hood –
A present from the Gentlemen, along o' being good!
          Five and twenty ponies
          Trotting through the dark –
          Brandy for the Parson,
          'Baccy for the Clerk.
Them that asks no questions isn't told a lie –
Watch the wall, my darling, while the Gentlemen go by!

Rikki-Tikki-Tavi

Rikki-Tikki-Tavi is a story from 'The Jungle Book' by Rudyard Kipling (1865–1936) who wrote many novels and short stories for adults and children. His parents worked in India and he was born there but went to school in England. Many of his stories are about Indian people and animals, such as 'The Jungle Book' and 'Just So Stories'. This story shows his knowledge of animals, especially the mongoose, and his understanding of small children.

THIS is the story of the great war that Rikki-tikki-tavi fought single-handed, through the bath-rooms of the big bungalow in Segowlee cantonment. Darzee, the tailor-bird, helped him, and Chuchundra, the musk-rat, who never comes out into the middle of the door, but always creeps round by the wall, gave him advice; but Rikki-tikki did the real fighting.

He was a mongoose, rather like a little cat in his fur and his tail, but quite like a weasel in his head and his habits. His eyes and the end of his restless nose were pink; he could scratch himself anywhere he pleased, with any leg, front or back, that he chose to use; he could fluff up his tail till it looked like a bottle-brush, and his war-cry, as he scuttled through the long grass, was: '*Rikk-tikk-tikki-tikki-tchk!*'

One day, a high summer flood washed him out of the burrow where he lived with his father and mother, and carried him, kicking and clucking, down a roadside ditch. He found a little wisp of grass floating there, and clung to it till he lost his senses. When he revived, he was lying in the hot sun on the middle of a garden path, very draggled indeed, and a small boy was saying: 'Here's a dead mongoose. Let's have a funeral.'

'No,' said his mother; 'let's take him in and dry him. Perhaps he isn't really dead.'

They took him into the house, and a big man picked him up

between his finger and thumb, and said he was not dead but half choked; so they wrapped him in cotton-wool, and warmed him, and he opened his eyes and sneezed.

'Now,' said the big man (he was an Englishman who had just moved into the bungalow); 'don't frighten him, and we'll see what he'll do.'

It is the hardest thing in the world to frighten a mongoose, because he is eaten up from nose to tail with curiosity. The motto of all the mongoose family is, 'Run and find out'; and Rikki-tikki was a true mongoose. He looked at the cotton-wool, decided that it was not good to eat, ran all round the table, sat up and put his fur in order, scratched himself, and jumped on the small boy's shoulder.

'Don't be frightened, Teddy,' said his father. 'That's his way of making friends.'

'Ouch! He's tickling under my chin,' said Teddy.

Rikki-tikki looked down between the boy's collar and neck, snuffed at his ear, and climbed down to the floor, where he sat rubbing his nose.

'Good gracious,' said Teddy's mother, 'and that's a wild creature! I suppose he's so tame because we've been kind to him.'

'All mongooses are like that,' said her husband. 'If Teddy doesn't pick him up by the tail, or try to put him in a cage, he'll run in and out of the house all day long. Let's give him something to eat.'

They gave him a little piece of raw meat. Rikki-tikki liked it immensely, and when it was finished he went out into the verandah and sat in the sunshine and fluffed up his fur to make it dry to the roots. Then he felt better.

'There are more things to find out about in this house,' he said to himself, 'than all my family could find out in all their lives. I shall certainly stay and find out.'

He spent all that day roaming over the house. He nearly drowned himself in the bath-tubs, put his nose into the ink on a writing table, and burnt it on the end of the big man's cigar, for he climbed up in the big man's lap to see how writing was done. At nightfall he ran into Teddy's nursery to watch how kerosene-lamps were lighted, and when Teddy went to bed Rikki-tikki climbed up too; but he was a restless companion, because he had to get up and attend to every noise all through the night, and find out what made it. Teddy's mother and father came in, the last thing, to look at their boy, and Rikki-tikki was awake on the pillow. 'I don't like that,' said Teddy's mother; 'he may bite the child.' 'He'll do no such thing,' said the father. 'Teddy's safer with that little beast than if he had a bloodhound to watch him. If a snake came into the nursery now —'

But Teddy's mother wouldn't think of anything so awful.

Early in the morning Rikki-tikki came to early breakfast in the verandah riding on Teddy's shoulder, and they gave him banana and some boiled egg; and he sat on all their laps one after the other, because every well-brought-up mongoose always hopes to be a house-mongoose some day and have rooms to run about in, and Rikki-tikki's mother (she used to live in the General's house at Segowlee) had carefully told Rikki what to do if ever he came across white men.

Then Rikki-tikki went out into the garden to see what was to be seen. It was a large garden, only half cultivated, with bushes as big as summer-houses of Marshal Niel roses, lime and orange trees, clumps of bamboos, and thickets of high grass. Rikki-tikki licked his lips. 'This is a splendid hunting-ground,' he said, and his tail grew bottle-brushy at the thought of it, and he scuttled up and down the garden, snuffing here and there till he heard very sorrowful voices in a thornbush.

It was Darzee, the tailor-bird, and his wife. They had made a beautiful nest by pulling two big leaves together and stitching them up the edges with fibres, and had filled the hollow with cotton and downy fluff. The nest swayed to and fro, as they sat on the rim and cried.

'What is the matter?' asked Rikki-tikki.

'We are very miserable,' said Darzee. 'One of our babies fell out of the nest yesterday, and Nag ate him.'

'H'm!' said Rikki-tikki, 'that is very sad – but I am a stranger here. Who is Nag?'

Darzee and his wife only cowered down in the nest without answering, for from the thick grass at the foot of the bush there came a low hiss – a horrid cold sound that made Rikki-tikki jump back two clear feet. Then inch by inch out of the grass rose up the head and spread hood of Nag, the big black cobra, and he was five feet long from tongue to tail. When he had lifted one-third of himself clear of the ground, he stayed balancing to and fro exactly as a dandelion-tuft balances in the wind, and he looked at Rikki-tikki with the wicked snake's eyes that never change their expression, whatever the snake may be thinking of.

'Who is Nag?' said he. '*I* am Nag. The great god Brahm put his mark upon all our people when the first cobra spread his hood to keep the sun off Brahm as he slept. Look, and be afraid!'

He spread out his hood more than ever, and Rikki-tikki saw the spectacle-mark on the back of it that looks exactly like the eye part of a hook-and-eye fastening. He was afraid for the minute; but it is impossible for a mongoose to stay frightened for any length of time, and though Rikki-tikki had never met a live cobra before, his mother had fed him on dead ones, and he knew that all a grown mongoose's business in life was to fight and eat snakes. Nag knew that too, and at the bottom of his cold heart he was afraid.

'Well,' said Rikki-tikki, and his tail began to fluff up again, 'marks or no marks, do you think it is right for you to eat fledglings out of a nest?'

Nag was thinking to himself, and watching the least little movement in the grass behind Rikki-tikki. He knew that mongooses in the garden meant death sooner or later for him and his family, but he wanted to get Rikki-tikki off his guard. So he dropped his head a little, and put it on one side.

'Let us talk,' he said. 'You eat eggs. Why should not I eat birds?'

'Behind you! Look behind you!' sang Darzee.

Rikki-tikki knew better than to waste time in staring. He jumped up in the air as high as he could go, and just under him whizzed by the head of Nagaina, Nag's wicked wife. She had crept up behind him as he was talking, to make an end of him; and he heard her savage hiss as the stroke missed. He came down almost across her back, and if he had been an old mongoose he

84

would have known that then was the time to break her back with one bite; but he was afraid of the terrible lashing return-stroke of the cobra. He bit, indeed, but did not bite long enough, and he jumped clear of the whisking tail, leaving Nagaina torn and angry.

'Wicked, wicked Darzee!' said Nag, lashing up as high as he could reach towards the nest in the thornbush; but Darzee had built it out of reach of snakes, and it only swayed to and fro.

Rikki-tikki felt his eyes growing red and hot (when a mongoose's eyes grow red, he is angry), and he sat back on his tail and hind legs like a little kangaroo, and looked all round him, and chattered with rage. But Nag and Nagaina had disappeared into the grass. When a snake misses its stroke, it never says anything or gives any sign of what it means to do next. Rikki-tikki did not care to follow them, for he did not feel sure that he could manage two snakes at once. So he trotted off to the gravel path near the house, and sat down to think. It was a serious matter for him.

If you read the old books of natural history, you will find they say that when the mongoose fights the snake and happens to get bitten, he runs off and eats some herb that cures him. That is not true. The victory is only a matter of quickness of eye and quickness of foot – snake's blow against mongoose's jump – and as no eye can follow the motion of a snake's head when it strikes, that makes things much more wonderful than any magic herb. Rikki-tikki knew he was a young mongoose, and it made him all the more pleased to think that he had managed to escape a blow from behind. It gave him confidence in himself, and when Teddy came running down the path, Rikki-tikki was ready to be petted.

But just as Teddy was stooping, something flinched a little in the dust, and a tiny voice said: 'Be careful. I am death!' It was Karait, the dusty brown snakeling that lies for choice on the dusty earth; and his bite is as dangerous as the cobra's. But he is so small that nobody thinks of him, and so he does the more harm to people.

Rikki-tikki's eyes grew red again, and he danced up to Karait with the peculiar rocking, swaying motion that he had inherited from his family. It looks very funny, but it is so perfectly balanced a gait that you can fly off from it at any angle you please; and in dealing with snakes this is an advantage. If Rikki-tikki had only known, he was doing a much more dangerous thing than fighting Nag, for Karait is so small, and can turn so quickly, that unless Rikki bit him close to the back of the head, he would get the return-stroke in his eye or lip. But Rikki did not know: his eyes were all red, and he rocked back and forth, looking for a good place to hold. Karait struck out. Rikki jumped sideways and tried to run in, but the wicked little dusty grey head lashed within a fraction of his shoulder, and he had to jump over the body, and the head followed his heels close.

Teddy shouted to the house: 'Oh, look here! Our mongoose is killing a snake'; and Rikki-tikki heard a scream from Teddy's mother. His father ran out with a stick, but by the time he came up, Karait had lunged out once too far, and Rikki-tikki had sprung, jumped on the snake's back, dropped his head far between his fore-legs, bitten as high up the back as he could get hold, and rolled away. That bite paralysed Karait, and Rikki-tikki was just going to eat him up from the tail, after the custom of his family at dinner, when he remembered that a full meal makes a slow mongoose, and if he wanted all his strength and quickness ready, he must keep himself thin.

He went away for a dust-bath under the castor-oil bushes, while Teddy's father beat the dead Karait. 'What is the use of that?' thought Rikki-tikki. 'I have settled it all.' And then Teddy's mother picked him up from the dust and hugged him, crying that he had saved Teddy from death, and Teddy's father said that he was a providence, and Teddy looked on with big scared eyes. Rikki-tikki was rather amused at all the fuss, which, of course, he did not understand. Teddy's mother might just as well have petted Teddy for playing in the dust. Rikki was thoroughly enjoying himself.

That night, at dinner, walking to and fro among the wine-glasses on the table, he could have stuffed himself three times over with nice things; but he remembered Nag and Nagaina, and though it was very pleasant to be patted and petted by Teddy's mother, and to sit on Teddy's shoulder, his eyes would get red from time to time, and he would go off into his long war-cry of '*Rikk-tikk-tikki-tikki-tchk!*'

Teddy carried him off to bed, and insisted on Rikki-tikki sleeping under his chin. Rikki-tikki was too well bred to bite or scratch, but as soon as Teddy was asleep he went off for his nightly walk round the house, and in the dark he ran up against Chuchundra, the muskrat, creeping round by the wall. Chuchundra is a broken-hearted little beast. He whimpers and cheeps all the night, trying to make up his mind to run into the middle of the room, but he never gets there.

'Don't kill me,' said Chuchundra, almost weeping. 'Rikki-tikki, don't kill me.'

'Do you think a snake-killer kills muskrats?' said Rikki-tikki scornfully.

'Those who kill snakes get killed by snakes,' said Chuchundra, more sorrowfully than ever. 'And how am I to be sure that Nag won't mistake me for you some dark night?'

'There's not the least danger,' said Rikki-tikki; 'but Nag is in the garden, and I know you don't go there.'

'My cousin Chua, the rat, told me –' said Chuchundra, and then he stopped.

'Told you what?'

'H'sh! Nag is everywhere, Rikki-tikki. You should have talked to Chua in the garden.'

'I didn't – so you must tell me. Quick, Chuchundra, or I'll bite you!'

Chuchundra sat down and cried till the tears rolled off his whiskers. 'I am a very poor man,' he sobbed. 'I never had spirit enough to run out into the middle of the room. H'sh! I mustn't tell you anything. Can't you *hear*, Rikki-tikki?'

Rikki-tikki listened. The house was as still as still, but he thought he could just catch the faintest *scratch-scratch* in the world – a noise as faint as that of a wasp walking on a window-pane – the dry scratch of a snake's scales on brickwork.

'That's Nag or Nagaina,' he said to himself; 'and he is crawling into the bath-room sluice. You're right, Chuchundra; I should have talked to Chua.'

He stole off to Teddy's bath-room, but there was nothing there, and then to Teddy's mother's bath-room. At the bottom of the smooth plaster wall there was a brick pulled out to make a sluice for the bathwater, and as Rikki-tikki stole in by the masonry curb where the bath is put, he heard Nag and Nagaina whispering together outside in the moonlight.

'When the house is emptied of people,' said Nagaina to her husband, '*he* will have to go away, and then the garden will be our own again. Go in quietly, and remember that the big man who killed Karait is the first one to bite. Then come out and tell me, and we will hunt for Rikki-tikki together.'

'But are you sure that there is anything to be gained by killing the people?' said Nag.

'Everything. When there were no people in the bungalow, did we have any mongoose in the garden? So long as the bungalow is empty, we are king and queen of the garden; and remember that as soon as our eggs in the melon-bed hatch (as they may tomorrow), our children will need room and quiet.'

'I had not thought of that,' said Nag. 'I will go, but there is no need that we should hunt for Rikki-tikki afterward. I will kill the big man and his wife, and the child if I can, and come away quietly. Then the bungalow will be empty, and Rikki-tikki will go.'

Rikki-tikki tingled all over with rage and hatred at this, and then Nag's head came through the sluice, and his five feet of cold body followed it. Angry as he was, Rikki-tikki was very frightened as he saw the size of the big cobra. Nag coiled himself up, raised his head, and looked into the bath-room in the dark, and Rikki could see his eyes glitter.

'Now, if I kill him here, Nagaina will know; and if I fight him on the open floor, the odds are in his favour. What am I to do?' said Rikki-tikki-tavi.

Nag waved to and fro, and then Rikki-tikki heard him drinking from the biggest water-jar that was used to fill the bath. 'That is good,' said the snake. 'Now, when Karait was killed, the big man had a stick. He may have that stick still, but when he comes in to bathe in the morning he will not have a stick. I shall wait here till he comes. Nagaina – do you hear me? – I shall wait here in the cool till daytime.'

There was no answer from outside, so Rikki-tikki knew Nagaina had gone away. Nag coiled himself down, coil by coil, round the bulge at the bottom of the water-jar, and Rikki-tikki stayed still as death. After an hour he began to move, muscle by muscle, towards the jar. Nag was asleep, and Rikki-tikki looked at his big back, wondering which would be the best place for a good hold. 'If I don't break his back at the first jump,' said Rikki, 'he can still fight; and if he fights – O Rikki!' He looked at the thickness of the neck below the hood, but that was too much for him; and a bite near the tail would only make Nag savage.

'It must be the head,' he said at last; 'the head above the hood; and when I am once there, I must not let go.'

Then he jumped. The head was lying a little clear of the water-jar, under the curve of it; and, as his teeth met, Rikki braced his back against the bulge of the red earthenware to hold down the head. This gave him just one second's purchase, and he made the most of it. Then he was battered to and fro as a rat is shaken by a dog – to and fro on the floor, up and down, and round in great circles; but his eyes were red, and he held on as the body cart-whipped over the floor, upsetting the tin dipper and the soapdish and the bath brush, and banged against the tin side of the bath. As he held he closed his jaws tighter and tighter, for he made sure he would be banged to death, and, for the honour of his family, he preferred to be found with his teeth locked. He was dizzy, aching, and felt shaken to pieces when something went off like a thunderclap just behind him; a hot wind knocked him senseless, and red fire singed his fur. The big man had been wakened by the noise, and had fired both barrels of a shot-gun into Nag just behind the hood.

Rikki-tikki held on with his eyes shut, for now he was quite sure he was dead; but the head did not move, and the big man picked him up and said: 'It's the mongoose again, Alice; the little chap has saved *our* lives now.' Then Teddy's mother came in with a very white face, and saw what was left of Nag, and Rikki-tikki dragged himself to Teddy's bedroom and spent half the rest of the night shaking himself tenderly to find out whether he really was broken into forty pieces, as he fancied.

When morning came he was very stiff, but well pleased with his doings. 'Now I have Nagaina to settle with, and she will be worse than five Nags, and there's no knowing when the eggs she spoke of will hatch. Goodness! I must go and see Darzee,' he said.

Without waiting for breakfast, Rikki-tikki ran to the thorn-bush where Darzee was singing a song of triumph at the top of his voice. The news of Nag's death was all over the garden, for the sweeper had thrown the body on the rubbish heap.

'Oh, you stupid tuft of feathers!' said Rikki-tikki angrily. 'Is this the time to sing?'

'Nag is dead – is dead – is dead!' sang Darzee. 'The valiant Rikki-tikki caught him by the head, and held fast. The big man brought the bang-stick, and Nag fell in two pieces! He will never eat my babies again.'

'All that's true enough; but where's Nagaina?' said Rikki-tikki, looking carefully round him.

'Nagaina came to the bath-room sluice and called for Nag,' Darzee went on; 'and Nag came out on the end of a stick – the sweeper picked him up on the end of a stick and threw him upon the rubbish-heap. Let us sing about the great, the red-eyed Rikki-tikki!' and Darzee filled his throat and sang.

'If I could get up to your nest, I'd roll all your babies out!' said Rikki-tikki. 'You don't know when to do the right thing at the right time. You're safe enough in your nest there, but it's war for me down here. Stop singing a minute, Darzee.'

'For the great, the beautiful Rikki-tikki's sake I will stop,' said Darzee. 'What is it, O Killer of the terrible Nag?'

'Where is Nagaina, for the third time?'

'On the rubbish heap by the stables, mourning for Nag. Great is Rikki-tikki with the white teeth.'

'Bother my white teeth! Have you ever heard where she keeps her eggs?'

'In the melon-bed, on the end nearest the wall, where the sun strikes nearly all day. She hid them there weeks ago.'

'And you never thought it worth while to tell me? The end nearest the wall, you said?'

'Rikki-tikki, you are not going to eat her eggs?'

'Not eat exactly; no. Darzee, if you have a grain of sense you will fly off to the stables and pretend that your wing is broken, and let Nagaina chase you away to this bush. I must get to the melon-bed, and if I went there now she'd see me.'

Darzee was a feather-brained little fellow who could never hold more than one idea at a time in his head; and just because he knew that Nagaina's children were born in eggs like his own, he didn't think at first that it was fair to kill them. But his wife was a sensible bird, and she knew that cobra's eggs meant young cobras later on; so she flew off from the nest, and left Darzee to keep the babies warm, and continue his song about the death of Nag. Darzee was very like a man in some ways.

She fluttered in front of Nagaina by the rubbish heap, and cried out, 'Oh, my wing is broken! The boy in the house threw a stone at me and broke it.' Then she fluttered more desperately than ever.

Nagaina lifted up her head and hissed, 'You warned Rikki-tikki when I would have killed him. Indeed and truly, you've chosen a bad place to be lame in.' And she moved towards Darzee's wife, slipping along over the dust.

'The boy broke it with a stone!' shrieked Darzee's wife.

'Well! It may be some consolation to you when you're dead to know that I shall settle accounts with the boy. My husband lies on the rubbish heap this morning, but before night the boy in the house will lie very still. What is the use of running away? I am sure to catch you. Little fool, look at me!'

Darzee's wife knew better than to do *that*, for a bird who looks at a snake's eyes get so frightened that she cannot move. Darzee's wife fluttered on, piping sorrowfully, and never leaving the ground, and Nagaina quickened her pace.

Rikki-tikki heard them going up the path from the stables, and he raced for the end of the melon-patch near the wall. There, in the warm litter about the melons, very cunningly hidden, he found twenty-five eggs, about the size of a bantam's eggs, but with whitish skin instead of shell.

'I was not a day too soon,' he said, for he could see the baby cobras curled up inside the skin, and he knew that the minute they were hatched they could each kill a man or a mongoose. He bit off the tops of the eggs as fast as he could, taking care to crush the young cobras, and turned over the litter from time to time to see whether he had missed any. At last there were only three eggs left, and Rikki-tikki began to chuckle to himself, when he heard Darzee's wife screaming.

'Rikki-tikki, I led Nagaina towards the house, and she has gone into the verandah, and – oh, come quickly – she means killing!'

Rikki-tikki smashed two eggs, and tumbled backward down the melon-bed with the third egg in his mouth, and scuttled to the verandah as hard as he could put foot to the ground. Teddy and his mother and father were there at early breakfast; but Rikki-tikki saw that they were not eating anything. They sat stone-still, and their faces were white. Nagaina was coiled up on the matting by Teddy's chair, within easy striking-distance of Teddy's bare leg, and she was swaying to and fro singing a song of triumph.

'Son of the big man that killed Nag,' she hissed, 'stay still. I am not ready yet. Wait a little. Keep very still, all you three. If you move I strike, and if you do not move I strike. Oh, foolish people, who killed my Nag!'

Teddy's eyes were fixed on his father, and all his father could do was to whisper, 'Sit still, Teddy. You mustn't move. Teddy, keep still.'

Then Rikki-tikki came up and cried: 'Turn round, Nagaina; turn and fight!'

'All in good time,' said she, without moving her eyes. 'I will settle my account with *you* presently. Look at your friends, Rikki-tikki. They are still and white; they are afraid. They dare not move, and if you come a step nearer I strike.'

'Look at your eggs,' said Rikki-tikki, 'in the melon-bed near the wall. Go and look, Nagaina.'

The big snake turned half round, and saw the egg on the verandah. 'Ah-h! Give it to me,' she said.

Rikki-tikki put his paws one on each side of the egg, and his eyes were blood-red. 'What price for a snake's egg? For a young cobra? For a young king-cobra? For the last – the very last of the brood? The ants are eating all the others down by the melon-bed.'

Nagaina spun clear round, forgetting everything for the sake of the one egg; and Rikki-tikki saw Teddy's father shoot out a big hand, catch Teddy by the shoulder, and drag him across the little table with the teacups, safe and out of reach of Nagaina.

'Tricked! Tricked! Tricked! *Rikk-tck-tck!*' chuckled Rikki-
tikki. 'The boy is safe, and it was I – I – I that caught Nag by the
hood last night in the bath-room.' Then he began to jump up and
down, all four feet together, his head close to the floor. 'He threw
me to and fro, but he could not shake me off. He was dead before
the big man blew him in two. I did it. *Rikki-tikki-tck-tck!* Come
then, Nagaina. Come and fight with me. You shall not be a
widow long.'

Nagaina saw that she had lost her chance of killing Teddy, and
the egg lay between Rikki-tikki's paws. 'Give me the egg, Rikki-
tikki. Give me the last of my eggs, and I will go away and never
come back,' she said, lowering her hood.

'Yes, you will go away, and you will never come back; for you
will go to the rubbish heap with Nag. Fight, widow! The big man
has gone for his gun! Fight!'

Rikki-tikki was bounding all round Nagaina, keeping just out
of reach of her stroke, his little eyes like hot coals. Nagaina
gathered herself together, and flung out at him. Rikki-tikki
jumped up and backward. Again and again and again she struck,
and each time her head came with a whack on the matting of the
verandah, and she gathered herself together like a watch-spring.
Then Rikki-tikki danced in a circle to get behind her, and
Nagaina spun round to keep her head to his head, so that the rustle
of her tail on the matting sounded like dry leaves blown along by
the wind.

He had forgotten the egg. It still lay on the verandah, and Nagaina came nearer and nearer to it, till at last, while Rikki-tikki was drawing breath, she caught it in her mouth, turned to the verandah steps, and flew like an arrow down the path with Rikki-tikki behind her. When the cobra runs for her life, she goes like a whiplash flicked across a horse's neck.

Rikki-tikki knew that he must catch her, or all the trouble would begin again. She headed straight for the long grass by the thorn-bush, and as he was running Rikki-tikki heard Darzee still singing his foolish little song of triumph. But Darzee's wife was wiser. She flew off her nest as Nagaina came along, and flapped her wings about Nagaina's head. If Darzee had helped they might have turned her; but Nagaina only lowered her hood and went on. Still, the instant's delay brought Rikki-tikki up to her, and as she plunged into the rathole where she and Nag used to live, his little white teeth were clenched on her tail, and he went down with her – and very few mongooses, however wise and old they may be, care to follow a cobra into its hole. It was dark in the hole; and Rikki-tikki never knew when it might open out and give Nagaina room to turn and strike at him. He held on savagely, and struck out his feet to act as brakes on the dark slope of the hot, moist earth.

Then the grass by the mouth of the hole stopped waving, and Darzee said: 'It is all over with Rikki-tikki! We must sing his death song. Valiant Rikki-tikki is dead! For Nagaina will surely kill him underground.'

So he sang a very mournful song that he made up on the spur of the minute, and just as he got to the most touching part the grass quivered again, and Rikki-tikki, covered with dirt, dragged himself out of the hole leg by leg, licking his whiskers. Darzee stopped with a little shout. Rikki-tikki shook some of the dust out of his fur and sneezed.

'It is all over,' he said. 'The widow will never come out again.' And the red ants that live between the grass stems heard him, and began to troop down one after another to see if he had spoken the truth.

Rikki-tikki curled himself up in the grass and slept where he was – slept and slept till it was late in the afternoon, for he had done a hard day's work.

'Now,' he said, when he awoke, 'I will go back to the house. Tell the Coppersmith, Darzee, and he will tell the garden that Nagaina is dead.'

The Coppersmith is a bird who makes a noise exactly like the beating of a little hammer on a copper pot; and the reason he is always making it is because he is the town crier to every Indian garden, and tells all the news to everybody who cares to listen. As Rikki-tikki went up the path, he heard his 'attention' notes like a tiny dinner-gong; and then the steady '*Ding-dong-tock!* Nag is dead – *dong!* Nagaina is dead! *Ding-dong-tock!*' That set all the birds in the garden singing, and the frogs croaking; for Nag and Nagaina used to eat frogs as well as little birds.

When Rikki got to the house, Teddy and Teddy's mother (she still looked very white, for she had been fainting) and Teddy's father came out and almost cried over him; and that night he ate all that was given him till he could eat no more, and went to bed on Teddy's shoulder, where Teddy's mother saw him when she came to look late at night.

'He saved our lives and Teddy's life,' she said to her husband. 'Just think, he saved all our lives!'

Rikki-tikki woke up with a jump, for all the mongooses are light sleepers.

'Oh, it's you,' said he. 'What are you bothering for? All the cobras are dead; and if they weren't, I'm here.'

Rikki-tikki had a right to be proud of himself; but he did not grow too proud, and he kept that garden as a mongoose should keep it, with tooth and jump and spring and bite, till never a cobra dared show its head inside the walls.

Swiss Family Robinson

The story of 'The Swiss Family Robinson' was originally told by Johann David Wyss (1743–1818) to his four sons. He later wrote it down so that he could read it aloud to them. When one of these sons, Johann Rudolf Wyss (1781–1830) grew up, he found the manuscript, revised it, and gave it to a publisher. It has been popular with children throughout the world ever since. In this part of the story the family have escaped from their wrecked ship to a desert island and now the father, the eldest son – Fred, and Turk, their dog, set off to explore the island.

WE rose at dawn, and my wife and I talked together as to our plans for the future. We both thought that the first thing to be done was to make a search for our lost comrades. We could not all, of course, go, and I proposed that Fred, as the eldest and strongest, should go with me, while the others stayed with their mother.

'We will leave Bill with you,' I said, 'and take Turk with us.'

Fred took a gun, a game-bag, and an axe, while we each carried a pair of pistols in our belt.

The banks of the stream were so steep and rocky that we had to go a long way up before we found a place where we could cross. When we reached the other side, we passed through very long grass, which was partly dried up by the sun, and we were very glad to turn down towards the beach again.

'If I were to fire my gun from time to time,' said Fred, 'the sailors might hear us, if any of them have taken shelter here about.'

'Very likely,' I answered, 'but at the same time you might bring a band of savages upon us.'

By and by we left the coast, and struck inland, coming, after two hours' heavy walking, to a grove of coconut palms, where we halted beside a clear stream that ran through the wood. Bright birds flew around, and chirped and sang, and played a thousand tricks.

Fred fancied he saw a monkey on one of the trees, and rose and went forward to watch it more closely. In doing so he stumbled over a small round ball on the ground, and fell.

'What is it?' he asked, as he brought the ball to me. 'Is it a bird's nest, or an ostrich's egg?'

'Your nest,' I answered, laughing, 'is simply a coconut.'

A blow from the axe cut through the outer husk and broke the shell. But we found that as the fruit was fully ripe, it was no longer good to eat.

'I always thought that coconuts were full of milk,' said Fred, as he looked at the kernel.

'The milk is found only in half-ripe nuts,' I told him. 'The riper the fruit gets the more the milk is used up, and the kernel is formed as the milk dries.'

We began to search for another coconut, and, after some time, we found one which we ate with pleasure.

A little farther on, Fred's keen eyes lighted on a great calabash-tree laden with fruit. But he could not understand what the curious swellings on the trunk were.

'Here is one,' he cried. 'I should say it is an ordinary gourd, only the rind appears much softer.'

'It is a kind of gourd,' I replied, 'and from the shell we shall be able to make cups, and plates, and bottles.'

'But you won't be able to cook in them, father,' said Fred. 'They will never stand the heat of the fire.'

'Oh,' said I, 'we can do as the savages do. They cut the gourds into halves, and to each half they attach a handle. Then they fill each half with water and put in whatever they wish to cook – flesh or fish, as the case may be – just as you would do into a saucepan. They then drop into the gourd red-hot stones till the water boils, and so the meat is cooked while the gourd is unharmed.'

As we talked, each of us tried to cut a calabash into some useful dish. But the tough skin was too much for Fred's knife, which often slipped when he tried to cut. Then I showed him how to do it by tying a piece of string tightly round the gourd and striking the fruit with the handle of my knife, when the nut broke up into two unequal parts. Soon we had as many soup-bowls as we could well carry.

'Fancy,' cried Fred, in his joy, 'we shall have plates, dishes, and cups. Will not mother be glad?'

Then he made a small spoon for his little brother, and two large dishes for Turk and Bill, and we filled them all with fine sand so as to keep them in proper shape while they dried. We buried the whole of this new kitchen ware in the sand, and marked the place where we left it, so as to be able to find it on our return.

We walked on for about four hours more, till we came to a little tongue of land which ran out into the sea, and on which was a hill from whose top we might have a wide view.

We climbed the hill and looked around. On every side Nature lay before us in all her beauty. The sunlight played on the rich green meadows, and on the wavelets of the now calm sea; but no trace of human being was to be seen anywhere.

'We must make up our minds,' I said, 'to live on this island, and to make ourselves as happy as possible.'

'Dear father,' cried Fred, 'we will never complain. So long as you and mother keep well, what can my brothers and I want more?'

Turning down a glade, we came to a clump of tall reeds, through which we made Turk lead the way, so as to warn us of any hidden danger. We each cut some of the reeds, and found our hands covered with a sweet sap.

'I have no doubt, Fred,' said I, 'that these reeds are sugar-canes. We will take a few back with us.'

'Won't mother be delighted?' cried Fred, who cut down more canes than he could carry.

'Make a small bundle,' I said, 'and then we shall go back to the palm-grove.'

We had no sooner seated ourselves under the shade, than a troop of large monkeys came out chattering and grinning at us on the coconut trees around.

'Now,' cried I, 'we will have some dessert.'

I gathered a handful of stones, and began to throw them at the monkeys, which got into a great rage, and, in return, pelted us with coconuts.

We opened the shells with an axe, and enjoyed the dessert which had been got with so little trouble. Then I took up such of the nuts as had long stalks, and threw them over my shoulder, while Fred lifted his sugar-canes and we set out for our tent.

ON our way back, Turk came suddenly upon another troop of monkeys, one of which he killed. All the rest ran off except a young one, which we took with us, and which we seated on Turk's back when we came near the tent.

'We shall return,' said I, 'like showmen at fairs; your brothers will be delighted at the sight.'

'Yes,' answered Fred; 'and Jack, who is so fond of making faces, will now have a model in the little monkey.'

We chatted away about monkeys and their funny ways till we came to the stream we had crossed in the morning. The first to greet us was Bill, whose deep bark was answered by Turk with such energy that the little monkey in fear sprang upon Fred's shoulder and showed no wish to get down again.

We had brought with us the nuts, and the canes, and the calabashes, and were quite glad when we got safe to the 'home' side of the stream.

The children jumped for joy at sight of the monkey, which still clung tightly to Fred.

'A monkey! A real live monkey!' they all cried at once. 'Where did you get it? What a nice little fellow he is!'

Jack took my gun, Ernest seized the coconuts, Frank carried the

calabashes, and my wife took charge of the game-bag. Fred, who
had the sugarcanes, placed the monkey once again on Turk's back.

When we reached the tent, we found signs of a good meal
waiting us. Fish were cooking on a wooden spit held up by two
forked sticks; on the other side of the fire a goose was roasting;
while over the flames hung an iron pot, which gave promise of
some excellent soup. My wife, too, had found in a chest we had
brought ashore a few Dutch cheeses packed in tin cases. Hungry
travellers could wish for no better welcome.

The sun went down almost as we finished our meal, and soon
we all turned into our tent to sleep. We had not been long asleep
when we were roused by the cackling of the hens overhead and
the loud barking of the dogs outside.

Rushing out with our guns, we saw by the light of the moon
that a whole troop of jackals had fallen upon our two brave dogs,
which snapped at their foes on all sides, and now and then dealt
blows with their paws.

'Now, Fred,' I cried, 'let us both fire together. Take good aim.'

Our shots rang out, two jackals rolled over on the sand dead,
and the others took to flight. We had peace for the rest of the
night.

Next morning it was agreed that Fred and I should pay a visit to
the wreck, in order to save, if possible, the livestock and the food
that were still on board. Before starting we set up a rough flagstaff
on the shore, and hoisted a spare piece of sail-cloth, which would
serve as a signal between the ship and the shore. If the flag were
pulled down, Fred and I would hasten to land with all speed.

We found that the animals we had left on board were alive, and

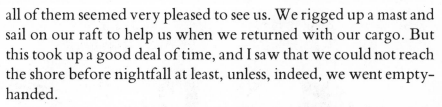

all of them seemed very pleased to see us. We rigged up a mast and sail on our raft to help us when we returned with our cargo. But this took up a good deal of time, and I saw that we could not reach the shore before nightfall at least, unless, indeed, we went empty-handed.

'Perhaps it would be better,' I said to Fred, 'to spend the night on board.'

'Then let us hoist a flag on the stump of the foremast,' said he, 'to let mother know that all is well.'

This done, we spent the rest of the day in throwing out the ballast from the tubs, and filling them with useful things. We spoiled the ship like Vandals, and soon gathered a large amount of booty. In the midst of what to us seemed priceless wealth, choice was very difficult.

First of all I made sure of a good supply of fire-arms, powder, and lead – to serve us in hunting, and to defend us against wild beasts. We took knives and forks, spoons, and cooking utensils, of which we had great need.

In the captain's cabin we found some silver covers, plates, and a hamper of good wine. From the storeroom we brought out hams, sausages, and several sacks of grain. To these we added a barrel of sulphur, some matches and cord, and a roll of canvas.

When night fell, a large fire burning on the rocks told us that all was well at home, and we, in turn, hung up the great ship lanterns to tell that we were safe.

Next morning we were early astir and on deck. Our first thought was as to ways and means of getting the animals ashore.

'Let us throw the sow into the water,' said Fred, 'her fat and her great size will buoy her up, and we can tow her afterwards.'

'That is all very well,' said I; 'but how about the sheep and the goats?'

'If we tie some empty kegs,' said Fred, 'and a few bits of wood to their sides, they should be able to swim to land.'

We tried the plan first with one of the sheep, to which we fastened two floats, and then flung it into the sea. The poor creature sank, and I thought it would never come up again. But at length it rose to the surface, swam a little, and then floated.

'Now,' I cried, when I saw this, 'we shall get them all ashore; we shall save the whole lot.'

But I wished very much to get back the sheep for the present. So Fred, taking a float, let himself down into the water. He threw a rope round the neck of the sheep and drew it to the side of the ship. We soon had it on board again, and we set to work with our plan.

After a deal of trouble, we got all the animals fitted with floats, and drove them into the water through a large hole in the side of the vessel, or shoved them over the bulwarks into the sea. They went into the water with a great splash and sank quickly, but they all came to the surface again, and floated between their casks.

We ourselves did not lose a moment, but jumped into our boat and cut the cables. We were soon right in the middle of our strange herd, and picked up the cords we had fastened to each animal. These we fixed to the stern of our craft, and thus drew the whole of them with us safely to land.

As we neared the shore a monster fish hove in sight, and, as I feared it was a shark and might seize some of the animals, I made Fred shoot at it. He fired with such good aim that the monster at once dived and made off, leaving a long trace of blood in his wake.

The wind carried us right to the little bay, and I steered to a spot where our animals could easily get ashore. We cut the cords, and the beasts gladly leaped on land, where Jack busied himself taking off their strange lifebuoys.

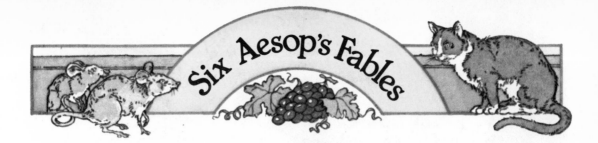

The Mice Meeting

ONCE upon a time a number of mice called a meeting to decide upon the best means of ridding themselves of a cat that had killed many of their relations.

Various plans were discussed and rejected, until at last a young mouse proposed that a bell should be hung round the tyrant's neck, in future, so that they would have warning of her movements and be able to escape.

The suggestion was received joyfully by nearly all, but an old mouse, who had sat silent for some time, got up and said: 'While I consider the plan to be a very clever one, and feel sure that it would prove to be quite successful if carried out, I should like to know who is going to put a bell on the cat?'

It is easier to make a suggestion than to carry it out.

The Town Mouse & the Country Mouse

ONCE upon a time a country mouse who had a friend in town invited him to pay him a visit in the country.

The invitation being duly accepted, the country mouse, though plain and rough in his habits of living, opened his heart in honour of an old friend. There was not a carefully stored-up morsel that he did not bring forth out of his larder – peas and barley, cheese-parings and nuts – hoping by quantity to make up what he feared was lacking in quality.

DAVID
FRANKLAND.

The town mouse, who was used to more dainty food, at first picked a bit here and a bit there, while the host sat nibbling a blade of barley straw.

At length he exclaimed, 'How is it, my good friend, that you can endure the dullness of this life? You are living like a toad in a hole. You can't really prefer these lonely rocks and woods to streets filled with shops and carriages and men! Believe me, you are wasting your time here. We must make the most of life while it lasts. A mouse, you know, does not live for ever. So come with me, and I'll show you life and the town.'

These fine words were too much for the simple country mouse, and he agreed to go with his friend to town.

It was late in the evening when the two crept into the city, and midnight before they reached the great house where the town mouse lived. Here were couches of crimson velvet, carvings in ivory, everything, in fact, that showed wealth and comfort. On the table were the remains of a splendid meal, and it was now the turn of the town mouse to play the host; he ran to and fro to supply his friend's wants, pressed dish upon dish and titbit upon titbit, as though he were waiting on a king.

The country mouse, for his part, tried to appear quite at home, and blessed the good fortune that had brought such a change in his way of life; when, in the midst of his enjoyment, as he was wondering how he could have been content with the poor food he was used to at home, suddenly the door opened and a party of ladies and gentlemen entered the room.

The two friends jumped from the table in the greatest fright, and hid themselves in the first corner they could reach. When the room was quiet again they ventured to creep out, but the barking of dogs drove them back in still greater terror than before.

At length, when all the household was asleep, the country mouse stole out from his hiding-place, and, bidding his host good-bye, whispered in his ear, 'My good friend, this fine mode of living may do for those who like it, but give me barley and bread in peace and security before the tastiest feast where fear and care lie in wait.'

*A humble life with peace and quiet
is better than a splendid one with danger and risk.*

The Fox & the Goat

ONE day a fox fell into a well, and wondered how he could get out again. At last a goat came along, and, feeling thirsty, he asked Reynard if the water was good.

The fox saw his chance, and, pretending that he was swimming for pleasure, replied, 'Yes come down, my friend; the water is so nice that I cannot drink enough of it, and there is plenty for both of us.' So the goat jumped in, and the artful fox, making use of his friend's horns, quickly sprang out.

When he was safely on top of the well, he coolly remarked to the poor goat, 'Had you half as much brains as you have beard, you would have looked before you leaped.'

Think before you act.

The Bees, the Drones & the Wasps

SOME bees built a comb in the hollow trunk of an oak-tree, but some drones claimed that they had built it, and that it belonged to them.

The case was brought into court before Judge Wasp, who, knowing the habits of both parties, addressed them thus:

'The plaintiffs and defendants are so much alike in shape and colour that it is difficult to say which are the rightful owners, and the case has very properly been brought before me. Now I think that justice will best be served now by following the plan which I propose. Let each party take a hive and build up a new comb, so that from the shape of the cells and the taste of the honey it will be quite clear to whom the comb in dispute belongs.'

The bees readily agreed to the wasp's plan, but the drones, on the other hand, would not do so.

Whereupon the wasp gave judgment: 'It is clear now who made the comb, and who cannot make it; the court gives judgment in favour of the bees.'

We may know a tree by its fruit.

The Fox & the Lion

WHEN a fox who had never seen a lion met one for the first time he was so terrified that he almost died of fright. When he met him the second time, however, he was still afraid, but managed to hide his fear. But when he saw him for the third time he felt so brave that he went up and began to talk to him as though they were old friends.

Familiarity breeds contempt.

The Charger & the Ass

A CHARGER, beautifully groomed and equipped, one day came galloping along a road, exciting the envy of a poor ass who was trudging along with a heavy load.

'Get out of my way!' cried the proud horse, 'or I shall trample you under my feet.'

The ass said nothing, but quietly moved to one side of the road.

Not long afterwards the charger went to the wars, and was badly wounded on the battlefield. Unfit for any further military service, he was sent home to work on the farm.

The ass saw him there painfully dragging a heavy wagon. 'Ah!' said he to himself, 'I need not have envied him in his pride; but for that he would have a true friend to help him in his need and lighten his load.'

He who despises a humble friend may be doing an ill turn to himself.

Rapunzel

ONCE upon a time there lived a man and his wife who very much wished to have a child, but for a long time in vain. Finally, the wife became pregnant. These people had a little window in the back part of their house, out of which they could see a beautiful garden, which was full of fine flowers and vegetables; but it was surrounded by a high wall, and no one dared to go in, because it belonged to a witch, who possessed great power, and who was feared by the whole world.

One day the woman stood at this window looking into the garden, and there she saw a bed which was filled with the most beautiful radishes, and which seemed so fresh and green that she felt quite glad, and a great desire to eat them seized her. This wish tormented her daily, and as she knew that she could not have them, she fell ill, and looked very pale and miserable. This frightened her husband, who asked her, 'What is the matter, my dear wife?'

'Ah!' she replied, 'if I cannot get any of those radishes to eat out of the garden behind the house, I shall die!'

Her husband, loving her very much, thought, 'rather than let my wife die, I must fetch her some radishes, whatever the cost.'

So, in the gloom of the evening, he climbed the wall of the witch's garden, and, snatching a handful of radishes in great haste, brought them to his wife, who made herself a salad with them, which she enjoyed very much. However, they were so nice and so well flavoured, that the next day after she felt the same desire for the third time, and could not get any rest, her husband was obliged to promise her some more.

So, in the evening, he made himself ready, and began clambering up the wall; but oh! how terribly frightened he was, for there he saw the old witch standing before him. 'How dare you,' she began, looking at him with a frightful scowl – 'how dare you climb over into my garden to take away my radishes like a thief? Evil shall happen to you for this.'

'Ah!' replied he, 'let pardon be granted before justice. I have only done this from a great necessity: my wife saw your radishes from her window, and took such a fancy to them that she would have died if she had not eaten them.' So then the witch ran after him in a fury, saying, 'If she behaves as you say, I will let you take away all the radishes you please; but I make one condition – you must give me your child. All shall go well with it, and I will care for it like a mother.'

In his anxiety the man consented, and when the child was born the witch appeared at the same time, gave the child the name 'Rapunzel,' and took it away with her.

Rapunzel grew to be the most beautiful child under the sun, and when she was twelve years old the witch shut her up in a tower, which stood in a forest, and had neither stairs nor door, and only one little window just at the top. When the witch wished to enter, she stood beneath, and called out:

'Rapunzel! Rapunzel!
Let down your hair.'

For Rapunzel had long and beautiful hair, as fine as spun gold, and, as soon as she heard the witch's voice, she unbound her tresses, opened the window, and then the hair fell down and the witch climbed up by it.

After a couple of years had passed away, it happened that the king's son was riding through the wood, and came by the tower. There he heard a song so beautiful that he stood still and listened.

It was Rapunzel, who, to pass the time of her loneliness away, was exercising her sweet voice. The king's son wished to ascend to her, and looked for a door in the tower, but he could not find one.

So he rode home, but the song had touched his heart so much that he went every day to the forest and listened to it; and as he stood one day behind a tree, he saw the witch come up, and heard her call out:

'Rapunzel! Rapunzel!
Let down your hair.'

Then Rapunzel let down her tresses, and the witch mounted up. 'Is that the ladder on which one must climb? Then I will try my luck too,' said the prince; and the following day, as he felt quite lonely, he went to the tower, and said:

> 'Rapunzel! Rapunzel!
> Let down your hair.'

Then the tresses fell down, and he climbed up.

Rapunzel was very much frightened at first when a man came in, for she had never seen one before; but the king's son talked in a loving way to her, and told how his heart had been so moved by her singing that he had no peace until he had seen her himself.

So Rapunzel lost her terror, and when he asked her if she would have him for a husband, and she saw that he was young and handsome, she thought, 'I would like to marry him.' So, saying 'Yes,' she put her hand within his. 'I will willingly go with you, but I know not how I am to descend. When you come, bring with you a skein of silk each time, out of which I will weave a ladder, and when it is ready I will come down by it, and you must take me upon your horse.'

Then they agreed that they should never meet till the evening, as the witch came in the daytime. The old woman found out nothing, until one day Rapunzel innocently said, 'Tell me, madam, how it happens you find it more difficult to come up to me than the king's young son, who climbs up in a moment!'

'Oh, you wicked child!' exclaimed the witch, 'what do I hear? I thought I had separated you from all the world, and yet you have deceived me.' And, seizing Rapunzel's beautiful hair in a fury, she gave her a couple of blows with her left hand, and, taking a pair of scissors in her right, *snip, snap*, she cut off all her beautiful tresses, and they fell upon the ground. Then she was so hard-hearted that she took the poor maiden into a great desert, and left her to die in great misery and grief.

But in the evening of the same day on which she had carried off Rapunzel, the old witch tied the shorn tresses so securely to the window-latch that when the king's son came, and called out:

> *'Rapunzel! Rapunzel!*
> *Let down your hair.'*

she let them down. The prince mounted, but when he got to the top he found, not his dear Rapunzel, but the witch, who looked at him with furious and wicked eyes.

'Aha!' she exclaimed scornfully, 'you would fetch your dear wife; but the beautiful bird sits no longer in her nest, singing; the cat has taken her away, and will now scratch out your eyes. To you Rapunzel is lost; you will never see her again.'

The prince lost his senses with grief at these words, and sprang out of the window of the tower in his bewilderment. He escaped with his life, but the thorns into which he fell put out his eyes. So he wandered, blind, in the forest, eating nothing but berries and roots, and doing nothing but weep and lament for the loss of his dear wife.

He wandered about in great misery, for some few years, and at last arrived at the desert where Rapunzel, who had given birth to

twins – a boy and girl – lived in great sorrow. Hearing a voice which he thought he knew, he followed in its direction, and, as he approached, Rapunzel recognised him, and fell into his arms and wept. Two of her tears moistened his eyes, and they became clear again, so that he could see as well as ever.

Then he led her away to his kingdom, where he was received with great demonstrations of joy, and where they lived for a long time, contented and happy.

What became of the old witch no one ever knew.

The Ballad of Jenny the Mare

I'LL sing you a song, and a merry, merry song,
  Concerning our Yorkshire Jen;
Who never yet ran with horse or mare,
  That ever she cared for a pin.

When first she came to Newmarket town,
  The sportsmen all view'd her around;
All the cry was, 'Alas, poor wench,
  Thou never can run this ground!'

When they came to the starting-post,
  The Mare look'd very smart;
And let them all say what they will,
  She never lost her start.

When they got to the two-mile post,
  Poor Jenny was cast behind:
She was cast behind, she was cast behind,
  All for to take her wind.

When they got to the three-mile post,
    The Mare look'd very pale –
SHE LAID DOWN HER EARS ON HER BONNY NECK,
    AND BY THEM ALL DID SHE SAIL;

'Come follow me, come follow me,
    All you that run so neat;
And ere that you catch me again,
    I'll make you all to sweat.'

When she got to the winning-post,
    The people all gave a shout;
And Jenny click'd up her lily-white foot,
    And jumped like any buck.

The Jockey said to her, 'This race you have run,
    This race for me you have got;
You could gallop it all over again,
    When the rest could hardly trot!'

The Twelve Labours of Hercules

The story of Hercules and his many adventures is one of the greatest in the tales of ancient Greece and Rome. Here it is retold by the American writer, Nathaniel Hawthorne (1804–1864), whose easy and readable versions of classical myths have helped generations of boys and girls to enjoy the adventure and excitement in those remarkable stories.

HERCULES was the son of Jupiter, king of the gods. Juno, queen of the goddesses, had children of her own, and she hated Hercules, from the moment of his birth, because Jupiter loved him more than he loved her children.

When he was eight months old she had two snakes put near him, to kill him. Hercules, however, strong as a man even in his babyhood, strangled the monsters before they could harm him. Juno then tried, as he grew up, to injure him in other ways. At last she brought upon him an illness that made him mad for a time, and when he was not in his right mind he offended the gods by some evil act.

But as soon as his senses returned to him the thought of what he had done filled him with deep sorrow.

'What can I do,' he cried in his great distress, 'to wash away the stain of this sin?'

Then a voice from heaven said to him: 'For twelve years you must obey the commands of a king named Eurystheus.

'You will have to do for him twelve very difficult and dangerous labours. When you have faithfully and patiently obeyed him you will be honoured among men, and rewarded at the end of your life with a place in heaven among the gods.'

On the very day that Hercules started on his journey in life along Virtue's pathway, a messenger came to order him to appear before Eurystheus. Hercules went boldly to the palace, and said he was ready to do all that was required of him. The crafty king received him with honour, and spoke kindly words to the young hero. But he had made up his mind to give Hercules such difficult tasks to do that he would either be killed in the attempt, or be laughed at by gods and men for failing.

The first of the twelve labours of Hercules was to kill the lion of Nemea that was ravaging a district in the east of Greece. Many an attempt had been made, but without success, to destroy this monster, for fear of which even armed men did not dare at night-time to wander away from their homes.

As soon as Hercules knew in what part the lion was last seen, he boldly went forth to do his duty. In a rocky valley he spied the creature. As he approached with his bow ready strung and an arrow fitted in its place, the animal lashed its tail to and fro in fury, while its roaring shook the ground and echoed among the mountain peaks.

Before the lion had time to spring, Hercules shot an arrow at it, and then, unfastening the club which hung at his side, advanced boldly. Roaring with pain from the wound of the arrow, the creature glared fiercely at him for a few moments, and then bounded away in the direction of its cave in the mountain side.

Hercules went after the lion in swift pursuit, and when he saw it enter the cave he followed. With no light to guide him, except the glare of two bright eyes shining like stars in the darkness, the hero rushed forward. Seizing the lion by the throat with one hand, with a few swift, powerful blows from the club he soon killed it. Thus did he bring the first of his labours to a successful close.

Then he placed the dead lion across his shoulders, and, amidst the joyous shouts of the citizens, walked boldly to the royal court and threw the huge body in triumph at the feet of the king. Eurystheus was amazed at this sign of the strength and courage of Hercules. He felt so much dread at the sight of one who could do so mighty a deed, that he gave orders for the hero never to be admitted again within the city gates. All directions for the future labours would be given him outside the walls. Further than this, the faint-hearted king made a house of brass, in which he could shut himself safely whenever Hercules drew near to the city.

The second labour of Hercules was to destroy the seven-headed Hydra. He first attacked it with arrows, but as these glanced off the monster's hide without causing a wound, he threw aside his bow and unslung his club. At each of his heavy, swinging blows he knocked off one of the Hydra's heads.

To his dismay, as soon as one head was destroyed, two others at once sprang up in its place. The more he wounded it the fiercer and stronger it grew. Then he called upon a friend who stood watching the combat to make an iron red hot, and, as each head was crushed, to burn the root at the neck. This plan succeeded, and Hercules was hailed joyfully as victor by the people whom he had delivered from the deadly monster.

THE third labour of Hercules was to capture alive a stag famous for its swiftness, its golden horns, and its feet of brass. For a whole year he followed it through the valleys, over the mountains, and across the rivers, hoping to make the animal lame by wounding it with an arrow. But he could never get within bowshot, and at last had to set a trap and wait patiently until the stag got entangled in it.

Hercules was now bidden to capture and carry away alive a wild boar which was causing great loss to life and property. The chase lasted for several hours, and was only ended when the creature tumbled into a snow-filled hollow and was caught in a noose of strong rope which Hercules threw over its head. King

Eurystheus was so terrified when he saw the hero approaching the royal city with the struggling, grunting boar on his back, that he shut himself up in his house of brass, and hid there for many days.

For the fifth task Hercules was ordered to make pure and sweet the stables of King Augeas, where three thousand oxen had lived for thirty-nine years without the place being once cleaned. It seemed impossible that the work could be done by one man. But Hercules, who was clever as well as strong, spent several months in cutting a new channel for the stream which flowed near to the stables. He changed the course of the river, so that it flowed as a rushing torrent right through the stables, carrying away to the sea the mountain-like heaps of refuse.

To the wonder of Augeas, the place was made clean and wholesome in a few hours. But when Hercules asked for the three hundred oxen which had been promised him if he did the work, the king refused to keep his word. He said that the stables had been cleansed by the river and not by Hercules.

The sixth and seventh labours were the killing of some terrible birds which fed on human flesh, and the capture of a wild bull which had gored to death many people in one of the islands of Greece. Then Hercules prepared for his eighth task. This was to seize the horses of a tyrant king named Diomedes, who for years had been a terror both to his own people and to strangers. Any visitor to the country was made prisoner, and thrown to be devoured by the king's horses, which fed on human flesh; and if one of his subjects chanced to offend him, the same horrible fate was his.

As soon as Hercules reached the palace of the tyrant, he challenged him to single combat. Killing him after a swift and sharp struggle, he threw the king's body into the stables to be devoured by his own horses. Then he boldly stepped into the midst of the fierce creatures, fastened them together by strong straps head to head, and drove them to the mountains. There, in course of time, many of them were killed by lions.

The ninth labour of Hercules was to conquer the Amazons, a nation of strong and warlike women, and to bring back as a sign of victory the girdle of gold and gems worn by their queen. These women warriors were feared by the best armies of men for their skill in the use of the bow and in throwing the javelin.

Hercules made it known all over Greece that he was going to fight the Amazons, and many brave men, eager for adventure, joined him. The Amazons fought on horseback, as was their custom, and the Greeks on foot. In the battle Hercules was successful, but, of all his labours, it proved one of the hardest and most dangerous.

The hero now set to work upon his tenth labour. This was to kill the three-headed giant known as Geryon, who was guarded by a dog as hideous as himself, and to drive away his numerous flocks, which fed upon human flesh. Before Hercules could begin this work he had to take a tiring journey, along the whole length of the Mediterranean and the Straits of Gibraltar, to the west coast of Africa. Months passed before he reached the land where Geryon lived. Even then he had to cross great mountains, and to follow the windings of long valleys, before he could find the monster.

But at last he was rewarded by seeing the terrible creature, with his dog by his side, sitting at the entrance to a great cavern. Both Geryon and his companion rushed upon Hercules so suddenly that he had not time to use his bow. A fearful struggle took place, the monster and the dog against the man. But soon the hideous two lay dead at the feet of their conqueror. The tenth labour of Hercules ended when he drove the flocks of Geryon to the mountain slopes, there to be devoured by the lions of Africa.

AFTER the slaying of Geryon and the dog, Hercules returned to Greece by way of the mainland of Europe, a long and toilsome journey. But he had no time to rest after his great labours, for, on the day of his arrival home, a messenger met him from King Eurystheus, with orders to start at once in search of the golden apples from the garden of the Hesperides.

The Hesperides were three beautiful maidens whose work was to guard the tree bearing the golden apples presented by Jupiter to the queen of the gods. The maidens were assisted in their task by a dragon, over whose huge body sprouted a hundred hideous heads.

It was a dangerous task, and the distance was great, for the apples grew in that far-off Africa from which Hercules had only just returned. But with a brave heart, not giving himself one day's rest, he set forth again to Africa to do his duty.

He had not the faintest idea in which part of Africa to look for the apples, but it was whispered to him by a friendly god that Nereus, one of the lesser gods, whose home was in the sea, could advise him in which direction to go. Now Nereus was very cunning, and, when he saw any one coming to ask him a question, it was his custom to take the form of a fish and swim far away beyond hearing.

But Hercules was lucky enough to catch Nereus when he was having a midday nap upon a rock, and he held him firmly until he had answered every question. Then, with a light heart, our hero travelled towards Africa. Having landed in the north, he was able, through what had been told him by Nereus, to reach the garden of the golden apples. How to get the treasures was now his chief difficulty; if he won the fight with the dragon, there still remained the three fair maidens to oppose him, and the greatest hero of his time could not very well lift a weapon against three girls.

While he was thus wondering what he had better do, he happened to meet a giant named Atlas. This giant was forced to carry the heavens upon his shoulders as a punishment for having once taken part in a battle against the gods.

'Tell me, great Atlas,' said he, 'how I may get into the garden where the golden apples grow.' 'Ah,' replied Atlas, 'all the guidance in the world would not bring you into that magic garden. But if you will carry my burden for a while, I will gladly go myself and obtain the golden apples for you.'

'That I will gladly do,' cried the hero; and, in a moment, the giant bent his knees and placed the load of the heavens upon the shoulders of Hercules. There he meant it to remain, for he was a cunning giant, and had grown tired of his weary burden. It did not take him long to reach the garden and pluck the golden apples. As soon as he had returned, he placed the sacred treasures in the hands of Hercules. Then, laughing with joy at being free from his heavy burden, he began to walk merrily away.

'Stay but for a little while,' shouted the astonished Hercules; 'if I am to carry your load, place it more comfortably upon my shoulders. It is only right that you should show me that kindness.'

The giant at once agreed to do what Hercules wished, and with

both hands he raised the load so that it might lie more easily. As soon as the hero felt the weight lifted from him, he ran swiftly to a distance. Then he turned round for one last look at the angry and disappointed Atlas, and laughed in triumph as he heard the cries of the giant, which sounded like the pealing of thunder.

Thus his eleventh labour was performed. The twelfth and last was to descend into the earth's depths and bring up the fearful three-headed dog, Cerberus, which was as big as an elephant. Each hair of the head of this awful creature was a snake, and earthquakes were caused whenever it barked. Hercules was not allowed by the ruler of the lower regions to have any weapons in his fight with the monster; he must use only his own bodily strength. After a struggle which lasted during a whole day, he conquered the dog, and carried it alive to King Eurystheus. Then he was ordered to take the creature back to its den in the rocky depths of the earth.

All this he did with as much success as in his other labours; and when the hero's tasks were done he won glory, both in heaven and on earth. When the end of his life came the gods promised that he should reign with them in glory for ever, as a reward for doing his duty so patiently and so bravely.

Four Aesop's Fables

The Wolf & the Crane

A WOLF had got a bone stuck in his throat, and in great pain ran howling up and down, begging every animal he met to relieve him, at the same time hinting at a handsome reward to the one who succeeded in getting it out.

A crane, feeling sorry for him, put her long beak down the wolf's throat and drew out the bone. She then modestly asked for the promised reward.

But the wolf, grinning and showing his teeth and pretending to feel hurt, replied, 'You ungrateful creature! Have I not given you your life? How many can say they have had their head in a wolf's jaws and brought it safely out again? And yet you are not content!'

Those who expect thanks from rascals are often disappointed.

The Hare & the Tortoise

A HARE met a tortoise one day and made fun of him for the slow and clumsy way in which he walked.

The tortoise laughed and said, 'I will run a race with you any time that you choose.'

'Very well,' replied the hare, 'we will start at once.'

The tortoise immediately set off in his slow and steady way without waiting a moment or looking back.

The hare, on the other hand, treated the matter as a joke and decided to take a little nap before starting, for he thought that it would be an easy matter to overtake his rival and win the race with plenty of time to spare.

The tortoise plodded on, and meanwhile the hare overslept with the result that he arrived at the winning-post only to see that the tortoise had got in before him.

Slow and steady wins the race.

The Astrologer & the Traveller

A CERTAIN astrologer, who was so interested in gazing at the stars that he forgot to watch his way, had the misfortune to fall into a ditch one dark night. His fellow-traveller, who had been watching the road and not the heavens and was therefore unharmed, said, 'Friend, take a lesson from your misfortune and let the stars go quietly on their course in future. It would serve you better if you kept your eye on the way you were going.'

Look where you're going.

The Cat & the Mice

A CAT grown feeble with age, and no longer able to hunt mice as she had done in her younger days, thought of a way to entice them within reach of her paws.

She suspended herself by the hind legs from a peg, thinking that the mice would mistake her for a bag, or for a dead cat at least, and would then venture to come near her.

An old mouse, who was wise enough to keep his distance, whispered to a friend, 'Many a bag have I seen in my time, but never one with a cat's head.'

'Hang there, good madam,' said the other, 'as long as you please, but I will not trust myself within reach of you. *You* are not clever enough for us.'

Wise men will not be fooled by old tricks.

The Settlers In Canada

As a young boy Frederick Marryat (1792–1848) longed for adventure, and when he reached the age of fourteen he finally managed to persuade his father to allow him to join the Royal Navy. In this book, one of the last he wrote, the Campbell family show some of that same spirit of adventure when they leave their home in England to face the dangers and rigours of the New World. At this point in the story Percival Campbell has been captured by unfriendly Red Indians.

IT was in the first week of June that Malachi, when he was out in the woods, perceived a young Indian, who came up to where he was, and took a seat by him, without saying a word.

'Is my son from the West?' said Malachi.

'The Young Otter is from the West,' replied the Indian. 'Does my father live with the white man?'

'He lives with the white man,' replied Malachi; 'he has no Indian blood in his veins.'

'Has the white man many in his lodge?' said the Indian.

'Yes; many young men and many rifles,' replied Malachi.

'Does not the cold kill the white man?' said the Indian.

'No; the white man can bear the winter's ice as well as an Indian.'

'Are all who came here with him now in the white man's lodge?'

'No, not at all; one white child slept in the snow, and is in the land of spirits,' replied Malachi.

Here there was a pause; at last the young Indian said –

'A little bird sang in my ear, and it said, "The white man's child is not dead; it wandered about in the woods and was lost, and the Indian found him, and took him to his wigwam in the Far West."'

'Did not the little bird lie to the Young Otter?' replied Malachi.

'No; the little bird sang what was true,' replied the Indian. 'The white boy is alive and in the lodge of the Indian.'

'There are many white men in the country who have children,' replied Malachi.

'The white boy had a rifle in his hand, and snowshoes on his feet.'

'So have all they who go out to hunt in the winter's snow,' replied Malachi.

'But the white boy was found near to the white man's lodge.'

'Is the Young Otter of a near tribe?'

'The lodges of our tribe are twelve days' journey to the westward,' replied the Indian.

'The chief of the Young Otter's band is a great warrior?'

'He is,' replied the Indian.

'Yes,' replied Malachi, 'the Angry Snake is a great warrior. Did he send the Young Otter to me to tell me that the white boy was alive, and in his wigwam?'

The Indian again paused. At last he said –

'It is many moons since the Angry Snake has taken care of the white boy, and has fed him with venison; many moons that he has hunted for him to give him food; and the white boy loves the Angry Snake as a father, and the Angry Snake loves the boy as his son. He will adopt him, and the white boy will be the chief of the tribe. He will forget the white men, and become red as an Indian.'

'The boy is forgotten by the white man, who has long numbered him with the dead,' replied Malachi.

'The white man has no memory,' replied the Indian, 'to forget so soon; but it is not so. He would make many presents to him who would bring back the boy.'

'And what presents could he make?' replied Malachi. 'The white man is poor.'

'The white man has powder, and lead, and rifles,' replied the Indian; 'more than he can use, locked up in his storehouse.'

'And will the Angry Snake bring back the white boy if the white man gives him powder, and lead, and rifles?' inquired Malachi.

'He will make a long journey, and bring the white boy,' replied the Indian; 'but first let the white man say what presents he will give.'

'He shall be spoken to,' replied Malachi, 'and his answer shall be brought. When the moon is at the full I will meet the Young

Otter after the sun is down, at the eastern side of the long prairie. Is it good?'

'Good,' replied the Indian, who rose, turned on his heel, and walked away into the forest.

The next day Malachi informed Alfred of his meeting with the Young Otter, and together they formed a plan for the purpose of taking him prisoner, and holding him as a hostage for Percival.

Three days passed, and Malachi, as the sun sank behind the lake, walked out to the end of the prairie. He had not been there ten minutes when the young Indian stood before him. He was armed, as before, with his tomahawk and bow and arrows; but Malachi had come out expressly without his rifle.

Malachi, as soon as he perceived the Indian, sat down, as is the custom among them when they hold a talk, and the Young Otter followed his example.

After conversing for some time, at a signal agreed upon by Malachi and the party, which lay concealed, the latter rushed forward and seized the Indian. The Young Otter sprang up in spite of their endeavours to keep him, and would certainly have escaped – for he had got his tomahawk clear, and was about to wield it around his head – had not Martin already passed one of the deer thongs round his ankle, by which the Indian was thrown again to the ground. His arms were then secured behind his back with other deerskin thongs, and another passed round his ankle and given to Alfred.

MARY Percival had one morning gone down to the Cedar Swamp to pick cranberries, and, some time after, her basket was found lying – with all the cranberries upset – on a hill by the side of the swamp; but she herself was not to be seen. Strawberry ran for Malachi, and said, 'Angry Snake.'

'Yes, Strawberry,' replied Malachi; 'but not a word at present. Follow me down to the Cedar Swamp; your eyes are younger than mine, and I shall want the use of them. We must find out how many Indians there were, and which way they have gone.'

'Here,' said Strawberry.

'I see, child; I see that and two more. That's her foot,' continued Malachi; 'the sole of a shoe cuts the grass sharper than a moccasin.'

'Here, again,' said Strawberry.

'Yes; you're right, child,' replied Malachi.

Malachi and the Strawberry continued to follow the almost imperceptible track till they arrived at the forest, when they heard the hallooing of Alfred and Martin, to which Malachi answered.

'What is it, Malachi?'

'Mary has been carried off,' replied Malachi, 'by the Snake.'

Alfred then said: 'Now, what is best to be done?'

'You must prepare a party, while Strawberry and I follow the trail. You must be off in three hours.'

'Then,' said Alfred, 'I'll ride off to the Fort. In two hours I will return with Captain Sinclair.'

'As quick as you please.'

Malachi and the Strawberry then continued to follow the trail, till they came upon a spot where a fire had been lighted.

'Here was the nest of the whole gang,' resumed Malachi.

The Strawberry said –

'Here is her foot again.'

'Yes, yes; it's clear enough that two of them have carried her off and brought her here to where the others were waiting for them. Now we have the new trail to find.'

The Strawberry pointed to a mark near where the fire had been lighted, and said, 'The moccasin of a squaw.'

'Right; then she is with them. So much the better,' replied Malachi, 'for, as she sent me that letter, she may serve us still.'

Alfred and Captain Sinclair soon arrived from the Fort, and brought with them two soldiers who were well used to the woods, and excellent shots; and the party of seven, which included two of the young new settlers whom Martin had hastily summoned, joined Malachi and the Strawberry. These two had not been idle; they had tracked the footmarks through the forest till they had come to a small rivulet. Here the trail was lost, and it was to be presumed that the Indians had walked in the water, either up or down, before they put their feet on the other side.

The Indian girl recovered the trail about three miles up the course of the stream, and they all started immediately. On their arrival at a clear spot in the woods, where the grass was very short and dry, they were again at fault. They went over to the other side of this heath, to see if they could again fall in with the trail, but could not discover it. Then they were summoned by a low whistle from the Strawberry, who had returned to the spot where the trail had been lost.

'They have turned back again,' said Strawberry; 'see, the track of the moccasins is both ways.'

'That's true,' said Malachi. 'Now then, Strawberry, to find out where they have left the old trail again.'

It was not till half an hour had elapsed that the spot was discovered; and then they started again, led by the Strawberry, until she stopped and spoke to Malachi, pointing to a small twig broken upon one of the bushes.

'That's true; let us see if it happens again.'

In a few moments Strawberry pointed out another.

'Then all's right,' said Malachi. 'The Indian woman who wrote the letter is our friend still. See, she has, whenever she has dared to do it, broken down a small twig, as a guide to us.'

They continued their course, through the woods until the sun went down, and they then lay down for the night under a large tree.

The next morning they resumed their task. The trail was now pretty clear, and was occasionally verified by the breaking of a twig. At the close of the day they arrived at the borders of a lake; the trail went right on to the shore of it, and then disappeared.

'Here they must have taken to the water,' said Alfred; 'but what means have they had to cross?'

'That we must discover,' replied Malachi. 'It is too dark now to attempt to find out; we must bring to for the night.'

They were sitting round the embers of the fire, when Martin sprang up, with his rifle ready to bring to his shoulder.

'What is it?' said Alfred, as Martin held up his finger as a sign for silence.

'There's somebody coming this way,' said Martin.

A low and singular sort of whistle between the teeth was heard, upon which the Strawberry gently put down Martin's rifle with her hand, saying –

'It is John.'

'John? Impossible!' said Alfred.

'It is,' replied Strawberry.

Strawberry stepped out from the group, calling John softly by name, and in a few seconds returned, leading John by the hand, who, without saying a word, quietly seated himself down by the fire.

'Well, John, how did you come here?' exclaimed Alfred.

'Followed trail,' replied John.

'But how – when did you leave home?'

'Yesterday,' replied John. 'Have you any meat?'

John having finished his supper, they all lay down to rest, one keeping watch.

Next day Strawberry discovered, at the edge of the lake, the mark of the bottom of a canoe which had been grounded. They recognised that the canoe had crossed over to the north point of the lake, and there they found it concealed in the bushes. They then followed the trail about two miles; but as the night was now closing in, they took up their quarters and retired to rest. At daybreak they again started, and made very rapid progress, for the twigs were now more frequently broken and bent than before. It was not far from dark, when the quick ears of the Strawberry were attracted by a noise like that of a person breathing heavily. She pointed with her finger to a bush; they advanced cautiously, and on the other side of it they found an Indian woman lying on the ground, bleeding profusely. They discovered that it was the Indian whom they had cured of the sprained ankle, and who, they presumed, had been then discovered breaking the twigs that they might follow the trail, for, on examination, they found that she had received a heavy blow on the head with a tomahawk. The Strawberry collected some herbs, with which she dressed the wound, and they again lay down to rest.

Acting on the advice of Malachi, they agreed to remain for two or three days till the woman was sufficiently recovered to travel, and show them the direct road to the lodges.

On the fifth day of their taking up their abode in the forest, the squaw said that she was able to travel if they walked slowly. On the sixth day they again proceeded – not to follow the trail, but, guided by the Indian woman, in a direct course for the lodges of the Indian band under the Angry Snake.

They continued their route till, as they drew up one night, the Indian stated that they were only three or four miles from the Indians' lodges. The night was passed very impatiently, and long before break of day they started, and were led by the squaw till they were within one hundred and fifty yards of the lodges, in a thick cluster of young spruce-firs, which completely secured them from discovery.

They had remained there about half an hour, when they perceived an Indian lad come out of one of the lodges. He was dressed in leggings and Indian shirt of deerskin, and carried in his hand his bow and arrows. An eagle's feather was stuck in his hair above the left ear, which marked him as the son of a chief.

'That's my brother Percival,' said John.

'Percival!' replied Alfred. 'Is it possible?'

'Yes,' whispered the Strawberry, 'it is Percival; but don't speak so loud.'

'Well, they have turned him into a regular Indian,' said Alfred; 'we shall have to make a pale face of him again.'

Percival, for he it was, looked round for some time, and at last, perceiving a crow flying over his head, he drew his bow, and the arrow brought the bird down at his feet.

They waited some little time longer, when an Indian woman, and then an old man – the Old Raven – came out, and, in a quarter of an hour afterwards, three more women and an Indian about twenty years old.

'I think we have the whole force now,' said Martin.

'They are going out to hunt – the old and the young Indian, and Percival; they have their bows and arrows,' said John.

'The boy is right,' said Malachi. 'We can now capture the men without the women's knowing anything about it.'

The party remained in their place of concealment for another quarter of an hour, till the two Indians and Percival had entered the woods. They then followed in a parallel direction through the woods for more than an hour, when a herd of deer darted past. The search party immediately stopped and crouched, to hide themselves. Hardly had they done so when one of the herd, which had been pierced by an arrow, followed, and, after a few bounds, fell to the earth. A minute or two afterwards the hunters made their appearance, and took out their knives to flay and cut up the expiring beast.

As the party gradually approached nearer and nearer to the Indians and Percival, the Old Raven appeared to be uneasy; he looked round and round him, and once or twice laid his ear to the ground.

'The Indian woman says that the Old Raven is sure some one is in the woods near him; and she thinks that she had better go to him,' said the Strawberry.

'Let her go,' said Captain Sinclair.

The woman walked up in the direction of the Indians, who immediately turned to her. She spoke to them, and occupied the attention of the Old Raven till the party were close up, when Malachi arose, and immediately all the others did the same, and rushed upon them. After a short struggle they were secured, but not before the younger Indian had wounded one of the soldiers by stabbing him with his knife. The thongs were already fast round the arms and legs of the Indians, when Percival, who had not been tied, again attempted to escape, and, by the direction of Malachi, he was bound as well as the other two.

His sojourn of nearly two years in the woods with the Indians had wholly obliterated, for the time, his recollections of his former life. To the questions of Alfred he returned no reply, and appeared not to understand him.

'Let me try him,' said Malachi; 'I will speak to him in the Indian tongue.'

Malachi spoke. Percival listened for some time, and at last replied in the Indian language.

'What does he say, Malachi?' said Alfred.

'He says he will sing his own death song; that he is the son of a warrior, and he will die like a brave.'

'Why, the boy is metamorphosed,' said Captain Sinclair.

Malachi called the Strawberry, and told her to speak to Percival. She sat down by Percival, and in her soft tones talked to him in her own tongue of his father and mother, of his cousins, and how he had been taken by the Indians when he was hunting; how his mother had wept for him, and all had lamented his loss. The Strawberry continued to talk to him for more than an hour, when Alfred again addressed him and said, 'Percival, don't you know me?'

'Yes,' replied Percival in English, 'I do; you are my brother Alfred.'

'All's right now,' said Malachi; 'only he must be kept fast. But the lad's coming to his senses again.'

At last they set off on their return to the Indian lodges. They arrived about an hour before dusk at their hiding-place, having taken the precaution to gag the two Indians for fear of their giving a whoop as notice of their capture.

Scarcely had they been five minutes again concealed among the spruce-fir trees, when they heard a distant whoop from the woods on the other side of the lodges. One of the Indian women from the lodges returned the whoop.

In about half an hour more the Angry Snake and his party were seen to emerge from the woods, and it was perceived that four of the Indians carried a litter made of branches between them.

'She could walk no farther,' said Malachi, 'so they are carrying her.'

The Indians were soon over the clearing, and stopped at one of the lodges. Mary Percival was lifted out, and was seen to walk with difficulty into the wigwam, followed by two of the Indian women.

A short parley took place between the Angry Snake and the other two women, and the chief and the rest of the party then went into another lodge.

'Let us attack immediately,' said Captain Sinclair.

'No; we have yet an hour and a half of daylight. We will wait one hour; for they, being tired, will soon go to sleep, as Indians always do.'

They remained for about half an hour more watching the lodges, but not a single person came out. Having examined the priming of the rifles, and leaving the prisoners to the charge of the Strawberry – who, with her knife drawn, stood over them – the whole party now crept softly towards the lodges. As soon as they had all arrived, they rose up and hastened to their allotted stations round the lodge of the Angry Snake and his followers.

'Let us first lead Miss Percival away to a place of safety,' whispered Captain Sinclair.

'Do you do it then,' said Alfred.

Captain Sinclair hastened to the lodge in which Miss Percival had been placed, and opened the door. Mary uttered a loud scream of delight, and, rising from the skins on which she had been laid, fell upon his neck. Captain Sinclair caught her in his arms, and was bearing her out of the lodge when an Indian woman caught him by the coat; but John, who had entered, putting the muzzle of his rifle into her face, she let go and retreated, and Captain Sinclair bore away Mary in his arms into the brushwood, where the Strawberry was standing over the Indian prisoners. Mary's scream had roused the Indians, who were in a sound sleep; but still no movement was to be heard in the lodge, and a debate between Malachi and Alfred whether they should enter the lodge or not was put an end to by a rifle being fired from the lodge, and the fall of one of the soldiers. Another shot followed, and Martin received a bullet in his shoulder; and then out bounded the Angry Snake, followed by his band, the chief whirling his tomahawk and springing upon Malachi, while the others attacked Alfred and Martin, who were nearest to the

door of the lodge. The rifle of Malachi met the breast of the Angry
Snake as he advanced, and the contents were discharged through
his body. The other Indians fought desperately; but, the whole of
the attacking party closing in, they were overpowered. Only two
of them, however, were taken alive, and these were seriously
wounded; they were tied and laid on the ground.

'He was a bad man,' said Malachi, who was standing over the
body of the Indian chief; 'but he will do no more mischief.'

'Are you much hurt, Martin?' inquired Alfred.

'No, not much. The ball has passed right through, and touched
no bone; so I am in luck. I'll go to the Strawberry and get her to
bind it up.'

Percival was now untied and suffered to walk about. The first
object which caught his eye was the body of the Angry Snake. He
looked on it for some time, and then sat down by its side. There he
remained for more than two hours without speaking, when, a
hole having been dug out by one of the party, the body was put in
and covered up. Percival remained a few minutes by the side of
the grave, and then turned to the two wounded Indians. He
brought them water, and spoke to them in the Indian tongue; but
while he was still with them, Mary sent for him to speak with
him. The sight of Mary appeared to have a powerful effect upon
the boy; he listened to her as she soothed and caressed him, and,
appearing to be overcome with a variety of sensations, he lay
down, moaned, and at last fell fast asleep.

Alfred and Malachi had resolved to set off the next morning on
their return home. They made a litter of boughs on which to carry
Mary, and, after a two days' march through the woods, they
reached a river which, the Indian woman told them, flowed into
Lake Erie. There they found two canoes, which had belonged to
the band of Indians, hauled up in the bushes on the bank.
Embarking on the canoes, they were soon gliding rapidly down
the stream. For four days they paddled their canoes, and on the
fifth day they entered the lake, about two hundred miles to the
west of the settlement.

On the sixth day they were delighted to perceive Fort Frontignac in the distance, and they knew that they were not above five miles from the settlement. In less than another hour they were abreast of the prairie, and landed at the spot where their own punt was moored. In order to prepare Mrs. Campbell a little for the appearance of her son, it was agreed that Percival should remain behind, and be taken up to Malachi's lodge to wait there with the Strawberry till they should come to fetch him. Having made this arrangement, to which Percival reluctantly consented, the others walked up towards the house.

When they were half-way from the beach, Mr. and Mrs. Campbell beheld the party advancing; they flew to meet them, and, as they caught Mary in their arms, all explanation was unnecessary – she was recovered, and that was sufficient for the time.

'It is very strange, mother,' said Alfred, when they reached the house, 'but we heard that the Indians had found a white boy in the woods.'

'Alas! not mine.'

'I have reason to believe that it was Percival.'

'Alfred, do not say so unless you have good cause.'

'Do you think, mother, that I would raise such hopes if I had not good reason to suppose that they would be realised?'

'Then you know that Percival is alive?'

'I am certain that he is alive.'

'God grant it!' said Mrs. Campbell. 'My heart is almost breaking with joy. Oh, where is he?'

'Percival is not far off,' said Alfred.

'Alfred, he is here! I am sure he is.'

'He is with Malachi and the Strawberry; in a minute I will bring him.'

Alfred left the house. In another minute he returned with Percival, and the mother embraced and wept over her long-lost child – and then gave him to his father's arms.

Lochinvar

O YOUNG Lochinvar is come out of the west,
Through all the wide border his steed was the best:
And save his good broadsword, he weapons had none,
He rode all unarmed, and he rode all alone.
So faithful in love, and so dauntless in war,
There never was knight like the young Lochinvar.

He staid not for brake, and he stopped not for stone,
He swam the Eske river where ford there was none;
But ere he alighted at Netherby gate,
The bride had consented, the gallant came late;
For a laggard in love, and a dastard in war,
Was to wed the fair Ellen of brave Lochinvar.

So boldly he entered the Netherby Hall,
Among bride's-men, and kinsmen, and brothers, and all:
Then spoke the bride's father, his hand on his sword,
(For the poor craven bridegroom said never a word),
'O come ye in peace here, or come ye in war,
Or to dance at our bridal, young Lord Lochinvar?'

'I long wooed your daughter, my suit you denied; –
Love swells like the Solway, but ebbs like its tide –
And now am I come, with this lost love of mine,
To lead but one measure, drink one cup of wine.
There are maidens in Scotland more lovely by far,
That would gladly be bride to the young Lochinvar.'

The bride kissed the goblet: the knight took it up,
He quaffed off the wine, and he threw down the cup.
She looked down to blush, and she looked up to sigh,
With a smile on her lips, and a tear in her eye.
He took her soft hand, ere her mother could bar, –
'Now tread we a measure!' said young Lochinvar.

So stately his form, and so lovely her face,
That never a hall such a galliard did grace;
While her mother did fret, and her father did fume,
And the bridegroom stood dangling his bonnet and plume;
And the bride-maidens whispered, ' 'Twere better by far,
To have matched our fair cousin with young Lochinvar.'

One touch to her hand, and one word in her ear,
When they reached the hall-door, and the charger stood near;
So light to the croupe the fair lady he swung,
So light to the saddle before her he sprung!
'She is won! we are gone, over bank, bush, and scaur;
They'll have fleet steeds that follow,' quoth young Lochinvar.

There was mounting 'mong Graemes of the Netherby clan;
Forsters, Fenwicks, and Musgraves, they rode and they ran:
There was racing and chasing on Cannobie Lee,
But the lost bride of Netherby ne'er did they see.
So daring in love, and so dauntless in war,
Have ye e'er heard of gallant like young Lochinvar?

The Seven Voyages of Sindbad

The First Voyage

LONG, long, ago, in the reign of the Caliph Haroun al Raschid, there dwelt in the city of Bagdad a poor man named Hindbad, who gained a living by carrying goods from place to place for other people; in fact, he was a porter.

Though, as a rule, he did not grumble with his lot, there were times when he was not content. One of these times happened to be, when, tired out by the weight of his load, he had sat down to rest outside the house of a very rich man whose name was Sindbad.

As the soft strains of music from the house reached his ears, and the scent of rare perfumes fell upon his senses, he was struck by the difference between his lot and that of the man whose name was so like his own.

'Why should I be so poor, and he so rich?' said Hindbad aloud; 'am I not as good a man as he?'

Sindbad, hearing the words without seeing the speaker, sent a servant to bring Hindbad before him, and the poor man, fearing he knew not what, went into the splendid hall where Sindbad was feasting with a number of his friends.

Pointing to a seat at his right hand, Sindbad gave his guest a share of the good things on the table, and the meal being at length finished, 'Tell me,' said he, 'why you were grumbling?'

'Pardon me, my lord,' replied Hindbad, 'I was weary and sad at heart.'

'Have no fear,' said Sindbad kindly, 'I do not blame you for your words; but, that you may know how hard I had to work to win the riches I now enjoy, let me tell you the story of my life.'

With these words he began as follows:

'When I was but a young man my father died, leaving me a very large fortune, nearly the whole of which I spent in enjoying myself. At last I began to think, unless I wished to become poor, I had better try to make some more money with the little left to me, so, having bought some goods, I set sail for the Persian Gulf, hoping to sell or exchange them at a profit.

The ship called at several small islands, where we did some good trading. One day, when the vessel could not move for want of wind to fill her sails, we saw what seemed to be a little green field peeping above the water. Thinking it very strange, a party of us rowed out to it, taking some wood for a fire, and food, so that we might hold a feast.

We had all landed, and were in the middle of our meal when we found to our horror that we were on the back of some huge sea-monster. The creature shook its great body, and lashed its tail so angrily that as many as could jumped into the boat, others into the sea, and soon all except myself were aboard the ship.

A fresh breeze had begun to blow, and the sails being set at once, away went the ship, leaving me still on the monster's back. Suddenly the huge creature dived under water, and I should have gone too, but that seizing a large piece of wood I kept myself afloat.

All through that day and through the night I was tossed about by the waves, but was at last thrown on to the shore of what was really an island. After a while the sun came out, warming me, and making me feel that if I wished to gain strength I must seek some food.

Dragging myself with great pain toward the middle of the island, I had the good fortune to find a few herbs. These I ate, drinking afterwards from a spring of clear, cool water.

Wishing to see on what sort of place I had been cast, I walked on until a man met me, who, hearing my strange story, took me to a cave in which were several other men. They were the servants of the ruler of the island, and had come to this part of it in order to fetch his horses back to the palace.

It was lucky for me that I met them that day; had it not been for this I should most likely have died, as I could never have found my way to the other side of the island, where the people lived, and to which the king's servants were returning next day.

They were very kind, giving me food to eat, and taking me with
them when they set out on their journey. As soon as we reached
the palace they took me before the king, who also treated me
with great kindness. He listened to my story, pitied my sad
state, and asked me to stay with him as long as I cared to.

Now the chief city of his kingdom, the city in which I made
my home, was built on the seashore. Every day ships came to it
from all parts of the world, and I, hoping to meet someone from
my own town, spent a great deal of time watching these ships,
and talking to the merchants who came and went in them.

I also grew friendly with some of the natives – Indians they
were, and very wise persons; but I never forgot to pay a daily
visit to the king, with whose chief men I had many pleasant talks
about the way in which their country and my own were governed.

Hearing one day of the island of Cassel, and of the sounds of
drums being beaten every night on the shore, I had a great wish
to visit it, which I did, seeing many large and curious fishes on
my voyage.

Shortly after my return from Cassel, the very ship in which I
had set out from Bussorah, and which had sailed away leaving
me struggling for life in the water, came into the harbour.
Among the many bundles of goods brought from this vessel to
the shore I saw those which I had bought, and on which my
name was clearly written. But, on telling the captain my name,
and that I wished to have my goods, he looked at me in surprise.

"How can you be Sindbad?" he asked, "when I myself saw him drowned. I fear you are not an honest man, though you look like one. I believe you are telling a lie in order to get these goods which do not belong to you."

I was at some pains to make him believe I spoke the truth, and, at last, on several of the sailors saying they were sure I was Sindbad, he let me have the goods.

Having looked through my bundle, I carried the very best of the goods to the kindly king, and asked him to take them as a gift. He seemed pleased with the gift, but not quite sure how I, a poor man cast up by the sea, had been able to get them.

I then told him of the coming of the ship, and the finding of my own bales of goods, on which he took my costly present with great pleasure, and gave me one worth far more in return. I next sold or exchanged the rest of my goods, and, having bidden his majesty good-bye, set sail for Bussorah, taking with me many articles made only on the island. These I sold for a large sum of money, for so much, indeed, that I had no further need to work.'

When Sindbad had finished the story of his first voyage, he ordered the band to play again, and spent the rest of the day with his guests. The poor porter, who never in all his life had been so well treated before, enjoyed himself greatly, and, when the rich man, on bidding him good-night, bade him come again the next day to hear more of his story, giving him at the same time a purse full of money, Hindbad was delighted at his good fortune.

The Second Voyage

'Although I had made up my mind to live quietly at home on the money gained by my first voyage,' said Sindbad, when he and his poor guest were once more seated together, 'I soon tired of doing nothing, and having bought a large number of useful articles, once more set out to sell them to the people who lived on the various islands.

The ship carried us safely to several places where I sold my own goods and bought others; but one day we reached what seemed to be a desert island. No living creature was to be seen, yet there were fruit-trees and flowers, and meadows, and running streams, all of which looked so tempting, that we felt obliged to land, if only to walk a little in the pleasant-looking fields.

Having no wish to wander about with the rest, I took some food and wine, found a nice, shady spot beside a stream, ate a good meal, and then fell fast asleep, wakening only when the others had returned to the vessel, and sailed away without me.

I blamed myself over and over again for my stupidity, but, as this was not likely to help me much, I climbed a high tree in order to get a good view of the island. Far away in the distance I saw something white, and to this I went with all speed.

It was a curious thing, very large, very smooth, and rounded like a dome. While I stood wondering what it could be, all around grew dark. It was late in the day, and the sun would set in a little while, but the sky seemed to be hidden all at once by a thick cloud.

To my surprise this was not so, but the cloud was really a huge bird, bigger than I had ever dreamed a bird could be. I thought it must be the wonderful roc of which I had heard the sailors talk, and the great white dome must be its egg.

Thinking it likely the bird was coming to sit on her egg, I crept under it, and, as soon as she was settled, tied myself firmly to one of her big, strong legs.

Thus I lay until the morning, when the bird, rising high, carried me so swiftly through the air that I became dizzy, and lost my senses. On coming to myself some time later I was lying on the ground, but still tied to the leg of the huge bird.

Not wishing to go through such a terrible journey again, I made haste to get free from the bird's leg, and it was well I did so, for almost the next moment she seized a huge snake in her bill and flew away.

I could not tell where she had carried me. All around were mountains so high that they seemed to touch the sky, and so steep that no one could climb them. I was no better off here than on the island. Suddenly I forgot my trouble for a time, for, looking at the ground, I found it was covered with diamonds, big shining diamonds.

But, alas, there were other things besides, things that filled my heart with fear, and made me wish more than ever to find some way out of the lonely valley. These were snakes, so large that they could swallow an elephant quite easily.

As the day grew brighter, however, they hid away in their homes, for fear, I suppose, of the roc, but when the night drew near they came out again in large numbers. Feeling it would be dreadful to spend the dark night in terror in case I should be swallowed by one of the great creatures, I looked about for some place in which to take shelter till the day dawned.

At length I found a cave, the entrance to which was so small that I could block it with a large stone. Though now feeling safer I could still not sleep; the hissing of the snakes outside was too frightening.

As soon as it was light I left the cave, and walked a short distance through the valley, feeling far too miserable to touch the diamonds under my feet. The food I had brought from the ship kept me from starving, but I was so weary that at last I felt obliged to lie down and sleep.

Hardly had I begun to doze, however, when I was startled by something heavy falling near me. Opening my eyes quickly I saw a large piece of raw meat lying at my feet. Another piece fell, and another, and several more, and as they fell heavily upon the diamonds, the lovely stones stuck firmly into the meat.

This made me think again of the sailors' stories, and I knew that the meat was being thrown into the valley by men on the mountains, in the hope that it would be fetched back by the eagles to feed their young ones, when the diamonds could be taken from their nests.

Now I thought I could see a way of escape by tying a piece of meat firmly to my back, and waiting till an eagle carried me up out of the dreadful valley. This I did, but not until I had first filled my bag with the precious stones.

I had not long to wait. One of a number of eagles picking me up bore me to his nest on the top of the mountains, where I was found by a merchant who had frightened the eagle away. At first he looked at me in surprise, and then said I had no right to steal his diamonds.

"If you will listen to me," I said gently "you will find I am no thief, though having enough diamonds to make both myself and you rich for life. I got them from the valley, and chose the very best to be found."

The other merchants now crowded round, and all showed great surprise at my story. They wondered much at the trick I had played, but they wondered still more when I showed them the stones.

Though I begged him to take several, the merchant who had found me would take only the smallest of them, which he said was a good fortune in itself. They agreed to let me spend that night in their camp, which I did, and was then taken to the merchant's house, where I told my strange story again to his wife and children.

In the course of time I once more reached my home, and settled down to a life of ease, and made glad the hearts of my poor neighbours, by sharing my riches with them.'

This being the end of Sindbad's second story, he gave Hindbad another purse of money, and asked him to return the next day.

'My third voyage,' said Sindbad the next day, 'was hardly begun when a very great storm arose, and the captain told us the ship was being driven towards an island, which was the home of numbers of little hairy savages not more than a metre high. He said they were very fierce, and we had better not make them angry in case they became dangerous.

As our vessel neared the land a swarm of them swam out, dragged it ashore, made us all get out, and then took the ship away with them to another island. As it was useless to stand and look after them, we walked on until we reached a beautiful palace, the courtyard of which we entered.

The yard led to a room where we saw a heap of men's bones, and a large number of spits, or long, steel skewers, on which joints of meat are roasted. As we stood looking at these things, a truly terrible ogre came into the room, making a loud noise.

In the very middle of his forehead was a huge eye, the only one he had; his mouth was like that of a horse, and his ears flapped down on his shoulders like an elephant's. He was as tall as a high

tree, and one glance at him was enough to make us all nearly die with fright.

Having taken a good look at us, the horrid ogre picked me up by my neck, and turned me round and round, but seemed to think me too thin, for, indeed, I was little more than skin and bone. Then he seized the captain, who was the fattest of us all, roasted, and ate him.

After this he went to sleep, and troubled us no more till the next day, when he roasted and ate another of our crew. On the third day he ate another, and we then made up our minds to kill him and try to escape. There were ten of us left, and each one taking a spit, and making its point red hot, we stuck them all together into the one eye of our terrible enemy.

Mad with pain he tried to seize us; but we got out of the way of his fearful claw-like hands, and ran off to the shore. Here we made some rafts, but had not got afloat when two giants came in sight leading the terrible ogre who we had fondly hoped was dead.

Jumping on to the rafts we pushed off from the shore, but the giants wading into the water as far as they dared, threw after us some huge stones which, falling upon the rafts, sank them all but the one on which I stood with two other men. Happily we got out of their reach quickly and, after beating about on the sea for many hours, came to another island, where we found some very good fruit.

Being now tired out we lay down to sleep, but were soon awakened by a rustling sound which, to our horror, we found was made by a huge snake. Before we could get away, the creature swallowed one of my comrades, and then went back to his den. The next night he came again, and caught the second of my comrades, as he was following me up a tree, where he had hoped to be quite safe.

All night I lay on one of the boughs, afraid to sleep in case the cruel monster should come back. As soon as day broke I slid down, gathered all the brushwood near, and making it into bundles placed some of them round the tree; the others I tied to the topmost branches. When the sky began to darken in the evening, I lit them, and kept myself safe all night, for, though the snake came, he feared to cross my circle of fire.

In the morning, feeling very miserable, I made up my mind to drown myself, but, on reaching the shore, I saw some distance off a ship passing slowly by. Unrolling my turban I waved it aloft, while shouting loudly, until the captain sent a boat to fetch me to the ship.

Good fortune now met me once again, for this was the very captain who had sailed away without me on my second voyage. As soon as he learned who I was, he told me how glad he was to have been able to make up for that fault, by saving me now from what might have proved a worse fate.

He had taken care of my goods left on the ship, and now returned them to me with much pleasure. On reaching port I sold them at a fair price, and again returned to Bussorah with a large sum of money.

From Bussorah I went to Bagdad and bought another fine house with splendid grounds all round it. As I had done each time before, so I did now, giving a great deal of money to poor people of the city, and settling down for some time to a quiet life. But this I found very difficult to do, and at last went to sea for the fourth time, when again many wonderful things happened to me.'

Hindbad went home that night with a glad heart, for he was no longer poor. In his hand he held a purse of money, and it seemed as if his rich friend meant to give him the same, every day he spent with him.

The Fourth Voyage

As soon as dinner was over, Sindbad began the story of his fourth voyage. 'Having set all my affairs straight,' he said, 'I travelled through a great part of Persia, buying and selling. At last, reaching the coast, I went aboard a ship, which, after calling at several places on the mainland, stood out to sea.

But soon a great storm arose; the sails were torn to shreds, the ship was blown upon the land, and many of the passengers and sailors were drowned.

With a few of the others I clung to a plank, which was washed ashore on an island, where we found fruit and water, of which we ate and drank freely. The next morning we set out to explore the island, but before getting far were met by some islanders who carried us to their homes.

They seemed very kind and gave us a tasty dish to eat.

Though feeling as hungry as my comrades, I ate none of this dish, fearing it might do me some harm. In this I was wise, for I was the only one who kept his senses. The others became dazed, and ate freely of the rice with which they were daily fed, becoming at last very fat, when the islanders killed and ate them.

The horror of the whole thing, together with the very little food I ate, kept me so thin that the islanders took no notice of me, which gave me the chance of going here and there without being watched. One day, when all the people except one old man had gone out, I walked slowly till some distance away from the village, when I set off running as fast as I could, taking no notice of the old man's cries.

Resting a while now and then, I hurried on until night came. For seven days I met no one; on the eighth I had the good fortune to come upon some men gathering pepper, which was plentiful on the island. On hearing my story they seemed very much surprised that I had got away with my life.

They treated me with much kindness and, when their work was done, took me with them to their own island, where the king gave me some new clothes and bade his people take great care of me. I became a great favourite with every one, and at last found a way of paying back a little of their kindness.

Seeing that all of them, even the king, rode upon the bare backs of their horses, I thought out a plan for making a saddle and bridle and stirrups. This, with the help of two workmen, I did, and gave the first set, when finished, to the king. So many costly presents were given me by those for whom I made saddles that I was soon a rich man again.

One day the king, as a token of his love, gave me a wife, thinking I should be more likely to settle down in his country, and not wish to return to my own. At first I was pleased enough to stay, but after a time I began to long for my own home in Bagdad. Therefore, keeping my eyes open, I waited for a chance to escape, which came about in a very curious manner.

My wife, who for some time had not been strong, fell sick and died, when, according to the custom of the country, I was buried with her in a deep pit on the side of a mountain near the sea.

My coffin was an open one, and when the mouth of the pit had been blocked by a huge rock, and the king with the other mourners had gone away, I rose, and by the aid of a little light that came through the corners not covered by the stone, looked about me.

The pit or long cave, as it really was, seemed full of dead bodies, which smelt so horribly that I was forced to hold my nose. At first I wished I had died in one of the storms at sea; then I was filled with a keen desire to live. Taking some of the bread and water placed in the coffin, I groped about to find some outlet from the cave, but failed to do so.

My food was nearly all gone, when, one day, the mouth of the cave was uncovered, and I saw another burial taking place. The dead body was that of a man, and his wife being buried with him, the usual seven small loaves and a pitcher of water had been placed in her coffin. The poor woman, however, soon died, so I took the bread and water, which lasted me for several days.

Then, one morning, hearing a strange sound, I was able to follow it, until I came upon an opening in the cave, through which I crawled, and found myself on the seashore. The sound I had heard proved to be the heavy breathing of some creature that had come into the cave to feed upon the dead bodies.

Feeling sure now of being able to get away from my living tomb, I went back to the cave in order to get the precious stones, and jewels, and costly stuffs buried with the dead bodies, and also to bring away my bread and water. On again reaching the shore I made several neat bundles of the goods, and then settled down to wait for the passing of some ship in the hope of being picked up.

On the third day, a vessel sailed slowly out from the harbour, and I, waving the linen of my turban, shouted loudly, which at last caused the sailors to look toward me. In a few minutes a boat was lowered and three men rowed ashore to fetch me.

To account for being in so strange a place, I told them I had been shipwrecked, but had got safely to land with a portion of my goods. The story was really a very poor one, but they seemed not to notice it, being far too busy with their own affairs.

The ship called at several ports on the islands and the mainland, where I made another large fortune by the sale of the articles brought from the cave, and at length I reached my home in safety.

As an act of thankfulness for having come safely through my troubles, I gave large sums of money to the church, to the poor, and to my own kindred, who listened in wonder to the story of my latest adventures.'

Here Sindbad wished his guests good-night, bidding them all dine with him next day, and giving Hindbad the usual purse of one hundred sequins.

The Fifth Voyage

'The pleasures of my home,' said Sindbad the next evening, 'made me forget past dangers, so, when the longing for travel came upon me, I bought many costly articles with which to carry on my trade, and sent them to the seaport town where a vessel was being built for my use.

The ship being larger than I needed for my own goods, I agreed to take several other merchants with me, and we set out in great hope of doing good business at the ports where we meant to call.

But, alas! coming one day to a desert island, where we found a young roc just ready to break from its shell, the merchants roasted and ate it, and thus brought about the deaths of every one except myself.

Just as my comrades had finished their meal, for I would by no means join in it, we saw the parent birds coming. The captain, fearing the anger of the great creatures, who looked like two large clouds floating in the sky, hurried us aboard and sailed away with all speed.

As soon as the old birds found what had been done, they swept down with a great noise, took up two huge stones, and flew after us. Stopping just above us they dropped the stones, one of which fell upon the ship, smashing it to pieces, and killing most of the sailors and merchants. Some, myself among them, sank into the water.

On coming to the surface I caught hold of a plank with one hand, and swam with the other, changing them at times, until the tide carried me to an island, the shore of which was so steep that some further toil was needed before I reached a place of safety.

In the morning, after eating the fruits which grew in plenty, and drinking the fresh, cool water of a brook, I wandered about, looking with pleasure at the beauty of the place.

After a time I saw a little old man making signs to me to carry him on my back over the brook. Having pity on his age, I did so, but, when I would have pulled him down on the other side, he twisted his legs so tightly round my neck, that I fell to the ground half choked.

Though he saw how faint I was he made no sign of getting off, but, opening his legs a little to let me breathe better, he dug his feet into my stomach to make me rise and carry him farther. Day after day, and night after night, he clung to me, until by good luck I got rid of him.

Coming to a spot where, a few days before, I had left the juice of some grapes in a container, I drank the juice which in the meantime had become very good wine. This gave me fresh strength, and, instead of dragging myself wearily along, I danced and sang with great good-will.

The old man, seeing how light-hearted the wine had made me, signed to me to give him some. He took a deep drink, and soon became so merry that he loosed his hold on my shoulders, when I tossed him off, and stunned him with a stone, in case he should make me his victim once more.

Some sailors whom I met shortly afterwards, their ship having put into the island for water, said I was the first person they had ever known to escape from the old man of the sea, who for years had been a terror to those obliged to visit the island.

One of the merchants on board, taking pity on my state, gave me a large bag, and advised me to go picking cocoa-nuts with some men whom we met in a place much visited by foreign traders. I kept close to the party, as he had bidden me, until we reached the place where the cocoa-nuts grew.

The trees were so tall that I wondered how we should get the nuts, when the men, picking up some stones, threw them at the monkeys of whom there were many on the branches. These creatures in return, pelted us with cocoa-nuts, throwing them down so quickly that we soon filled our bags.

Day after day this was done until at length we had enough to fill the ship which waited for us in the harbour. Then, bidding the friendly merchant good-bye, I went aboard, and in due time arrived in Bagdad, none the worse for my adventures. I had done well, too, with my cocoa-nuts, having changed them for pearls and spices in the places at which we had called.'

Giving Hindbad another hundred sequins, Sindbad wished him goodnight, and asked him to return next day to hear the story of his sixth voyage.

The Sixth Voyage

'You will perhaps wonder why, after meeting with so many dangers, I should again venture forth, when I might have stayed quietly at home,' said Sindbad, taking up his story where he had left off the day before. 'I wonder myself, now, yet at the time I was quite willing and eager to set out.

Travelling by way of Persia and the Indies, I at length took passage on a vessel bound on a long voyage. After being many days at sea the captain and pilot lost their way. They had no idea where we were, until the captain found his ship had got into a most dangerous current which, unless God took pity on us, would surely carry us to our death.

Almost mad with grief he left his place on deck, and went to see that his orders were carried out; but, as the men set about changing the sails, the ropes broke, and the vessel, now quite helpless, was carried ashore and wrecked, yet not so badly, for we were able to save our lives, our goods, and our provisions.

But even such comfort as was left us was taken away by the captain. 'We may as well set about digging our graves,' said he, 'for no one ever escapes from this terrible place.'

And, indeed, this seemed true, the shore being covered with wrecks, and goods of great value, and, worst of all for men in our position to see, the bones of those who had already died there, as we were only too likely to do.

The coast was very steep, and there seemed no way of climbing up, but under the hills, through a great cave, ran the very current that had brought us ashore. For some days we wandered about, heedless of the precious stones under our feet, thinking only of our sad fate. The most careful ate only a little of their share of food each day, so that some lived longer than others; but at last I was the only one left, and, maddened by my foolishness in leaving home, I began to dig my grave, fully believing that now at least there was no more hope.

Yet it pleased God again to spare me. As I stood, lonely and miserable, looking upon the currents that had wrought our ruin, an idea came into my head. With all speed I made a raft with the pieces of timber on the shore, loaded it with the precious stones

and costly stuffs lying here and there, and stepped aboard, trusting that the stream would carry me to some place where men lived, and so give me a chance of escape. If I lost my life, I should be no worse off than in staying on the coast to die.

With two small oars I guided the raft, leaving it to be carried by the current. Several days passed, and still the raft floated on in total darkness through the long tunnel. At length my food being all eaten, I sank down in a state of drowsiness, and awoke to find myself once more in the light, and surrounded by a number of black men.

Full of joy at my good fortune I rose, and gave thanks aloud to God, who had brought me to a place of safety. One of the blacks, understanding my words, stepped forward and asked how I had reached their country. They had seen my raft floating in the river, he said, and had tied it to the bank till I should awake. After eating a little food I told them of my strange adventures, the man who had first spoken to me telling the others what I said, he being the only one who understood my speech.

They looked at me in wonder, and placing me on a horse took me straight to their king. He thought my story so strange that he had it written down in letters of gold, and put away with the important papers of the kingdom. The sight of my raft and bales of goods, which the natives had taken care to bring with them, was a still further surprise. He thought my treasures very beautiful, but most of all the emeralds, of which he himself had none.

Seeing this, I begged him to accept the whole of my goods, as a token of my thankfulness to him and his people, but this he would by no means do. He said that instead of taking my riches he meant to add to them, and meanwhile, I was placed in the care of one of his chief men, who treated me with great kindness.

Though the time passed pleasantly, I could not but long to return to my home. Going therefore to pay my daily visit to the king, I told him of my wish, and begged that he would let me return to Bagdad. He agreed at once, and, giving me many valuable gifts, asked that I would carry a message of friendship to the Caliph Haroun al Raschid, together with a costly present, and a letter written upon a skin of great value. Then, sending for the captain in whose ship I was to sail, and the merchant who was to travel with me, he charged them to treat me well on the journey.

Reaching Bagdad in the course of time, I set out to fulfil my promise to the king. His gift to the Caliph was made up of four things – a beautiful cup cut out of a large ruby and filled with pearls; the skin of a snake supposed to keep any one who lay upon it from becoming ill; a large quantity of wood of aloes, and of camphor; and a beautiful slave whose clothing was rich with jewels.

The Caliph, astonished at the richness of the gift, could not keep from asking many questions about the king who had given it into my care. After telling him all he wished to know, I was free to return home, and to settle down again, this time, as I thought, for good.'

The story being finished, Hindbad went away, taking with him another purse of gold; but the next day he returned to dine with Sindbad, who, after the meal, told the story of his seventh and last voyage in these words.

The Seventh Voyage

'I was one day enjoying myself with some friends, when a slave from the palace came with a message that I should go to the Caliph at once. His Highness, having written a reply to the letter from the King of the Indies, wished me to carry it to him, together with a suitable present.

Now, though it would have given me great pleasure to serve my sovereign in any other way, I felt quite unable to face again the dangers of the sea, and, to let him know why, I told him of all the misery through which I had passed. In reply he said that though he felt very sorry for me, yet I must bear this letter and gift to the King of the Indies.

"You have but to sail to Serendib," said he, "and present my gifts to his Majesty: after that you are free to return to Bagdad."

Seeing that he would not change his mind, I at last agreed to go, and, after a fair and pleasant voyage, arrived at the king's court. The gift was a very costly one, and his Majesty showed great pleasure when it was handed to him.

After a short stay in the island I begged leave to depart, but the king gave his consent only after much pressing on my part. I went on board the vessel, taking with me a splendid gift, and hoping to have a speedy and pleasant voyage.

We had been at sea, however, only about three days, when the ship being seized by pirates, I was taken with several others and sold as a slave. The rich merchant, who bought me, treated me well, and, finding I was able to shoot with a bow, took me out with him to shoot elephants of which there were numbers in the forest.

Having told me to climb a tree and to wait for the animals to pass by, he gave me a supply of food, and went back to the town.

No elephants passed during the night, but in the morning I shot one out of a large herd. As soon as the others had gone, I ran quickly to my master, who, praising me highly, came back to the forest and helped to bury the huge creature. This he did to get the tusks, when the flesh had rotted away from them.

Every day for two whole months I shot an elephant; then one morning as I waited in the tree for them, instead of passing by they came toward it, and looked at me steadily for a few moments. I trembled with fear, for the creatures were many in number, and seemed bent on taking my life in revenge for the death of their friends.

One great animal at last tore up the tree in which I was by the roots, lifted me from the ground where I had fallen, placed me

on his back, and, closely followed by the others, carried me to a field, some distance away, which I found afterwards to be covered with the bones and teeth of dead elephants.

Having laid me on the ground they all went away, leaving me lost in wonder at their wisdom. It seemed as if they knew it was only their teeth I wanted, and they had brought me to their burying-place, so that I could get all I wished without killing any more of their number.

Here, indeed, was a great treasure, and I went quickly to tell my master of my good fortune. As I met no elephants on the way, I felt sure they had gone farther into the forest in order to leave the road open. My master, wondering why I was so long away, had meanwhile gone to the tree and found it torn from the ground, so he was overjoyed to see me, having feared the creatures had killed me in their anger.

The next day we rode to the spot on an elephant whom we loaded with as many tusks as it could carry, and on getting back home my master said that as he had become a rich man through me, I should be a slave no longer.

"The merchants of this city," he said, "have had many slaves killed by the elephants, who are indeed very cunning animals. But it has pleased God to spare your life, and to show how every one of us may become rich without the loss of any more lives. I have no doubt that when the people of this city hear about this they will all wish to help in making you a rich man, but I would rather do this by myself. I will not only set you free, I will give you enough money to live on for the rest of your life."

Having thanked the merchant for his kindness, I said, "Sir, I have no wish to take so great a gift from you. Give me leave to return to my own country a free man, and I shall be well content."

This he was quite willing to do, saying that as soon as the wind was fair, he would send me home in one of the ships that would then come to carry away the ivory.

While waiting for the ships I made several journeys to the hill with the friendly merchant, bringing home so many tusks that the storehouses were soon full of ivory. The vessels came at last, and the merchant himself, choosing the one in which I was to sail, filled it with ivory, the half of which he said was mine. Besides this splendid present he gave me a number of things found or made only in that island, and enough food to last the whole voyage: he also paid the cost of my journey.

The voyage was a good one, yet, knowing the dangers of the ocean, and how quickly storms arise, I landed at the first port we reached on the mainland, taking with me my share of the ivory which soon sold for a great deal of money.

Having bought some rare gifts for my family, I set out for Bagdad with a party of merchants. The way was long and tiring, but reaching the city at length, I went straight to the Caliph, in order to let him know that his commands had been properly carried out.

I had been so long away that he feared some danger had befallen me, so I made bold to tell him of my adventures. The story of the elephants filled him with wonder; indeed, had he not known me to be a truthful man, he would not have believed it.

As it was he gave orders that this story, as well as all the others I had told, should be written in letters of gold, and kept in a safe place for all time.

My family, my kindred, and all my friends welcomed my return with great joy. Since that, my last voyage, I have lived a quiet life, doing much good.'

'Now, friend,' he added, turning to Hindbad, 'I think you will agree I have earned the riches I enjoy, and the pleasures that fill my life.'

'Sir,' replied Hindbad, as he rose and kissed his host's hand, 'I must own that your troubles have been greater than mine. You richly deserve all you have, and I hope you will from now live a happy and peaceful life.'

Although he had no more stories to tell, Sindbad begged the poor porter to come to dine with him every day. 'You need not do any more rough work,' said he, wishing him good-night, and putting into his hand another full purse, 'for Sindbad the Sailor will be your friend for the rest of your life.'

The Dog in the Manger

A DOG once made his bed in a manger, and lay snarling and growling to keep the horses away from their food. 'What a miserable cur he is!' said one of the animals. 'He cannot eat the corn himself, nor will he let us eat it who are hungry.'

Live and let live.

The Fox & the Stork

A FOX one day invited a stork to dinner, and amused himself at the expense of his guest, by providing nothing for him to eat but some thin soup in a shallow dish.

This the fox lapped up very quickly, while the stork, unable to gain a mouthful with her long, narrow bill, was as hungry at the end of the dinner as when she began.

The fox expressed his regret at seeing her eat so sparingly, and feared that the dish was not seasoned to her liking.

The stork said but little, but begged that the fox would do her the honour of returning the visit next day, which invitation Reynard the fox readily accepted.

The fox kept the appointment, and, having greeted his hostess, turned his attention to the dinner placed before them.

To his dismay Reynard saw that the meal was served in a narrow-necked vessel, and, while the stork was able to thrust in her long bill and take her fill, he was obliged to content himself with licking the outside of the jar.

Unable to satisfy his hunger, he retired with as good grace as he could, knowing that he could hardly find fault with his hostess, for she had only paid him back in his own coin.

Those who love practical jokes must be prepared to laugh at themselves.

Beddgelert

BEDDGELERT lies near Snowdon in the county of Gwynedd, about 12 kilometres inland from the sea. 'Bedd' is the Welsh word for 'grave,' so Beddgelert means the 'Grave of Gelert.'

This is the story of how it came to be so called.

Many years ago there lived a brave chieftain, called Llewellyn, in Snowdonia. Now Llewellyn had a faithful dog, Gelert which had been presented to him by King John of England, and this dog was the leader of all Llewellyn's pack. At home he was as gentle as a lamb but in the hunt he was fierce and brave.

One day when Llewellyn and his men had assembled on the mountainside ready for hunting the hare, the huntsman blew a loud blast on his horn to rally the pack of hounds. To the huntsman's surprise, Gelert, the leader of the pack, was not there. So he blew again upon his horn. Still Gelert did not come. 'It seems very strange that Gelert does not come in answer to my call,' said the huntsman.

But they could not wait for him any longer and the huntsmen and the rest of the pack went on without him.

But somehow or other things went wrong that day. The chase was poor and the hound failed to run their quarry to earth.

At twilight Llewellyn rode sadly towards his castle. He was wondering greatly where Gelert had been all day. Just then he heard the familiar sound of his barking.

'Ah! Bad dog! Why did you fail me to-day? Where have you been?' Llewellyn began. But as he rode nearer he could see that something was wrong.

The dog did not bound forward to greet him as he usually did. He crouched low and licked his lips. Then, looking more closely at him, Llewellyn perceived that Gelert's coat was tangled and matted with clots of blood.

'What is the matter? Where did all this blood come from?' cried his master.

Here, there and everywhere the ground was smeared with it. Llewellyn dismounted hastily and ran into the castle. Here there were signs everywhere of a struggle. Blood, freshly-spilled, lay all over the floor. No servants were there to answer to his call. Gelert followed at his master's heels, dragging his hind legs somewhat.

Quickly Llewellyn's gaze travelled to the cradle in which he had left his baby son. He rushed up to it. The baby was not there! The coverlet was torn and smeared with blood. All was in disorder. Llewellyn had only one thought at the time. 'Cruel monster!' he cried to the dog. 'You have betrayed my trust and devoured my son!'

The poor dumb creature's eyes searched his master's face.

'If only I could speak!' he seemed to say. He crouched low and tried to lick his master's feet. But Llewellyn was furious.

'You, too, shall die, treacherous hound!' And so saying he plunged his sword into Gelert's side.

His dying yelp was heard from afar. It woke Llewellyn's sleeping child who murmured and cried out.

The chieftain searched in the direction from which the sound came. There, in another room, quite safe and sound, beneath a heap of bloodstained clothes, lay the child.

At his side, torn and mangled, but quite dead, lay an enormous wolf!

Now the truth was made clear to Llewellyn. The gallant dog had fought with the wolf and had killed him, in order to save the life of the child he so jealously guarded.

Llewellyn's grief was pitiful to behold. 'The desperate deed which laid you low, this heart shall ever regret,' said he.

So Gelert was buried with ceremony and there beneath a mound of stones, his grave can still be seen to this day.

The Thirty-nine Steps

This exciting story by John Buchan (1875–1940) is set in the sparsely populated countryside of the Scottish Borders. Richard Hannay had, quite unwittingly, been involved in an international political intrigue. Now he was being hunted by men who had already killed and would stop at nothing to dispose of him. And because he was already – though wrongly – implicated in a murder, Hannay could not turn to the police. In this chapter we see how formidable an opposition he faces.

I SAT down on the very crest of the pass and took stock of my position.

Behind me was the road climbing through a long cleft in the hills, which was the upper glen of some notable river. In front was a flat space of maybe a mile, all pitted with bog holes and rough with tussocks, and then beyond it the road fell steeply down another glen to a plain whose blue dimness melted into the distance. To left and right were round-shouldered green hills as smooth as pancakes, but to the south – that is, the left hand – there was a glimpse of high heathery mountains, which I remembered from the map as the big knot of hill which I had chosen for my sanctuary. I was on the central boss of a huge upland country, and could see everything moving for miles. In the meadows below the road half a mile back a cottage smoked, but it was the only sign of human life. Otherwise there was only the calling of plovers and the tinkling of little streams.

It was now about seven o'clock, and as I waited I heard once again that ominous beat in the air. Then I realized that my vantage-ground might be in reality a trap. There was no cover for a tomtit in those bald green places.

I sat quite still and hopeless while the beat grew louder. Then I saw an aeroplane coming up from the east. It was flying high, but as I looked it dropped several hundred feet and began to circle round the knot of hill in narrowing circles, just as a hawk wheels before it pounces. Now it was flying very low, and now the observer on board caught sight of me. I could see one of the two occupants examining me through glasses.

Suddenly it began to rise in swift whorls, and the next I knew it was speeding eastward again till it became a speck in the blue morning.

That made me do some savage thinking. My enemies had located me, and the next thing would be a cordon round me. I didn't know what force they could command, but I was certain it would be sufficient. The aeroplane had seen my bicycle, and would conclude that I would try to escape by the road. In that case there might be a chance on the moors to the right or left. I wheeled the machine a hundred yards from the highway, and plunged it into a moss-hole, where it sank among pond weed and water buttercups. Then I climbed to a knoll which gave me a view of the two valleys. Nothing was stirring on the long white ribbon that threaded them.

I have said there was not cover in the whole place to hide a tomtit. As the day advanced it was flooded with soft fresh light till it had the fragrant sunniness of the South African veld. At other times I would have liked the place, but now it seemed to suffocate me. The free moorlands were prison walls, and the keen hill air was the breath of a dungeon.

I tossed a coin – heads right, tails left – and it fell heads, so I turned to the north. In a little I came to the brow of the ridge which was the containing wall of the pass. I saw the high road for maybe ten miles, and far down it something that was moving, and that I took to be a motor-car. Beyond the ridge I looked on a rolling green moor, which fell away into wooded glens. Now my life on the veld has given me the eyes of a kite, and I can see things for which most men need a telescope. . . . Away down the slope, a couple of miles away, several men were advancing like a row of beaters at a shoot. . . .

I dropped out of sight behind the skyline. That way was shut to me, and I must try the bigger hills to the south beyond the highway. The car I had noticed was getting nearer, but it was still a long way off with some very steep gradients before it. I ran hard, crouching low except in the hollows, and as I ran I kept scanning the brow of the hill before me. Was it imagination, or did I see figures – one, two, perhaps more – moving in a glen beyond the stream?

If you are hemmed in on all sides in a patch of land there is only one chance of escape. You must stay in the patch, and let your enemies search it and not find you. That was good sense, but how on earth was I to escape notice in that table-cloth of a place? I would have buried myself to the neck in mud or lain below water or climbed the tallest tree. But there was not a stick of wood, the bog holes were little puddles, the stream was a slender trickle. There was nothing but short heather, and bare hill bent, and the white highway.

Then, in a tiny bight of road, beside a heap of stones, I found the roadman.

He had just arrived, and was wearily flinging down his hammer. He looked at me with a fishy eye and yawned.

'Confoond the day I ever left the herdin'!' he said, as if to the world at large. 'There I was my ain maister. Now I'm a slave to the Government, tethered to the roadside, si' sair een, and a back like a suckle.'

He took up the hammer, struck a stone, dropped the implement with an oath, and put both hands to his ears. 'Mercy on me! My heid's burstin'!' he cried.

He was a wild figure, about my own size but much bent, with a week's beard on his chin, and a pair of big horn spectacles.

'I canna dae't,' he cried again. 'The Surveyor maun just report me. I'm for my bed.'

I asked him what was the trouble, though indeed that was clear enough.

'The trouble is that I'm no sober. Last nicht my dochter Merran was waddit, and they danced till fower in the byre. Me and some ither chiels sat down to the drinkin', and here I am. Peety that I ever lookit on the wine when it was red!'

I agreed with him about bed.

'It's easy speakin',' he moaned. 'But I got a post-caird yestreen sayin' that the new Road Surveyor would be round the day. He'll come and he'll no find me, or else he'll find me fou, and either way I'm a done man. I'll awa' back to my bed and say I'm no weel, but I doot that'll no help me, for they ken my kind o' no-weel-ness.'

Then I had an inspiration. 'Does the new Surveyor know you?' I asked.

'No him. He's just been a week at the job. He rins about in a wee motor-cawr, and wad speir the inside oot o' a whelk.'

'Where's your house?' I asked, and was directed by a wavering finger to the cottage by the stream.

'Well, back to your bed,' I said, 'and sleep in peace. I'll take on your job for a bit and see the Surveyor.'

He stared at me blankly; then, as the notion dawned on his fuddled brain, his face broke into the vacant drunkard's smile.

'You're the billy,' he cried. 'It'll be easy eneuch managed. I've finished that bing o' stanes, so you needna chap ony mair this forenoon. Just take the barry, and wheel eneuch metal frae yon quarry doon the road to mak anither bing the morn. My name's Alexander Trummle, and I've been seeven year at the trade, and twenty afore that herdin' on Leithen Water. My freens ca' me Ecky, and whiles Specky, for I wear glesses, being weak i' the sicht. Just you speak the Surveyor fair, and ca' him Sir, and he'll be fell pleased. I'll be back or midday.'

I borrowed his spectacles and filthy old hat; stripped off coat, waistcoat, and collar, and gave him them to carry home; borrowed, too, the foul stump of a clay pipe as an extra property. He indicated my simple tasks, and without more ado set off at an amble bedwards. Bed may have been his chief object, but I think there was also something left in the foot of a bottle. I prayed that he might be safe under cover before my friends arrived on the scene.

Then I set to work to dress for the part. I opened the collar of my shirt – it was a vulgar blue-and-white check such as ploughmen wear – and revealed a neck as brown as any tinker's. I rolled up my sleeves, and there was a forearm which might have been a blacksmith's, sunburnt and rough with old scars. I got my boots and trouser-legs all white from the dust of the road, and hitched up my trousers, tying them with string below the knee. Then I set to work on my face. With a handful of dust I made a water-mark round my neck, the place where Mr. Turnbull's Sunday ablutions might be expected to stop. I rubbed a good deal of dirt also into the sunburn of my cheeks. A roadman's eyes would no doubt be a little inflamed, so I contrived to get some dust in both of mine, and by dint of vigorous rubbing produced a bleary effect.

The sandwiches Sir Harry had given me had gone off with my coat, but the roadman's lunch, tied up in a red handkerchief, was at my disposal. I ate with great relish several of the thick slabs of scone and cheese and drank a little of the cold tea. In the handkerchief was a local paper tied with string and addressed to Mr. Turnbull – obviously meant to solace his midday leisure. I did up the bundle again, and put the paper conspicuously beside it.

My boots did not satisfy me, but by dint of kicking among the stones I reduced them to the granite-like surface which marks a roadman's footgear. Then I bit and scraped my finger-nails till the edges were all cracked and uneven. The men I was matched against would miss no detail. I broke one of the bootlaces and retied it in a clumsy knot, and loosed the other so that my thick grey socks bulged over the uppers. Still no sign of anything on the road. The motor I had observed half an hour ago must have gone home.

My toilet complete, I took up the barrow and began my journeys to and from the quarry a hundred yards off.

I remember an old scout in Rhodesia, who had done many queer things in his day, once telling me that the secret of playing a part was to think yourself into it. You could never keep it up, he said, unless you could manage to convince yourself that you were *it*. So I shut off all other thoughts and switched them on to the road-mending. I thought of the little white cottage as my home, I recalled the years I had spent herding on Leithen Water, I made my mind dwell lovingly on sleep in a box-bed and a bottle of cheap whisky. Still nothing appeared on that long white road.

Now and then a sheep wandered off the heather to stare at me.

A heron flopped down to a pool in the stream and started to fish, taking no more notice of me than if I had been a milestone. On I went, trundling my loads of stone, with the heavy step of the professional. Soon I grew warm, and the dust on my face changed into solid and abiding grit. I was already counting the hours till evening should put a limit to Mr. Turnbull's monotonous toil.

Suddenly a crisp voice spoke from the road, and looking up I saw a little Ford two-seater, and a round-faced young man in a bowler hat.

'Are you Alexander Turnbull?' he asked. 'I am the new County Road Surveyor. You live at Blackhopefoot, and have charge of the section from Laidlawbyres to the Riggs? Good! A fair bit of road, Turnbull, and not badly engineered. A little soft about a mile off, and the edges want cleaning. See you look after that. Good morning. You'll know me the next time you see me.'

Clearly my get-up was good enough for the dreaded Surveyor. I went on with my work, and as the morning grew towards noon I was cheered by a little traffic. A baker's van breasted the hill, and sold me a bag of ginger biscuits which I stowed in my trouser-pockets against emergencies. Then a herd passed with sheep, and disturbed me somewhat by asking loudly, 'What has become o' Specky?'

'In bed wi' the colic,' I replied, and the herd passed on. . . .

Just about midday a big car stole down the hill, glided past and drew up a hundred yards beyond. Its three occupants descended as if to stretch their legs, and sauntered towards me.

Two of the men I had seen before from the window of the Galloway inn – one lean, sharp, and dark, the other comfortable and smiling. The third had the look of a countryman – a vet, perhaps, or a small farmer. He was dressed in ill-cut knicker-bockers, and the eye in his head was as bright and wary as a hen's.

' 'Morning,' said the last. 'That's a fine easy job o' yours.'

I had not looked up on their approach, and now, when accosted, I slowly and painfully straightened my back, after the manner of roadmen; spat vigorously, after the manner of the low Scot; and regarded them steadily before replying. I confronted three pairs of eyes that missed nothing.

'There's waur jobs and there's better,' I said sententiously. 'I wad rather hae yours, sittin' a' day on your hinderlands on thae cushions. It's you and your muckle cawrs that wreck my roads! If we a' had oor richts, ye sud be made to mend what ye break.'

The bright-eyed man was looking at the newspaper lying beside Turnbull's bundle.

'I see you get your papers in good time,' he said.

I glanced at it casually. 'Aye, in gude time. Seein' that that paper cam' out last Setterday I'm just sax days late.'

He picked it up, glanced at the superscription, and laid it down again. One of the others had been looking at my boots, and a word in German called the speaker's attention to them.

'You've a fine taste in boots,' he said. 'These were never made by a country shoemaker.'

'They were not,' I said readily. 'They were made in London. I got them fraw the gentleman that was here last year for the shootin'. What was his name now?' And I scratched a forgetful head.

Again the sleek one spoke in German. 'Let us get on,' he said. 'This fellow is all right.'

They asked one last question.

'Did you see anyone pass early this morning? He might be on a bicycle or he might be on foot.'

I very nearly fell into the trap and told a story of a bicyclist hurrying past in the grey dawn. But I had the sense to see my danger. I pretended to consider very deeply.

'I wasna up very early,' I said. 'Ye see, my dochter was merrit last nicht, and we keepit it up late. I opened the house door about seeven and there was naebody on the road then. Since I cam' up here there has just been the baker and the Ruchill herd, besides you gentlemen.'

One of them gave me a cigar, which I smelt gingerly and stuck in Turnbull's bundle. They got into their car and were out of sight in three minutes.

My heart leaped with an enormous relief, but I went on wheeling my stones. It was as well, for ten minutes later the car returned, one of the occupants waving a hand to me. Those gentry left nothing to chance.

I finished Turnbull's bread and cheese, and pretty soon I had finished the stones. The next step was what puzzled me. I could not keep up this road-making business for long. A merciful Providence had kept Mr. Turnbull indoors, but if he appeared on the scene there would be trouble. I had a notion that the cordon was still tight round the glen, and that if I walked in any direction I should meet with questioners. But get out I must. No man's nerve could stand more than a day of being spied on.

I stayed at my post till about five o'clock. By that time I had resolved to go down to Turnbull's cottage at nightfall and take my chance of getting over the hills in the darkness. But suddenly a new car came up the road, and slowed down a yard or two from me. A fresh wind had risen, and the occupant wanted to light a cigarette.

It was a touring car, with the tonneau full of an assortment of baggage. One man sat in it, and by an amazing chance I knew him. His name was Marmaduke Jopley, and he was an offence to creation. He was a sort of blood stockbroker, who did his business by toadying eldest sons and rich young peers and foolish old ladies. 'Marmie' was a familiar figure, I understood, at balls and polo-weeks and country houses. He was an adroit scandal-monger, and would crawl a mile on his belly to anything that had a title or a million. I had a business introduction to his firm when I came to London, and he was good enough to ask me to dinner at his club. There he showed off at a great rate, and pattered about his duchesses till the snobbery of the creature turned me sick. I asked a man afterwards why nobody kicked him, and was told that Englishmen reverenced the weaker sex.

Anyhow there he was now, nattily dressed, in a fine new car, obviously on his way to visit some of his smart friends. A sudden daftness took me, and in a second I had jumped into the tonneau and had him by the shoulder.

'Hallo, Jopley,' I sang out. 'Well met, my lad!'

He got a horrid fright. His chin dropped as he stared at me. 'Who the devil are you?' he gasped.

'My name's Hannay,' I said. 'From Rhodesia, you remember.'

'Good God, the murderer!' he choked.

'Just so. And there'll be a second murder, my dear, if you don't do as I tell you. Give me that coat of yours. That cap, too.'

He did as he was bid, for he was blind with terror. Over my dirty trousers and vulgar shirt I put on his smart driving coat, which buttoned high at the top and thereby hid the deficiencies of my collar. I stuck the cap on my head, and added his gloves to my get-up. The dusty roadman in a minute was transformed into one of the neatest motorists in Scotland. On Mr. Jopley's head I clapped Turnbull's unspeakable hat, and told him to keep it there.

Then with some difficulty I turned the car. My plan was to go back the road he had come, for the watchers, having seen it before, would probably let it pass unremarked, and Marmie's figure was in no way like mine.

'Now, my child,' I said, 'sit quite still and be a good boy. I mean you no harm. I'm only borrowing your car for an hour or two. But if you play me any tricks, and above all if you open your mouth, as sure as there's a God above me I'll wring your neck. Savez?'

I enjoyed that evening's ride. We ran eight miles down the valley, through a village or two, and I could not help noticing several strange-looking folk lounging by the roadside. These were the watchers who would have had much to say to me if I had come in other garb or company. As it was, they looked incuriously on. One touched his cap in salute, and I responded graciously.

As the dark fell I turned up a side glen which, as I remember from the map, led into an unfrequented corner of the hills. Soon the villages were left behind, then the farms, and then even the wayside cottages. Presently we came to a lonely moor where the night was blackening the sunset gleam in the bog pools. Here we stopped, and I obligingly reversed the car and restored to Mr. Jopley his belongings.

'A thousand thanks,' I said. 'There's more use in you than I thought. Now be off and find the police.'

As I sat on the hillside, watching the tail-light dwindle, I reflected on the various kinds of crime I had now sampled. Contrary to general belief, I was not a murderer, but I had become an unholy liar, a shameless impostor, and a highwayman with a marked taste for expensive motor-cars.

The Blue Light

A SOLDIER had served a king his master many years, till at last he was dismissed without pay or reward. How he should earn his living he did not know, so he set out and journeyed homeward all day in a very downcast mood until in the evening he came to the edge of a deep wood. As the road led that way, he pushed forward, but had not gone far before he saw a light glimmering through the trees, towards which he made his way; and soon came to a hut where no one lived but an old witch. The poor fellow begged for a night's lodging and something to eat and drink; but she would listen to nothing: however, he was not easily got rid of, and at last she said, 'I think I will take pity on you this once: but if I do you must dig over all my garden for me in the morning.' The soldier agreed very willingly to anything she asked, and he became her guest.

The next day he kept his word and dug the garden very neatly. The job lasted all day, and in the evening, when his mistress would have sent him away, he said, 'I am so tired of my work that I must beg you to let me stay another night.' The old lady vowed at first she would not do any such thing, but after a great deal of talk he carried his point, agreeing to chop up a whole cart-load of wood for her the next day.

This task too was duly ended, but not till towards night; and then he found himself so tired, that he begged a third night's rest. And this too was given, but only on his pledging his word that the next day he would fetch the witch the blue light that burnt at the bottom of the well.

When morning came she led him to the well's mouth, tied him to a long rope, and let him down. At the bottom sure enough he found the blue light as the witch had said, and at once made the signal for her to draw him up again. But when she had pulled him up so near to the top that she could reach him with her hands, she said; 'Give me the light, I will take care of it,' – meaning to play him a trick, by taking it for herself and letting him fall again to the bottom of the well. But the soldier saw through her wicked thoughts, and said: 'No, I shall not give you the light till I find myself safe and sound out of the well.' At this she became very angry, and dashed him, with the light she had longed for for many years, down to the bottom. And there lay the poor soldier for a while in despair, on the damp mud below, and feared that his end had come. But his pipe happened to be in his pocket still half-full, and he thought to himself, 'I may as well make an end of smoking you out; it is the last pleasure I shall have in this world.' So he lit it at the blue light, and began to smoke.

Up rose a cloud of smoke, and suddenly a peculiar black dwarf was seen making his way through the midst of it. 'What do you want with me, soldier?' said he. 'I have no business with you,' he answered. But the dwarf said, 'I am bound to serve you in everything, as lord and master of the blue light.' 'Then first of all be so good as to help me out of this well.' No sooner said than done: the dwarf took him by the hand and drew him up, and the blue light, of course, with him. 'Now do me another piece of kindness,' said the soldier: 'Pray let that old lady take my place in the well.' When the dwarf had done this, and lodged the witch safely at the bottom, they began to ransack her treasures; and the soldier carried off as much of her gold and silver as he could. Then the dwarf said, 'If you should chance at any time to want me, you have nothing to do but to light your pipe at the blue light, and I will soon be with you.'

The soldier was greatly pleased at his good luck, and went into the best inn in the first town he came to, and ordered some fine clothes to be made and a handsome room to be got ready for him. When all was ready, he called his little man to him, and said, 'The king sent me away penniless, and left me to hunger and need: I have a mind to show him that it is my turn to be master now; so bring me his daughter here this evening, that she may wait upon me, and do what I bid her.' 'That is rather a dangerous task,' said the dwarf. But away he went, took the princess out of her bed, fast asleep as she was, and brought her to the soldier.

Very early in the morning he carried her back: and as soon as she saw her father, she said, 'I had a strange dream last night: I thought I was carried away through the air to a soldier's house, and there I waited upon him as his servant.' Then the king wondered greatly at such a story, but told her to make a hole in her pocket and fill it with peas, so that if it were really as she said, and the whole was not a dream, the peas might fall out in the streets as she passed through, and leave a clue to tell where she had been taken. She did so; but the dwarf had heard the king's

plot; and when evening came, and the soldier said he must bring him the princess again, he strewed peas over several of the streets, so that the few that fell from her pocket were not known from the others; and the people amused themselves all the next day picking up peas, and wondering where so many came from.

When the princess told her father what had happened to her the second time, he said, 'Take one of your shoes with you, and hide it in the room you are taken to.' The dwarf heard this also; and when the soldier told him to bring the king's daughter again he said, 'I cannot save you this time; it will be an unlucky thing for you if you are found out – as I think you will.' But the soldier would have his own way. 'Then you must take care and make the best of your way out of the city gate very early in the morning.'

The princess kept one shoe on her as her father bid her, and hid it in the soldier's room. And when she got back to her father, he ordered it to be sought for all over the town, and at last it was found where she had hid it. The soldier had run away, it is true, but he had been too slow, and was soon caught and thrown into a strong prison. What was worse, in the hurry of his flight, he had left behind him his great treasure, the blue light and all his gold, and had only one coin in his pocket.

As he was standing very sorrowful at the prison grating, he saw one of his comrades, and calling out to him said, 'if you will bring me a little bundle I left in the inn, I will give you a silver coin.' His comrade thought this very good pay for such a job: so he went away, and soon came back bringing the blue light and the gold. Then the soldier soon lit his pipe: up rose the smoke, and with it came his old friend the little dwarf. 'Do not fear, master,' said he: 'keep up your heart at your trial and leave everything to take its course; only mind to take the blue light with you.' The trial soon came. The prisoner was found guilty, and was ordered to be hanged on the gallows tree.

But as he was let out, he said he had one favour to beg of the king. 'What is it?' said His Majesty. 'That you will let me smoke one pipe on the road.' 'Two, if you like,' said the king. Then he lit his pipe at the blue light, and the black dwarf was before him in a moment. 'Be so good as to kill, slay, or put to flight all these people,' said the soldier, 'and as for the king, you may cut him into three pieces.' Then the dwarf began to lay about him, and soon got rid of the crowd: but the king begged hard for mercy, and to save his life, agreed to let the soldier have the princess for his wife, and to make him his heir.

The Old Hound

A HOUND who had been most skilled and faithful to his master in the hunting-field at last became too old to continue to play his part as in his younger days.

One day, when hunting a wild boar, he seized the creature by the ear, but not having sufficient strength to retain his hold, he allowed the boar to escape.

At that moment his master rode up and, seeing what had happened, severely scolded the dog, and would have beaten him had he not sadly cried:

'Spare your old servant! Although my heart is willing my limbs are feeble. Remember what I was rather than what I am now.'

Faithful service should be long remembered.

The Leopard & the Fox

O NE day a leopard, feeling very proud of his beautiful spots, went so far as to ask himself why even the lion should be thought greater than he, who had so rare a skin. Indeed, so proud did he become that he made up his mind to have nothing to do with other beasts of the forest.

This, of course, was soon noticed, and the fox, feeling very hurt and annoyed, went boldly up to the leopard and told him that he was foolish in having such a good opinion of himself.

'You may think yourself very fine,' said Reynard the fox, 'but, depend upon it, people value a bright brain far more than a handsome body.'

Beauty is only skin-deep.

The Frog & the Ox

N ox, grazing in a swampy meadow, happened to put his foot on a family of young frogs and crushed most of them to death.

Now, one that escaped ran off to tell his mother.

'Oh, Mother!' he said, 'while we were playing, such a big four-footed beast trod on us.'

'Big?' asked the old frog; 'how big? Was it as big' – and she puffed herself out very much – 'as big as this?'

'Oh!' said the little one, 'a great deal bigger than that.'

'Well, was it so big?' and she swelled herself out further still.

'Yes, Mother, it was; and if you were to swell till you burst yourself you would never be half its size.'

Annoyed with her little one for doubting her powers, the old frog tried yet again, and this time burst herself in the vain attempt to be what she was not.

Men may be ruined by attempting to change the work of Nature.

The Ass, the Fox & the Lion

HE ass and the fox entered into partnership together to protect each other, and swore eternal friendship. Soon after, they went hunting, but before they had gone far a lion crossed their path. The fox saw the lion first, and, pointing him out to the ass, said: 'We must make terms with this lion and get him to be friendly with us.' So saying, he went boldly up to the lion and offered to help him trap the ass, provided that his own life should be spared. The lion was quite willing to promise this, whereupon the fox induced the ass to follow him to a deep pit, into which he managed to push him. As soon as the lion saw that the ass was trapped he sprang upon the fox and made a meal of him, leaving the ass to be eaten at his leisure.

Those who betray their friends
must not expect others to keep faith with them.

The Ugly Duckling

IT was beautiful in the country – it was summer-time – the wheat was yellow, the oats were green, the hay was stacked up in the green meadows, and the stork paraded about on his long red legs talking in Egyptian, which language he had learned from his mother. The fields and meadows were skirted by thick woods, and a deep lake lay in the midst of the woods.

Yes, it was indeed beautiful in the country! The sunshine fell warm on an old mansion, surrounded by deep canals, and from the walls down to the water's edge there grew large burdock-leaves, so high that children could stand upright among them without being seen.

This place was as wild and unfrequented as the thickest part of the wood, and a duck had chosen to make her nest there. She was sitting on her eggs; but the pleasure she had felt at first was now almost gone, because she had been there so long, and had so few visitors, for the other ducks preferred swimming on the canals to sitting among the burdock-leaves gossiping with her.

At last the eggs cracked one after another, 'Tchick, tchick!' All the eggs were alive, and one little head after another appeared. 'Quack, quack,' said the duck, and all got up as well as they could; they peeped about from under the green leaves, and as green is good for the eyes, their mother let them look as long as they pleased.

'How large the world is!' said the little ones, for they found their present situation very different from their former one, while they were in the egg-shells.

'Do you imagine this to be the whole of the world?' said the mother. 'It extends far beyond the other side of the garden, to the pastor's field; but I have never been there. Are you all here?' And then she got up. 'No, I have not got you all; the largest egg is still here. How long will this last? I am so weary of it!' and then she sat down again.

'Well, and how are you getting on?' asked an old duck, who had come to pay her a visit.

'This one egg keeps me so long,' said the mother, 'it will not break; but you should see the others! They are the prettiest little ducklings I have seen in all my days; they are all like their father – the good-for-nothing fellow! He has not been to visit me once.'

'Let me see the egg that will not break,' said the old duck; 'depend upon it, it is a turkey's egg. I was cheated in the same way once myself, and I had such trouble with the young ones; for they were afraid of the water, and I could not get them there. I called and scolded, but it was all of no use. But let me see the egg – ah yes! to be sure, that is a turkey's egg. Leave it, and teach the other little ones to swim.'

'I will sit on it a little longer,' said the duck. 'I have been sitting so long, that I may as well spend the harvest here.'

'It is no business of mine,' said the old duck, and away she waddled.

The great egg burst at last, 'Tchick, tchick,' said the little one and out it tumbled – but oh! how large and ugly it was! The duck looked at it. 'That is a great, strong creature,' said she, 'none of the others is at all like it; can it be a young turkey-cock? Well, we shall soon find out; it must go into the water, though I push it in myself.'

The next day there was delightful weather, and the sun shone warmly upon all the green leaves when mother-duck with her family went down to the canal; 'plump' she went into the water. 'Quack, quack,' cried she, and one duckling after another jumped in. The water closed over their heads, but all came up again, and swam together in the pleasantest manner; their legs moved without effort. All were there, even the ugly grey one.

'No! it is not a turkey,' said the old duck; 'only see how prettily it moves its legs, how upright it holds itself; it is my own child! It is also really very pretty when one looks more closely at it; quack, quack, now come with me; I will take you into the world, introduce you in the duck-yard; but keep close to me, or some one may tread on you, and beware of the cat.'

So they came into the duck-yard. There was a horrid noise; two families were quarrelling about the remains of an eel, which in the end was grabbed by the cat.

'See, my children, such is the way of the world,' said the mother-duck, wiping her beak, for she too was fond of roasted eels. 'Now use your legs,' said she, 'keep together, and bow to the old duck you see over there. She is the most distinguished of all the fowls present, and is of Spanish blood, which accounts for her dignified appearance and manners. And look, she has a red rag on her leg; that is considered extremely handsome, and is the greatest distinction a duck can have. Don't turn your feet inwards; a well-educated duckling always keeps his legs far apart, like his father and mother, just so – look! Now bow your necks, and say "Quack!"'

And they did as they were told. But the other ducks who were in the yard looked at them and said aloud, 'Only see, now we have another brood, as if there were not enough of us already; and how ugly that one is, we will not endure it;' and immediately one of the ducks flew at him, and bit him in the neck.

'Leave him alone,' said the mother, 'he is doing no one any harm.'

'Yes, but he is so large, and so strange-looking, and therefore he shall be teased.'

'Those are fine children that our good mother has,' said the old duck with the red rag on her leg. 'All are pretty except one, and that has not turned out well.'

'That cannot be, please your highness,' said the mother. 'Certainly he is not handsome, but he is a very good child, and swims as well as the others, indeed rather better. I think he will grow like the others all in good time, and perhaps will look smaller. He stayed so long in the egg-shell, that is the cause of the difference;' and she scratched the duckling's neck, and stroked his whole body. 'Besides,' she added, 'he is a drake; I think he will be very strong, therefore it does not matter so much, as he will fight his way through.'

'The other ducks are very pretty,' said the old duck. 'Do make yourselves at home, and if you find an eel's head you can bring it to me.'

And so they made themselves at home.

But the poor little duckling who had come last out of its egg-shell, and who was so ugly, was bitten, pecked, and teased by both ducks and hens. 'It is so large,' they all said. And the turkey-cock, who had come into the world with spurs on, and therefore fancied he was an emperor, puffed himself up like a ship in full sail, and marched up to the duckling quite red with rage. The poor little thing scarcely knew what to do; he was quite distressed, because he was so ugly, and because he was the joke of the poultry-yard.

So passed the first day, and afterwards matters grew worse and worse; the poor duckling was scorned by all. Even his brothers and sisters behaved unkindly, and were constantly saying, 'I wish the cat would catch you, you nasty creature!' The mother said, 'Ah, if you were only far away!' The ducks bit him, the

hens pecked him, and the girl who fed the poultry kicked him.

He ran over the hedge; the little birds in the bushes were terrified. 'That is because I am so ugly,' thought the duckling, shutting his eyes, while he ran on. At last he came to a wide moor, where lived some wild ducks; here he lay the whole night, tired and comfortless.

In the morning the wild ducks flew up and noticed their new companion. 'Who are you?' they asked; and our little duckling turned himself in all directions, and greeted them as politely as possible.

'You are really very ugly,' said the wild ducks; 'however, that does not matter to us, provided you do not marry into our families.' Poor thing! he had never thought of marrying; he only begged permission to lie among the reeds, and drink the water of the moor.

There he lay for two whole days; on the third day there came two wild geese, or rather ganders, who had not been long out of their egg-shells, which accounts for their impertinence.

'Listen,' they said, 'you are so ugly that we like you very much. Will you come with us, and be a bird of passage? On another moor, not far from this, are some dear, sweet, wild geese, as lovely creatures as have ever said "hiss, hiss." You are truly in the way to make your fortune, ugly as you are.'

Bang! a gun went off all at once, and both wild geese were stretched dead among the reeds. Bang! a gun went off again, whole flocks of wild geese flew up from among the reeds, and another report followed.

There was a grand hunting party; the hunters lay in ambush all around; some were even sitting in the trees, whose huge branches stretched far over the moor. The blue smoke rose through the thick trees like a mist, and was dispersed as it fell over the water; the hounds splashed about in the mud, the reeds and rushes bent in all directions. How frightened the poor little duck was! He turned his head, thinking to hide it under his wings; and in a moment a most frightening looking dog stood close to him, his tongue hanging out of his mouth, his eyes sparkling fearfully. He

opened his jaws wide at the sight of our duckling, showed him his sharp white teeth, and, splash, splash? he was gone – gone without hurting him.

'Well! let me be thankful,' he sighed. 'I am so ugly that even the dog will not eat me.'

And now he lay still, though the shooting continued among the reeds, shot following shot.

The noise did not cease till late in the day, and even then the poor little thing dared not stir; he waited several hours before he looked around him, and then hurried away from the moor as fast as he could. He ran over fields and meadows, though the wind was so strong that he had some difficulty in proceeding.

Towards evening he reached a poor little hut – so poor that it knew not on which side to fall, and therefore remained standing. The wind blew violently, so that our poor little duckling was obliged to support himself on his tail in order to stand against it; but it became worse and worse. He then saw that the door had lost one of its hinges, and hung so much awry that he could creep through the crevice into the room – which he did.

In this room lived an old woman, with her tom-cat and her hen; and the cat, whom she called her little son, knew how to set up his back and purr; indeed he could even emit sparks when stroked the wrong way. The hen had very short legs, and was therefore called 'Cuckoo Shortlegs'; she laid very good eggs, and the old woman loved her as her own child.

The next morning the new guest was noticed; the cat began to mew, and the hen to cackle.

'What is the matter?' asked the old woman, looking round; however, her eyes were not good, and so she took the young duckling to be a large duck who had lost her way. 'This is a great catch,' said she; I shall now have duck's eggs, if it is not a drake; we must try at any rate.'

And so the duckling was put to the test for three weeks, but no eggs made their appearance.

Now the cat was the master of the house and the hen was the mistress, and they used always to say, 'We and the world,' for they imagined themselves to be not only the half of the world, but also by far the better half. The duckling thought it was possible to be of a different opinion, but that the hen would not allow.

'Can you lay eggs?' asked she.

'No.'

'Well, then, hold your tongue.'

And the cat said, 'Can you set up your back? Can you purr?'

'No.'

'Well, then, you should have no opinion when reasonable persons are speaking.'

So the duckling sat alone in a corner, and was in a very bad temper; however, he happened to think of the fresh air and bright sunshine, and these thoughts gave him such a strong desire to swim again that he could not help telling it to the hen.

'What's the matter with you?' said the hen. 'You have nothing to do, and, therefore, brood over these fancies; either lay eggs, or purr, then you will forget them.'

'But it is so delicious to swim,' said the duckling; 'so delicious when the waters close over your head, and you plunge to the bottom.'

'Well, that is a queer sort of a pleasure,' said the hen; 'I think you must be crazy. Ask the cat – he is the most sensible animal I know – whether he would like to swim or to plunge to the bottom of the water. Ask our mistress, the old woman – there is no one in the world wiser than she – do you think she would take pleasure in swimming and in the waters closing over her head?'

'You do not understand me,' said the duckling.

'What! we do not understand you! So you think yourself wiser than the cat and the old woman, not to mention myself. Do not fancy any such thing, child, but be thankful for all the

kindness that has been shown you. Are you not lodged in a warm room, and have you not the advantage of society from which you can learn something? But you are a simpleton, and it is tiring to have anything to do with you. Believe me, I wish you well. I tell you unpleasant truths, but it is thus that real friendship is shown. Come, for once give yourself the trouble to learn to purr, or to lay eggs.'

'I think I will go out into the wide world again,' said the duckling.

'Well, go,' answered the hen.

So the duckling went. He swam on the surface of the water, he plunged beneath, but all animals passed him by, on account of his ugliness. And the autumn came, the leaves turned yellow and brown, the wind caught them and danced them about; the air was very cold, the clouds were heavy with hail or snow, and the raven sat on the hedge and croaked. The poor duckling was certainly not very comfortable!

One evening, just as the sun was setting with unusual brilliancy, a flock of large beautiful birds rose from out of the brushwood; the duckling had never seen anything so beautiful before; their plumage was of a dazzling white, and they had long slender necks. They were swans; they uttered a strange cry, spread out their long, splendid wings, and flew away from these cold regions to warmer countries across the open sea. They flew so high, so very high! and the little ugly duckling's feelings were so strange; he turned round and round in the water like a mill-wheel, strained his neck to look after them, and sent forth such a loud and strange cry that it almost frightened himself.

Ah! he could not forget them, those noble birds! those happy birds! When he could see them no longer, he plunged to the bottom of the water, and when he rose again, was almost beside himself. The duckling did not know what the birds were called, or where they were flying, yet he loved them as he had never before loved anything. He did not envy them; it would never have occurred to him to wish such beauty for himself; he would have been quite contented if the ducks in the duck-yard had only endured his company – the poor ugly animal.

And the winter was so cold, so cold! The duckling was obliged to swim round and round in the water, to keep it from freezing; but every night the opening in which he swam became smaller and smaller. It froze so that the crust of ice crackled; the duckling

was obliged to make good use of his legs to prevent the water from freezing entirely; at last, tired out, he lay stiff and cold in the ice.

Early in the morning there passed by a peasant who saw him, broke the ice in pieces with his wooden shoe, and brought him home to his wife.

He now revived; the children would have played with him, but our duckling thought they wished to tease him, and in his terror jumped into the milk-pail, so that the milk was spilled about the room. The good woman screamed and clapped her hands; he flew then into the pan where the butter was kept, and then into the flour, and out again, and then how strange he looked!

The woman screamed, and struck at him with her spoon; the children ran races with each other trying to catch him, and laughed and screamed as well. It was as well for him that the door stood open; he jumped out among the bushes into the new fallen snow, and lay there in a daze.

But it would be too sad to relate all the trouble and misery that he was obliged to suffer during the severity of the winter. He was lying on a moor among the reeds, when the sun began to shine warmly again; the larks sang, and spring arrived.

And once more he shook his wings. They were stronger than before, and carried him forwards quickly; and before he was well aware of it, he was in a large garden where the apple-trees stood in full bloom, where the syringas sent forth their fragrance and hung their long green branches down into the winding canal! Oh! everything was so lovely, so full of the freshness of spring! And out of the thicket came three beautiful white swans. They displayed their feathers so proudly, and swam so lightly, so lightly! The duckling knew the glorious creatures, and was seized with a strange sadness.

'I will fly to them, those kingly birds!' he said. 'They will kill me, because I, ugly as I am, have presumed to approach them; but it doesn't matter. Better to be killed by them than to be bitten by the ducks, pecked by the hens, kicked by the girl who feeds the poultry, and to have so much to suffer during the winter!' He flew into the water, and swam towards the beautiful creatures; they saw him and shot forward to meet him. 'Only kill me,' said the poor animal, and he bowed his head low, expecting death. But what did he see in the water? He saw beneath him his own form, no longer that of a plump, ugly grey bird – it was that of a swan.

It doesn't matter if one has been born in a duck-yard, if one has been hatched from a swan's egg.

The good creature felt himself really elevated by all the troubles and adversities he had experienced. He could now rightly estimate his own happiness, and the larger swans swam round him, and stroked him with their beaks.

Some little children were running about in the garden; they threw grain and bread into the water, and the youngest exclaimed, 'There is a new one!' The others also cried out, 'Yes, a new swan has come!' and they clapped their hands and danced around. They ran to their father and mother, bread and cake were thrown into the water, and everyone said: 'The new one is the best, so young, and so beautiful!' and the old swans bowed before him.

The young swan felt quite ashamed, and hid his head under his wings; he scarcely knew what to do, he was so happy, but still not proud – for a good heart is never proud.

He remembered how he had been persecuted and scorned, and he now heard every one say he was the most beautiful of all beautiful birds. The syringas bent down their branches towards him low into the water, and the sun shone warmly and brightly. He shook his feathers, stretched his slender neck, and in the joy of his heart said, 'How little did I dream of so much happiness when I was the despised ugly duckling!'

The Adventures of Huckleberry Finn

Mark Twain is the pen-name of Samuel Langhorne Clemens (1835–1910). Readers of his books will first have come across Huckleberry Finn in 'The Adventures of Tom Sawyer'. But in this book the story centres on Huck, and has added appeal because it is, to a large extent, the story of the young Mark Twain himself.

YOU don't know about me, without you have read a book by the name of *The Adventures of Tom Sawyer*, but that ain't no matter. That book was made by Mr. Mark Twain, and he told the truth, mainly. There was things which he stretched, but mainly he told the truth. That is nothing. I never seen anybody but lied, one time or another, without it was Aunt Polly, or the widow, or maybe Mary. Aunt Polly – Tom's Aunt Polly, she is – and Mary, and the Widow Douglas, is all told about in that book – which is mostly a true book; with some stretchers, as I said before.

Now the way that the book winds up, is this: Tom and me found the money that the robbers hid in the cave, and it made us rich. We got six thousand dollars apiece – all gold. It was an awful sight of money when it was piled up. Well, Judge Thatcher, he took it and put it out at interest, and it fetched us a dollar a day apiece, all the year round – more than a body could tell what to do with. The Widow Douglas, she took me for her son, and allowed she would sivilize me; but it was rough living in the house all the time, considering how dismal regular and decent the widow was in all her ways; and so when I couldn't stand it no longer, I lit out. I got into my old rags and my sugar-hogshead again, and was free and satisfied. But Tom Sawyer he hunted me up and said he was going to start a band of robbers, and I might join if I would go back to the widow and be respectable. So I went back.

The widow she cried over me, and called me a poor lost lamb, and she called me a lot of other names, too, but she never meant no harm by it. She put me in them new clothes again, and I couldn't do nothing but sweat and sweat, and feel all cramped up. Well, then, the old thing commenced again. The widow rung a bell for supper, and you had to come to time. When you got to the table you couldn't go right to eating, but you had to wait for the widow to tuck down her head and grumble a little over the victuals, though there warn't really anything the matter with them. That is, nothing only everything was cooked by itself. In a barrel of odds and ends it is different; things get mixed up, and the juice kind of swaps around, and the things go better.

After supper she got out her book and learned me about Moses and the Bulrushers; and I was in a sweat to find out all about him; but by-and-by she let it out that Moses had been dead a considerable long time; so then I didn't care no more about him; because I don't take no stock in dead people.

Pretty soon I wanted to smoke, and asked the widow to let me. But she wouldn't. She said it was a mean practice and wasn't clean, and I must try to not do it any more. That is just the way with some people. They get down on a thing when they don't know nothing about it. Here she was a-bothering about Moses, which was no kin to her, and no use to anybody, being gone, you see, yet finding a power of fault with me for doing a thing that had some good in it. And she took snuff too; of course, that was all right, because she done it herself.

Her sister, Miss Watson, a tolerable slim old maid, with goggles on, had just come to live with her, and took a set at me now, with a spelling-book. She worked me middling hard for about an hour, and then the widow made her ease up. I couldn't stood it much longer. Then for an hour it was deadly dull, and I was fidgety. Miss Watson would say, 'Don't put your feet up there, Huckleberry'; and, 'Don't scrunch up like that, Huckleberry – set up straight'; and pretty soon she would say, 'Don't gap and stretch like that, Huckleberry – why don't you try to behave?' Then she told me all about the bad place, and I said I wished I was there. She got mad, then, but I didn't mean no harm. All I wanted was to go somewhere; all I wanted was a change, I warn't particular. She said it was wicked to say what I said; said she wouldn't say it for the whole world; *she* was going to live so as to go to the good place. Well, I couldn't see no advantage in going where she was going, so I made up my mind I wouldn't try for it. But I never said so, because it would only make trouble, and wouldn't do no good.

Now she had got a start, and she went on and told me all about the good place. She said all a body would have to do there was to go around all day long with a harp and sing for ever and ever. So I didn't think much of it. But I never said so. I asked her if she reckoned Tom Sawyer would go there, and she said, not by a considerable sight. I was glad about that, because I wanted him and me to be together.

Miss Watson she kept pecking at me, and it got tiresome and

lonesome. By-and-by they fetched the niggers in and had prayers, and then everybody was off to bed. I went up to my room with a piece of candle and put it on the table. Then I set down in a chair by the window and tried to think of something cheerful, but it warn't no use. I felt so lonesome I most wished I was dead. The stars was shining; and the leaves rustled in the woods ever so mournful; and I heard an owl, away off, who-whooing about somebody that was dead, and a whippowill and a dog crying about somebody that was going to die; and the wind was trying to whisper something to me and I couldn't make out what it was, and so it made the cold shivers run over me. Then away out in the woods I heard that kind of a sound that a ghost makes when it wants to tell about something that's on its mind and can't make itself understood, and so can't rest easy in its grave and has to go about that way every night grieving. I got so downhearted and scared, I did wish I had some company. Pretty soon a spider went crawling up my shoulder, and I flipped it off and it lit in the candle; and before I could budge it was all shrivelled up. I didn't need anybody to tell me that that was an awful bad sign and would fetch me some bad luck, so I was scared and most shook the clothes off of me. I got up and turned around in my tracks three times and crossed my breast every time; and then I tied up a little lock of my hair with a thread to keep witches away. But I hadn't no confidence. You do that when you've lost a horse-shoe that you've found, instead of nailing it up over the door, but I hadn't ever heard anybody say it was any way to keep off bad luck when you'd killed a spider.

I set down again, a-shaking all over, and got out my pipe for a smoke; for the house was all as still as death, now, and so the widow wouldn't know. Well, after a long time I heard the clock away off in the town go boom – boom – boom – twelve licks – and all still again – stiller than ever. Pretty soon I heard a twig snap, down in the dark amongst the trees – something was a-stirring. I set still and listened. Directly I could just barely hear a 'me-yow! me-yow!' down there. That was good! Says I, 'me-yow! me-yow!' as soft as I could, and then I put out the light and scrambled out of the window on to the shed. Then I slipped down to the ground and crawled in amongst the trees, and sure enough there was Tom Sawyer waiting for me.

WE went tip-toeing along a path amongst the trees back towards the end of the widow's garden, stooping down so as the branches wouldn't scrape our heads. When we was passing the kitchen I fell over a root and made a noise. We crouched down and laid still. Miss Watson's big nigger, named Jim, was setting in the kitchen door; we could see him pretty clear, because there was a light behind him. He got up and stretched his neck out about a minute, listening. Then he says:

'Who dah?'

He listened some more; then he come tip-toeing down and

stood right between us; we could a touched him, nearly. Well, likely it was minutes and minutes that there warn't a sound, and we all there so close together. There was a place on my ankle that got to itching; but I dasn't scratch it; and then my ear begun to itch; and next my back, right between my shoulders. Seemed like I'd die if I couldn't scratch. Well, I've noticed that thing plenty of times since. If you are with the quality, or at a funeral, or trying to go to sleep when you wain't sleepy – if you are anywheres where it won't do for you to scratch, why you will itch all over in upwards of a thousand places. Pretty soon Jim says:

'Say – who is you? Whar is you? Dog my cats ef I didn' hear sumf'n. Well, I knows what I's gwyne to do. I's gwyne to set down here and listen tell I hears it agin.'

So he set down on the ground betwixt me and Tom. He leaned his back up against a tree, and stretched his legs out till one of them most touched one of mine. My nose begun to itch. It itched till the tears come into my eyes. But I dasn't scratch. Then it begun to itch on the inside. Next I got to itching underneath. I didn't know how I was going to set still. This miserableness went on as much as six or seven minutes; but it seemed a sight longer than that. I was itching in eleven difference places now. I reckoned I couldn't stand it more'n a minute longer, but I set my teeth hard and got ready to try. Just then Jim begun to breathe heavy; next he begun to snore – and then I was pretty soon comfortable again.

Tom he made a sign to me – kind of a little noise with his mouth – and we went creeping away on our hands and knees. When we was ten foot off, Tom whispered to me and wanted to tie Jim to the tree for fun; but I said no; he might wake and make a disturbance, and then they'd find out I warn't in. Then Tom said he hadn't got candles enough, and he would slip in the kitchen and get some more. I didn't want him to try. I said Jim might wake up and come. But Tom wanted to resk it; so we slid in there and got three candles, and Tom laid five cents on the table for pay. Then we got out, and I was in a sweat to get away; but nothing would do Tom but he must crawl to where Jim was, on his hands and knees, and play something on him. I waited, and it seemed a good while, everything was so still and lonesome.

As soon as Tom was back, we cut along the path, around the garden fence, and by and by fetched up on the steep top of the hill the other side of the house. Tom said he slipped Jim's hat off his head and hung it on a limb right over him, and Jim stirred a little, but he didn't wake. Afterwards Jim said the witches bewitched him and put him in a trance, and rode him all over the State, and then set him under the trees again and hung his hat on a limb to show who done it. And next time Jim told it he said they rode him down to New Orleans; and after that, every time he told it he spread it more and more, till by and by he said they rode him all over the world, and tired him most to death, and his back was all over saddle-boils. Jim was monstrous proud about it, and he got so he wouldn't hardly notice the other niggers. Niggers would come miles to hear Jim tell about it, and he was more looked up to than any nigger in that country. Strange niggers would stand with their mouths open and look him all over, same as if he was a wonder. Niggers is always talking about witches in the dark by the kitchen fire; but whenever one was talking and letting on to know all about such things, Jim would happen in and say, 'Hm! What you know 'bout witches?' and that nigger was corked up and had to take a back seat. Jim always kept that five-center piece around his neck with a string, and said it was a charm the devil give to him with his own hands and told him he could cure anybody with it and fetch witches whenever he wanted to, just by saying something to it; but he never told what it was he said to it. Niggers would come from all around there and give Jim anything they had, just for a sight of that five-center piece; but they wouldn't touch it, because the devil had had his hands on it. Jim was most ruined, for a servant, because he got so stuck up on account of having seen the devil and been rode by witches.

Well, when Tom and me got to the edge of the hill-top, we looked away down into the village and could see three or four lights twinkling, where there was sick folks, maybe; and the stars over us was sparkling ever so fine; and down by the village was the river, a whole mile broad, and awful still and grand. We went down the hill and found Jo Harper, and Ben Rogers, and two or three more of the boys, hid in the old tanyard. So we unhitched a skiff and pulled down the river two mile and a half, to the big scar on the hill-side, and went ashore.

We went to a clump of bushes, and Tom made everybody swear to keep the secret, and then showed them a hole in the hill, right in the thickest part of the bushes. Then we lit the candles and crawled in on our hands and knees. We went about two hundred yards, and then the cave opened up. Tom poked about amongst the passages and pretty soon ducked under a wall where you wouldn't a noticed that there was a hole. We went along a narrow place and got into a kind of room, all damp and sweaty and cold, and there we stopped. Tom says:

'Now we'll start this band of robbers and call it Tom Sawyer's Gang. Everybody that wants to join has got to take an oath, and write his name in blood.'

Everybody was willing. So Tom got out a sheet of paper that he had wrote the oath on, and read it. It swore every boy to stick to the band, and never tell any of the secrets; and if anybody done anything to any boy in the band, whichever boy was ordered to kill that person and his family must do it, and he mustn't eat and he mustn't sleep till he had killed them and hacked a cross in their breasts, which was the sign of the band. And nobody that didn't belong to the band could use that mark, and if he did he must be sued; and if he done it again he must be killed. And if anybody that belonged to the band told the secrets, he must have this throat cut, and then have his carcass burnt up and the ashes scattered all around, and his name blotted off of the list with blood and never mentioned again by the Gang, but have a curse put on it and be forgot, for ever.

Everybody said it was a real beautiful oath, and asked Tom if he got it out of his own head. He said, some of it, but the rest was out of pirate books, and robber books, and every gang that was high-toned had it.

Some thought it would be good to kill the *families* of the boys that told the secrets. Tom said it was a good idea, so he took a pencil and wrote it in. Then Ben Rogers says:

'Here's Huck Finn, he hain't got no family – what you going to do 'bout him?'

'Well, hain't he got a father?' says Tom Sawyer.

'Yes, he's got a father, but you can't never find him, these days. He used to lay drunk with the hogs in the tanyard, but he hain't been seen in these parts for a year or more.'

They talked it over, and they was going to rule me out, because they said every boy must have a family or somebody to kill, or else it wouldn't be fair and square for the others. Well, nobody could think of anything to do – everybody was stumped, and set still. I was most ready to cry; but all at once I thought of a way, and so I offered them Miss Watson – they could kill her. Everybody said:

'Oh, she'll do, she'll do. That's all right. Huck can come in.'

Then they all stuck a pin in their fingers to get blood to sign with, and I made my mark on the paper.

'Now,' says Ben Rogers, 'what's the line of business of this Gang?'

'Nothing only robbery and murder,' Tom said.

'But who are we going to rob? Houses – or cattle – or –'

'Stuff! Stealing cattle and such things ain't robbery, it's burglary,' says Tom Sawyer. 'We ain't burglars. That ain't no sort of style. We are highwaymen. We stop stages and carriages on the road, with masks on, and kill the people and take their watches and money.'

'Must we always kill the people?'

'Oh, certainly. It's best. Some authorities think different, but mostly it's considered best to kill them. Except some that you bring to the cave here and keep them till they're ransomed.'

'Ransomed? What's that?'

'I don't know. But that's what they do. I've seen it in books; and so, of course, that's what we've got to do.'

'But how can we do it if we don't know what it is?'

'Why blame it all, we've *got* to do it. Don't I tell you it's in the books? Do you want to go to doing different from what's in the books, and get things all muddled up?'

'Oh, that's all very fine to *say*, Tom Sawyer, but how in the nation are these fellows going to be ransomed if we don't know how to do it to them? That's the thing *I* want to get at. Now, what do you *reckon* it is?'

'Well, I don't know. But per'aps if we keep them till they're ransomed, it means that we keep them till they're dead.'

'Now, that's something *like*. That'll answer. Why couldn't you said that before? We'll keep them till they're ransomed to death – and a bothersome lot they'll be, too, eating up everything and always trying to get loose.'

'How you talk, Ben Rogers. How can they get loose when there's a guard over them, ready to shoot them down if they move a peg?'

'A guard. Well, that *is* good. So somebody's got to set up all night and never get any sleep, just so as to watch them. I think that's foolishness. Why can't a body take a club and ransom them as soon as they get here?'

'Because it ain't in the books so – that's why. Now, Ben Rogers, do you want to do things regular, or don't you? – that's the idea. Don't you reckon that the people that made the books knows what's the correct thing to do? Do you reckon *you* can learn 'em anything? Not by a good deal. No, sir, we'll just go on and ransom them in the regular way.'

'All right. I don't mind; but I say it's a fool way, anyhow. Say – do we kill the women, too?'

'Well, Ben Rogers, if I was as ignorant as you I wouldn't let on. Kill the women? No – nobody ever saw anything in the books like that. You fetch them to the cave, and you're always as polite as pie to them; and by-and-by they fall in love with you and never want to go home any more.'

'Well, if that's the way, I'm agreed, but I don't take no stock in it. Mighty soon we'll have the cave so cluttered up with women, and fellows waiting to be ransomed, that there won't be no place for the robbers. But go ahead, I ain't got nothing to say.'

Little Tommy Barnes was asleep, now, and when they waked him up he was scared, and cried, and said he wanted to go home to his ma, and didn't want to be a robber any more.

So they all made fun of him, and called him cry-baby, and that made him mad, and he said he would go straight and tell all the secrets. But Tom give him five cents to keep quiet, and said we would all go home and meet next week and rob somebody and kill some people.

Ben Rogers said he couldn't get out much, only Sundays, and so he wanted to begin next Sunday; but all the boys said it would be wicked to do it on Sunday, and that settled the thing. They agreed to get together and fix a day as soon as they could, and then we elected Tom Sawyer first captain and Jo Harper second captain of the Gang, and so started home.

I clumb up the shed and crept into my window just before day was breaking. My new clothes was all greased up and clayey, and I was dog-tired.

WELL, I got a good going-over in the morning, from old Miss Watson, on account of my clothes; but the widow she didn't scold, but only cleaned off the grease and clay, and looked so sorry that I thought I would behave a while if I could. Then Miss Watson she took me in the closet and prayed, but nothing come of it. She told me to pray every day, and whatever I asked for I would get it. But it warn't so. I tried it. Once I got a fish-line, but no hooks. It warn't any good to me without hooks. I tried for the hooks three or four times, but somehow I couldn't make it work. By-and-by, one day, I asked Miss Watson to try for me, but she said I was a fool. She never told me why, and I couldn't make it out no way.

I set down, one time, back in the woods, and had a long think about it. I says to myself, if a body can get anything they pray for, why don't Deacon Winn get back the money he lost on pork? Why can't the widow get back her silver snuff-box that was stole? Why can't Miss Watson fat up? No, says I to myself, there ain't nothing in it. I went and told the widow about it, and she said the thing a body could get by praying for it was 'spiritual gifts'. This was too many for me, but she told me what she meant – I must help other people, and do everything I could for other people, and look out for them all the time, and never think about myself. This was including Miss Watson, as I took it. I went out in the woods and turned it over in my mind a long time, but I couldn't see no advantage about it – except for the other people – so at last I reckoned I wouldn't worry about it any more, but just let it go. Sometimes the widow would take me one side and talk about Providence in a way to make a body's mouth water; but maybe next day Miss Watson would take hold and knock it all down again. I judged I could see that there was two Providences, and a poor chap would stand considerable show with the widow's Providence, but if Miss Watson's got him there warn't no help for him any more. I thought it all out, and reckoned I would belong to the widow's, if he wanted me, though I couldn't make out how he was agoing to be any better off then than what he was before, seeing I was so ignorant and so kind of low-down and ornery.

Pap he hadn't been seen for more than a year, and that was comfortable for me; I didn't want to see him no more. He used to always whale me when he was sober and could get his hands on me; though I used to take to the woods most of the time when he was around. Well, about this time he was found in the river drowned, about twelve mile above town, so people said. They judged it was him, anyway; said this drowned man was just his size, and was ragged, and had uncommon long hair – which was all like pap – but they couldn't make nothing out of the face, because it had been in the water so long it warn't much like a face at all. They said he was floating on his back in the water. They took him and buried him on the bank. But I warn't comfortable long, because I happened to think of something. I knowed mighty well that a drownded man don't float on his back, but on his face. So I knowed, then, that this warn't pap, but a woman dressed up in a man's clothes. So I was uncomfortable again. I judged the old man would turn up again by-and-by, though I wished he wouldn't.

We played robbers now and then about a month, and then I resigned. All the boys did. We hadn't robbed nobody, we hadn't killed any people, but only just pretended. We used to hop out of the woods and go charging down on hog-drovers and women in carts taking garden stuff to market, but we never hived any of them. Tow Sawyer called the hogs 'ingots', and he called the turnips and stuff 'julery', and we would go to the cave and pow-wow over what we had done and how many people we had killed and marked. But I couldn't see no profit in it. One time Tom sent a boy to run about town with a blazing stick, which he called a slogan (which was the sign for the Gang to get together), and then he said he had got secret news by his spies that next day a whole parcel of Spanish merchants and rich A-rabs was going to camp in Cave Hollow with two hundred elephants, and six hundred camels, and over a thousand 'sumter' mules, all loaded down with di'monds, and they didn't have only a guard of four hundred soldiers, and so we would lay in ambuscade, as he called it, and kill the lot and scoop the things. He said we must slick up our swords and guns, and get ready. He never could go after even a turnip-cart but he must have the swords and guns all scoured up for it; though they was only lath and broomsticks, and you might scour at them till you rotted, and then they warn't worth a mouthful of ashes more than what they was before. I didn't believe we could lick such a crowd of Spaniards and A-rabs, but I wanted to see the camels and elephants, so I was on hand next day, Saturday, in the ambuscade; and when we got the word, we rushed out of the woods and down the hill. But there warn't no Spaniards and A-rabs, and there warn't no camels nor no elephants. It warn't anything but a Sunday-school picnic, and only a primer-class at that. We busted it up, and chased the children up the hollow; but we never got anything but some doughnuts and jam, though Ben Rogers got a rag doll, and Jo Harper got a hymn-book and a tract; and then the teacher charged in and made us drop everything and cut. I didn't see no di'monds, and I told Tom Sawyer so. He said there was loads of them there, anyway; and he said there was A-rabs there too, and elephants and things. I said, why couldn't we see them, then? He said if I warn't so ignorant, but had read a book called *Don Quixote*, I would know without asking. He said it was all done by enchantment. He said there was hundreds of soldiers there, and elephants and treasure, and so on, but we had enemies which he called magicians, and they had turned the whole thing into an infant Sunday-school, just out of spite. I said all right, then the thing for us to do was to go for the magicians. Tom Sawyer said I was a numskull.

'Why,' says he, 'a magician could call up a lot of genies, and they would hash you up like nothing before you could say Jack Robinson. They are as tall as a tree and as big around as a church.'

'Well,' I says, 's'pose we got some genies to help *us* – can't we lick the other crowd then?'

'How you going to get them?'

'I don't know. How do *they* get them?'

'Why, they rub an old tin lamp or an iron ring, and then the genies come tearing in, with the thunder and lightning a-ripping around and the smoke a-rolling, and everything they're told to do they up and do it. They don't think nothing of pulling a shot-tower up by the roots, and belting a Sunday-school superintendent over the head with it – or any other man.'

'Who makes them tear around so?'

'Why! whoever rubs the lamp or the ring. They belong to whoever rubs the lamp or the ring, and they've got to do whatever he says. If he tells them to build a palace forty miles long, out of di'monds, and fill it full of chewing-gum, or whatever you want, and fetch an emperor's daughter from China for you to marry, they've got to do it – and they've got to do it before sun-up next morning too. And more – they've got to waltz that palace around over the country wherever you want it, you understand.'

'Well,' says I, 'I think they are a pack of flatheads for not keeping the palace themselves 'stead of fooling them away like that. And what's more – if I was one of them I would see a man in Jericho before I would drop my business and come to him for the rubbing of an old tin lamp.'

'How you talk, Huck Finn. Why, you'd *have* to come when he rubbed it, whether you wanted to or not.'

'What, and I as high as a tree and as big as a church? All right, then: I *would* come; but I lay I'd make that man climb the highest tree there was in the country.'

'Shucks, it ain't no use to talk to you, Huck Finn. You don't seem to know anything, somehow – perfect sap-head.'

I thought all this over for two or three days, and then I reckoned I would see if there was anything in it. I got an old tin lamp and an iron ring and went out in the woods and rubbed and rubbed till I sweat like an Injun, calculating to build a palace and sell it; but it warn't no use, none of the genies come. So then I judged that all that stuff was only just one of Tom Sawyer's lies. I reckoned he believed in the A-rabs and the elephants, but as for me I think different. It had all the marks of a Sunday-school.

Lorna Doone

The Doones are a family of thieves and murderers who live in the Doone Valley in Somerset in the seventeenth century. When they murder a local farmer his son, John Ridd, seeks revenge. But John is in love with Lorna Doone and will do nothing that might place her at risk. At this point in the classic adventure story by Richard Doddridge Blackmore (1825–1900), John has taken Lorna to live with his family. Counsellor Doone, the head of the Doones, has come to visit the farm and talk with John, and the Ridds – despite their many differences with the Doones – have offered him hospitality.

JEREMY Stickles was gone south, ere ever the frost set in, for the purpose of mustering forces to attack the Doone Glen. But, of course, this weather had put a stop to every kind of movement; for even if men could have borne the cold, they could scarcely be brought to face the perils of the snow-drifts.

Although it was the longest winter ever known in our parts (never having ceased to freeze for a single night, and scarcely for a single day, from the middle of December till the second week in March), to me it was the very shortest and the most delicious; and verily I do believe it was the same to Lorna. But when the Ides of March were come, lo, there were increasing signals of a change of weather. The fog, which had hung about, vanished, and the shrouded hills shone forth with brightness manifold. When the first of the rain began, and the old familiar softness spread upon the window glass, and ran a little way in channels, knowing at once the difference from the short sharp thud of snow, we all ran out, and filled our eyes and hearts with gazing.

In truth it was time for me to work; for the rain was now coming down in earnest; and all outlets being blocked with ice set up like tables, it threatened to flood everything. It was not long before I managed to drain off this threatening flood, by opening the old sluice-hole; but I had much harder work to keep the stables, and the cowhouse, and the other sheds from flooding.

At first the rain made no impression on the bulk of snow, but ran from every sloping surface and froze on every flat one, through the coldness of the earth; and so it became impossible for any man to keep his legs without the help of a shodden staff. After a good while, however, the air growing very much warmer, this state of things began to change, and a worse one to succeed it; for now the snow came thundering down from roof, and rock, and ivied tree, and floods began to roar and foam in every trough and gulley.

It was now high time to work very hard, both to make up for the farmwork lost during the months of frost and snow, and also to be ready for a great and vicious attack from the Doones, who would burn us in our beds at the earliest opportunity.

Now in spite of the floods, and the state of the roads most perilous, Squire Faggus came at last, riding his famous strawberry mare. There was a great ado between him and Annie, as you may well suppose, after some four months of parting.

Tom Faggus had very good news to tell. He had taken up his purchase from old Sir Roger Bassett of a nice bit of land, to the south of the moors, and in the parish of Molland. When the lawyers knew thoroughly who he was, and how he had made his money, they behaved uncommonly well to him, and showed great sympathy with his pursuits. Now this farm of Squire Faggus was of the very finest pasture, when it got good store of rain. And Tom saw at once that it was fit for – the breeding of fine cattle. Then he pressed us both on another point, the time for his marriage to Annie; and mother looked at me to say when, and I looked back at mother. However, knowing something of the world, and unable to make any further objection, by reason of his prosperity, I said that we must even do as the fashionable people did, and allow the maid herself to settle when she would leave home and all. But Tom paid little heed to this, and left the room to submit himself to Annie.

Upon this I went in search of Lorna, to tell her of our cousin's arrival, and to ask whether she would think fit to see him, or to dine by herself that day; for she should do exactly as it pleased her in everything, while remaining still our guest. But Lorna had some curiosity to know what this famous man was like, and declared that she would by all means have the pleasure of dining with him, if he did not object to her company on the ground of the Doones' dishonesty.

Accordingly she turned away, with one of her very sweetest smiles, saying that she must not meet a man of such fashion and renown in her common gardening frock; but must try to look as nice as she could, if only in honour of dear Annie. And truth to tell, when she came to dinner, everything about her was the neatest and prettiest that can possibly be imagined.

Two things caught Squire Faggus's eyes, and he kept his bright bold gaze first on one, and then on the other, until my darling was hot with blushes. The two objects were first, Lorna's face, and secondly, the ancient necklace restored to her by Sir Ensor Doone.

Now when the young maidens were gone – for we had quite a high dinner of fashion that day, with Betty Muxworthy waiting, and Gwenny Carfax at the gravy – Squire Faggus said quite suddenly, and perhaps on purpose to take us aback, in case of our hiding anything.

'What do you know of the history of that beautiful maiden, good mother?'

'Not half so much as my son does,' mother answered, with a soft smile at me; 'and when John does not choose to tell a thing, wild horses will not pull it out of him.'

'Bravo, our John Ridd!' he answered; 'fools will be fools till the end of the chapter; and I might be as big a one, if I were in thy shoes, John. Nevertheless, in the name of God, don't let that helpless child go about with a thing worth half the county on her.'

'She is worth all the country herself,' said I; 'but she has nothing worth half a rick of hay upon her.'

'Tush,' Tom Faggus cried, 'the necklace, you great oaf, the necklace is worth all your farm put together, and your Uncle

Ben's fortune to the back of it; ay, and all the town of Dulverton.'

'What,' said I, 'that common glass thing, which she has had from her childhood!'

'Glass indeed! They are the finest brilliants ever I set eyes on.'

'Surely,' cried mother, now flushing as red as Tom's own cheeks, with excitement, 'you must be wrong, or the young mistress would herself have known it.'

'Trust me,' answered Tom, 'trust me, good mother, and simple John, for knowing brilliants when I see them. I would have stopped an eight-horse coach, with four carabined outriders, for such a booty.'

'Master Faggus,' began my mother, with a manner of some dignity, 'you have won my daughter's heart somehow; and you have won my consent to the matter through your honest sorrow, and manly undertaking to lead a different life, and touch no property but your own. Annie is my eldest daughter, and the child of a most upright man. I love her best of all on earth, next to my boy John here, and I will not risk my Annie's life with a man who yearns for the highway.'

Having made this very long speech (for her), mother came home upon my shoulder, and wept so that (but for heeding her) I would have taken Tom by the nose, and thrown him, and Winnie, his horse, over our farmyard gate. Now, as nothing very long abides, it cannot be expected that a woman's anger should last very long, if she be at all of the proper sort. And my mother being one of the very best, could not long retain her wrath against the Squire Faggus. And, as Annie put the case, Tom deserved the greater credit for vanquishing so nobly these yearnings of his nature; and it seemed very hard to upbraid him, considering how good his motives were. But how my mother contrived to know, that because she had been too hard upon Tom, he must be right about the necklace, is a point which I never could clearly perceive, though no doubt she could explain it.

To prove herself right in the conclusion, she went herself to fetch Lorna, that the trinket might be examined, before the day grew dark. She laid the glittering circlet in my mother's hands, and Tom Faggus took it eagerly, and bore it to the window.

'What will you take for it, Mistress Lorna? At a hazard, say now.'

'I am not accustomed to sell things, sir,' replied Lorna. 'What is it worth, in your opinion?'

'There are twenty-five diamonds in it, and twenty-five large brilliants that cannot be matched in London. How say you, Mistress Lorna, to a hundred thousand pounds?'

My darling's eyes so flashed at this, brighter than any diamonds, and she took the necklace quietly from the hands of Squire Faggus, and went up to my mother with the sweetest smile I ever saw.

'Dear kind mother, I am so glad,' she said in a whisper. 'Now you will have it, won't you, dear? And I shall be so happy; for a thousandth part of your kindness no jewels in the world can match.'

Mother knew not what to say. Of course, she would never dream of taking such a gift as that; and she called me to help her. But knowing that my eyes were full, I pretended not to hear my mother,. but to see a wild cat in the dairy.

Therefore I cannot tell what mother said in reply to Lorna; for when I came back, behold Tom Faggus had gotten again the necklace which had such charms for him, and was delivering all around a dissertation on precious stones, and his sentiments on those in his hand.

He said that the necklace was made in Amsterdam, two or three hundred years ago, and on the gold clasp he found some letters, done in some inverted way; also a bearing of some kind, which he believed was a mountain-cat. We said no more about the necklace for a long time afterwards, and Tom Faggus took his departure the day after his arrival.

SCARCELY was he out of sight when in came Master Jeremy Stickles, splashed with mud from head to foot, and not in the very best of humours, though happy to get back again.

'Curse those fellows!' he cried. 'A pretty plight you may call this, for His Majesty's Commissioner to return to his headquarters in! Well, this is better than being chased over the moors for one's life, John. All the way from Landacre Bridge, I had ridden a race for my precious life, at the peril of my limbs and neck with three great Doones galloping after me.'

The weather had been against him bitterly, closing all the roads around him. It had taken him eight days, he said, to get from Exeter to Plymouth; whither he found that most of the troops had been drafted off from Exeter. When all were told, there was but a battalion of one of the King's horse regiments, and two companies of foot soldiers; and their commanders had orders, later than the date of Jeremy's commission, on no account to quit the southern coast and march inland. Therefore, although they would gladly have come for a brush with the celebrated Doones, it was more than they durst attempt, in the face of their instructions.

Jeremy made no doubt he might manage, with the help of his own men, to force the stranghold of the enemy; but the truth was that the officers, knowing how hard it would be to collect their men at that time of the year, and in that state of the weather, began with one accord to make every possible excuse. And so it came to pass that the King's Commissioner returned without any army whatever; but with promise of two hundred men when the roads should be more passable. And meanwhile, what were we to do, abandoned as we were to the mercies of the Doones, with only our own hands to help us? And herein I grieved at my own folly in having let Tom Faggus go, whose wit and courage would have been worth at least half a dozen men to us. Upon this matter I held council with my friend Stickles; telling him all about Lorna's presence, and what I knew of her history. He agreed with me that we could not hope to escape an attack from the outlaws and recommended that a watch must be maintained at night. He thought it wise that I should go to Lynmouth and fetch every one of his mounted troopers who might now be quartered there.

Knowing how fiercely the floods were out, I resolved to travel the higher road, by Cosgate and through Countisbury; therefore I swam my horse through the Lynn, and thence galloped up and along the hills. I could see all the inland valleys ribboned with broad waters; and in every winding crook, the banks of snow that fed them; while on my right the turbid sea was flaked with April showers.

I followed the bank of the flood to the beach, and there had the luck to see Will Watcombe on the opposite side, caulking an old boat. Though I could not make him hear a word, I got him to understand that I wanted to cross over. Upon this he fetched another man, and the two of them launched a boat and, paddling well out to sea, fetched round the mouth of the frantic river. The other man proved to be Stickles' chief mate; and so he went back and fetched his comrades, bringing their weapons, but leaving their horses behind. There were but four of them, but I started again for my home, and the men would follow afoot, crossing our river high up on the moorland.

It was lucky that I came home so soon; for I found the house in a great commotion, and all the women trembling. When I asked what the matter was, Lorna answered that it was all her fault. She had stolen out to the garden towards dusk, to watch some favourite hyacinths just pushing up, when she descried two glittering eyes glaring at her steadfastly, and then a calm, cruel face appeared; and she knew it was the face of Carver Doone.

The maiden could neither shriek nor fly, but only gaze, as if bewitched. Then Carver Doone lifted his gun and pointed full at Lorna's heart. Then he lowered the muzzle. When it pointed to the ground, he pulled the trigger, and the bullet flung the mould all over her. While she leaned there, quite unable yet to save herself, Carver came to the brink of the flood.

'I have spared you this time,' he said in his deep voice, 'only because it suits my plans. But unless you come back tomorrow, and teach me to destroy that fool who has destroyed himself for you, your death is here, where it has long been waiting.' Then he turned away and Lorna saw his giant figure striding across the meadowland.

Now expecting a sharp attack that night, we prepared a great quantity of food. For we would almost surrender rather than keep our garrison hungry. We sent all the women to bed quite early, except Gwenny Carfax and our old Betty. It was not likely that the Doones could bring more than eight or ten men against us, while their homes were in danger from flood, and to meet these we had eight good men, including Jeremy and myself, besides our three farm-servants and the parish-clerk and the shoemaker. I was not content to abide within the house, or go the rounds with the troopers; but betook myself to the rick-yard, knowing that the Doones were likely to begin there.

The robbers rode into our yard as coolly as if they had been invited, having lifted the gate from the hinges first on account of its being fastened. I could see our troopers round the corner from where the Doones were, and expecting the order to fire. But Jeremy Stickles wisely kept them in readiness, until the enemy should advance upon them.

'Two of you lazy fellows go,' it was the voice of Carver Doone, 'and make us a light to cut their throats by. Only one thing, once again. If any man touches Lorna, I will stab him where he stands. Now for our rights. We have borne too long the insolence of these yokels. Kill man and child, and burn the cursed place down.'

While I was hesitating a blaze of fire lit up the house and brown smoke hung around it. Six of our men had let go at the Doones, by Jeremy Stickles' order. Being unable any longer to contain myself, I came across the yard, and went up to Carver Doone, and took him by the beard and said, 'Do you call yourself a man?'

And with that word, I laid him flat upon his back in our straw-yard. Seeing him down, the others ran, and some of them got their horses, before our men came up; and some went away without them. And among these last was Captain Carver.

POSSIBLY I may have mentioned that little Ruth Huckaback had promised to spend her Christmas with us. I was begged over and over again to go and see Ruth, and make all things straight. So one beautiful spring morning, up the lane I stoutly rode, well armed and well provided.

When I came home my sister Eliza met me and said, 'Don't go in there John,' pointing to mother's room, 'until I have had a talk with you.'

'In the name of Moses,' I inquired, 'what are you at now?'

'It is nothing we are at,' she answered; 'neither may you make light of it. It is something very important about Lorna Doone.'

'Let us have it at once,' I cried.

'Do you know a man nearly as broad as he is long, and with a length of snow-white hair, and a thickness also, as the copses were last winter?'

I was almost sure that the man who was come must be the Counsellor himself, of whom I felt much keener fear than of his son Carver. And knowing that his visit boded ill to me and Lorna, I went and sought her and led her to meet our dreadful visitor. Mother was standing by the door, listening to a long harangue delivered by the Counsellor.

Feeling that I must speak first, I took my darling round the waist and led her up to the Counsellor.

'Now, Sir Counsellor Doone,' I said, 'you know right well that Sir Ensor Doone gave approval.'

'Approval of what, good rustic John?'

'To the love betwixt me and Lorna, which your story shall not break without more evidence than your word.'

The Counsellor looked with great wrath in his eyes. 'Young people of the present age,' said he severely, 'have no right feeling of any sort, upon the simplest matter. Lorna Doone, stand forth and state in your own voice whether you regard this as a pleasant trifle.'

'You know without any words of mine,' she answered softly, 'that if John will have me I am his for ever.'

This speech was too much for her, and the Counsellor beckoned to me to come away.

After breakfast the next morning, the Counsellor followed Annie into the dairy, to see how we managed the clotted cream, and thereupon they talked a little; and Annie thought him a fine old gentleman, for he had nobly condemned the people who spoke against Tom Faggus.

'Have you ever heard,' asked the Counsellor, 'that if you pass across the top, without breaking the surface, a string of beads, the cream will set three times as solid, and in thrice the quantity?'

'No, sir, I have never heard that,' said Annie. 'I will get my coral necklace; it will not be witchcraft, will it, sir?'

'Certainly not,' the old man replied; 'but coral will not do, my child. The beads must be of plain common glass; but the brighter they are the better.'

'Then I know the very thing,' cried Annie; 'dearest Lorna has a necklace of some old glass-beads.'

'Bring it here, Annie, if you know where it is.'

'To be sure I do,' she answered.

Now as luck would have it Lorna had taken it into her head that I was far too valuable to be trusted with her necklace. So she had led me to give it up. Therefore Annie found it sparkling in the secret hole, near the head of Lorna's bed, which she herself had recommended for its safer custody; and without a word to any one she brought it down, and danced it in the air before the Counsellor, for him to admire its lustre.

'Now,' he said, in a stern whisper, 'not a word of this to a soul; neither must you nor any other enter this place for three hours. By that time the charm will have done its work. Put the bauble under this pannikin; which none must lift for a day and a night. Have no fear, not a breath of harm shall come to you, if you obey my orders.'

'Oh, sir, that I will, if you will only tell me what to do.'

'Go to your room, without so much as a single word to any one. Bolt yourself in, and for three hours read the Lord's Prayer backwards.'

Poor Annie was only too glad to escape, upon these conditions. Meanwhile the Counsellor was gone. He bade our mother adieu, with so much dignity of bearing, and such high-bred courtesy of the old school, that when he had gone, dear mother fell back on the chair which he had used last night, as if it would teach her the graces.

'Oh, the wickedness of the world! Oh, the lies that are told of people because a man is better born, or has better manners! Oh, Lizzie, you have read me beautiful things about Sir Gallyhead, and the rest; but nothing to equal Sir Counsellor.'

'You had better marry him, madam,' said I, coming in very sternly; 'he can repay your adoration. He has stolen a hundred thousand pounds.'

'John,' cried my mother, 'you are mad!'

'Of course I am, mother. He has gone off with Lorna's necklace.'

Hereupon ensued grim silence. Mother looked at me, to know; and as for me, I could have stepped almost on the heart of any one. It was not the value of the necklace; it was my fury at the breach of hospitality.

The Starfish

T HERE was a princess once who knew nearly everything. If a leaf stirred in the forest, if a tiny fish cast one of its scales, if a feather fell from the wing of a bird – she knew of it. The secret of her knowledge lay in the topmost turret of her castle. There was a room there with twelve windows, each one clearer than the last, so that from the twelfth window she could see every detail of the whole wide world.

In consequence she thought herself very wise, and made up her mind that she would not marry anyone who was not as wise as she. She set her suitors a test. Each was told to hide himself where she would not be able to find him. If he succeeded he should have her hand; if he failed he must lose his head.

So far no one had succeeded, while ninety-seven heads had paid the penalty of their owners' rashness. Suitors were growing scarce, when one day three brothers appeared and made formal request for her hand. The eldest was given the first chance to hide. He lowered himself into a deep pit, thinking that there at least he would be safe from his lady's eye. But no! – the princess saw him and his fate was sealed. The second brother was more cunning; he hid himself in the lowest cellar of the royal castle, but he too was found and had his head chopped off.

The turn of the youngest came. He asked for a day to think things over, and then for three chances, so that if he failed once and twice he might still hope to succeed at the third attempt.

Because he was young and very handsome the princess agreed.

The next day he went out hunting. A black raven flew across his path and he raised his bow. 'Don't shoot!' croaked the raven. 'I may yet be able to help you!' The young man good-naturedly let him go. By and by he came to a lake and a fish jumped up. He made as though to catch it, but – 'Spare me!' the fish cried; 'I may yet be able to help you!' So he spared the fish also.

Before very long he met with a fox, limping along with a thorn in its foot. He shot and missed. 'Never mind,' the fox said. 'It will be more to your credit if you help me to take this thorn out of my foot!' And again the young man complied.

The next day he was to hide himself. He did not in the least know where to go, so he turned his steps to the forest and asked the raven's advice.

'One good turn deserves another,' the raven said. He took an egg from his nest, shut the youth inside it and replaced it in the nest.

The princess looked from her windows. One, two, three – not until she reached the eleventh did she see him. She sent someone to fetch the egg from the raven's nest, and when it was broken – there was the suitor, very much abashed.

'You have failed once,' the princess said, 'but you are forgiven. Tomorrow you may try again.'

When the next day dawned the young man was even more perplexed. He went to the lakeside and called on the fish to help him.

'There is one chance,' said the fish; 'I can swallow you and sink to the bottom of the lake.'

The princess looked from all her windows in turn. Only when she came to the twelfth did she find trace of him. Then she sent a fisherman to catch the fish and bring it to the castle. When it was opened – there was her suitor, quite covered with confusion!

'You have failed again,' she said, gravely. 'If you fail the third time you must die!'

The next day the youth sought his only other friend, the fox.

'You are so cunning,' he said. 'You know the holes in the earth and the crannies of the rock. Surely you will be able to hide me!'

The fox thought long and earnestly.

'I believe I know what to do,' he said at last. 'Come with me.'

Together they made their way to a bubbling spring. The fox dipped himself in it and came out as a respectable merchant. Then he dipped the young man in, and *he* emerged as a starfish. The merchant put the starfish in his pocket and took him to market.

Now it chanced that the princess also was at market that morning. When she saw the dainty little creature she wanted to buy it, and willingly paid the price the merchant asked. Before he gave it to her he managed to whisper in its ear, 'When the princess goes to the turret, hide in her hair!'

And that, a little later, was just what the starfish did! It crept beneath the thick braids of her yellow hair, and as she had not eyes in the back of her head she ran from window to window with never a glimpse of her suitor. And when she had looked in vain from the twelfth window she banged it down so hard that every window in the turret was shattered to atoms! The starfish was quite frightened, but the princess, feeling it among her tresses, shook it to the ground and bade it begone.

The little creature ran and ran until it came to the market-place, and there the merchant found it. His task over, he carried it at once to the magic spring. Having dipped themselves, the two resumed their proper shapes, the fox to receive the grateful thanks of his friend, and the suitor to find his way to the castle, where the princess was waiting to marry him.

With all her windows broken she was no wiser than anyone else, but at least she was wise enough to know that she had met her match. And as her husband never told her how he had out-witted her, she gave him her complete respect and a share of her kingdom, and lived with him happily to the end of her life.

John Gilpin

The Diverting History of John Gilpin;
showing how he went farther than he intended,
and came safe home again.

OHN Gilpin was a citizen
    Of credit and renown,
A train-band captain eke was he
    Of famous London town.

John Gilpin's spouse said to her dear,
    'Though wedded we have been
These twice ten tedious years, yet we
    No holiday have seen.

'Tomorrow is our wedding day
    And we will then repair
Unto the Bell at Edmonton
    All in a chaise and pair.

'My sister, and my sister's child,
    Myself and children three,
Will fill the chaise; so you must ride
    On horseback after we.'

He soon replied, 'I do admire
    Of womankind but one,
And you are she, my dearest dear,
    Therefore it shall be done.

'I am a linen-draper bold,
    As all the world doth know,
And my good friend the Calender
    Will lend his horse to go.'

Quoth Mrs. Gilpin, 'That's well said;
    And for that wine is dear,
We will be furnished with our own,
    Which is both bright and clear.'

John Gilpin kissed his loving wife;
   O'erjoyed was he to find
That, though on pleasure she was bent,
   She had a frugal mind.

The morning came, the chaise was brought,
   But yet was not allow'd
To drive up to the door, lest all
   Should say that she was proud.

So three doors off the chaise was stayed,
   Where they did all get in;
Six precious souls, and all agog
   To dash through thick and thin.

Smack went the whip, round went the wheels,
   Were never folk so glad,
The stones did rattle underneath,
   As if Cheapside were mad.

John Gilpin at his horse's side
   Seiz'd fast the flowing mane,
And up he got, in haste to ride,
   But soon came down again;

For saddle-tree scarce reached had he,
   His journey to begin,
When, turning round his head, he saw
   Three customers come in.

So down he came; for loss of time,
   Although it grieved him sore,
Yet loss of pence, full well he knew,
   Would trouble him much more.

'Twas long before the customers
   Were suited to their mind,
When Betty screaming came down stairs,
   'The wine is left behind!'

'Good lack,' quoth he, – 'yet bring it me,
  My leathern belt likewise,
In which I bear my trusty sword
  When I do exercise.'

Now Mistress Gilpin (careful soul!)
  Had two stone bottles found,
To hold the liquor that she loved,
  And keep it safe and sound.

Each bottle had a curling ear,
  Through which the belt he drew,
And hung a bottle on each side.
  To make his balance true.

Then over all, that he might be
  Equipp'd from top to toe,
His long red cloak, well brush'd and neat,
  He manfully did throw.

Now see him mounted once again
  Upon his nimble steed,
Full slowly pacing o'er the stones
  With caution and good heed.

But finding soon a smoother road
  Beneath his well-shod feet,
The snorting beast began to trot,
  Which galled him in his seat.

So, 'Fair and softly,' John he cried,
  But John he cried in vain;
That trot became a gallop soon,
  In spite of curb and rein.

So stooping down, as needs he must
  Who cannot sit upright,
He grasp'd the mane with both his hands,
  And eke with all his might.

His horse, who never in that sort
  Had handled been before,
What thing upon his back had got
  Did wonder more and more.

Away went Gilpin, neck or nought;
  Away went hat and wig;
He little dreamt, when he set out,
  Of running such a rig.

The wind did blow, the cloak did fly.
  Like streamer long and gay,
Till, loop and button failing both,
  At last it flew away.

Then might all people well discern
  The bottles he had slung;
A bottle swinging at each side,
  As hath been said or sung.

The dogs did bark, the children scream'd,
  Up flew the windows all;
And every soul cried out, 'Well done!'
  As loud as he could bawl.

Away went Gilpin – who but he?
  His fame soon spread around;
'He carries weight! he rides a race!
  'Tis for a thousand pound!'

And still, as fast as he drew near,
  'Twas wonderful to view,
How in a trice the turnpike-men
  Their gates wide open threw.

And now, as he went bowing down
  His reeking head full low,
The bottles twain behind his back
  Were shatter'd at a blow.

Down ran the wine into the road,
    Most piteous to be seen,
Which made his horse's flanks to smoke
    As they had basted been.

But still he seem'd to carry weight,
    With leathern girdle braced;
For all might see the bottle necks
    Still dangling at his waist.

Thus all through merry Islington
    These gambols he did play,
Until he came unto the Wash
    Of Edmonton so gay;

And there he threw the Wash about
    On both sides of the way,
Just like unto a trundling mop,
    Or a wild goose at play.

At Edmonton his loving wife
    From the balcony spied
Her tender husband, wond'ring much
    To see how he did ride.

'Stop, stop, John Gilpin! – Here's the house –'
    They all aloud did cry;
'The dinner waits, and we are tired':
    Said Gilpin – 'So am I!'

But yet his horse was not a whit
    Inclin'd to tarry there;
For why? – his owner had a house
    Full ten miles off, at Ware.

So like an arrow swift he flew,
    Shot by an archer strong;
So did he fly – which brings me to
    The middle of my song.

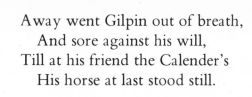

Away went Gilpin out of breath,
    And sore against his will,
Till at his friend the Calender's
    His horse at last stood still.

The Calender, amazed to see
    His neighbour in such trim,
Laid down his pipe, flew to the gate,
    And thus accosted him:

'What news? what news? your tidings tell;
    Tell me you must and shall –
Say why bare-headed you are come,
    Or why you come at all?'

Now Gilpin had a pleasant wit
    And loved a timely joke:
And thus unto the Calender
    In merry guise he spoke:

'I came because your horse would come;
    And, if I well forbode,
My hat and wig will soon be here,
    They are upon the road.'

The Calender, right glad to find
    His friend in merry pin,
Return'd him not a single word,
    But to the house went in;

Whence straight he came with hat and wig;
    A wig that flowed behind,
A hat not much the worse for wear,
    Each comely in its kind.

He held them up, and in his turn
    Thus show'd his ready wit:
'My head is twice as big as yours,
    They therefore needs must fit.

'But let me scrape the dirt away,
    That hangs upon your face;
And stop and eat, for well you may
    Be in a hungry case.'

Said John, 'It is my wedding-day,
    And all the world would stare,
If wife should dine at Edmonton,
    And I should dine at Ware.'

So turning to his horse, he said,
    'I am in haste to dine;
'Twas for your pleasure you came here,
    You shall go back for mine.'

Ah, luckless speech, and bootless boast
    For which he paid full dear;
For, while he spake, a braying ass
    Did sing most loud and clear;

Whereat his horse did snort, as he
    Had heard a lion roar,
And galloped off with all his might,
    As he had done before.

Away went Gilpin, and away
    Went Gilpin's hat and wig:
He lost them sooner than at first,
    For why? – they were too big.

Now Mistress Gilpin, when she saw
    Her husband posting down
Into the country far away,
    She pulled out half-a-crown;

And thus unto the youth she said,
    That drove them to the Bell:
'This shall be yours, when you bring back
    My husband safe and well.'

The youth did ride, and soon did meet
    John coming back amain!
Whom in a trice he tried to stop,
    By catching at his rein;

But not performing what he meant,
    And gladly would have done,
The frighted steed he frighted more,
    And made him faster run.

Away went Gilpin, and away
    Went post-boy at his heels,
The post-boy's horse right glad to miss
    The lumb'ring of the wheels.

Six gentlemen upon the road
    Thus seeing Gilpin fly,
With post-boy scampering in the rear.
    They raised the hue-and-cry:–

'Stop thief! stop thief! – a highwayman!'
    Not one of them was mute;
And all and each that passed that way
    Did join in the pursuit.

And now the turnpike gates again
    Flew open in short space;
The toll-men thinking as before,
    That Gilpin rode a race.

And so he did, and won it too,
    For he got first to town;
Nor stopped till where he had got up
    He did again get down.

Now let us sing, long live the King,
    And Gilpin, long live he;
And, when he next doth ride abroad,
    May I be there to see!

Gulliver's Travels

When Jonathan Swift (1667–1745) wrote 'Travels into Several Remote Nations of the World, by Lemuel Gulliver' he intended it as a satire on the politics of the day and on the behaviour of the human race. But to generations of young readers it has simply been a most enjoyable story – with some very unusual characters. On this, the first of his voyages, Gulliver visits the land of Lilliput.

THIS is the story of a man who lived many years ago, named Lemuel Gulliver, and of the many strange things that happened to him.

When Lemuel was fourteen his father sent him to college to learn how to be a doctor. He worked very hard, till at last he was able to become a doctor, and then he found a place as a ship-surgeon. After he had gone several voyages with the ship he became tired of the sea, and made up his mind to settle in London. He married a young lady in London, and for a time all went well. Then, little by little, his good fortune seemed to leave him, and he became very poor.

After a time he went as surgeon on board a sailing ship, called the *Antelope*, which was making a voyage to the South Seas. For many weeks the journey was safe and pleasant; but, at last, in a strange sea a great wind sprang up and the vessel was driven on a rock. Sad to say, the ship at once split in two, and all on board were lost, except six men who had been able to let down a small boat.

Among the six thus saved was our friend Gulliver. After they had rowed with all their might for some distance, they were unable to row any longer. So they all jumped into the sea and began to swim towards land. Gulliver was a strong swimmer and he swam with all his might.

At last, to his great joy, he felt his feet touch the bottom. By this he knew that he was near some shore. For some time he walked about to see if he could find any trace of living people, but there was nothing to be seen; not a house of any kind was in sight. Being now quite tired, and his eyes feeling as if they could keep open no longer, he laid himself down on the grass, which was soft and short. There he slept more soundly than ever he had done in his life before.

He slept for about nine hours, and then woke just as it was daybreak, but, to his great surprise, found himself unable to stir. He was on his back, and his legs and arms were, on each side, firmly fastened to the ground. His hair, too, which was long and thick, had been tied down to the ground in the same way. Across his body he felt several thin cords from his shoulder to his knees.

Here was a sad plight for him! Well might he wonder who it was had bound him in this way! Not being able to move his head, he could only look up, and the sun, which began to be hot, hurt his eyes. Close by he heard a slight noise, but as he could see nothing except the sky, he did not know what it was.

A short time had passed, when he felt something alive moving on his left leg, something that walked up his body, across his chest and to his chin.

To his great surprise, he saw that it was a tiny human creature, not six inches in height. In his hand this small man carried a tiny bow and arrow, ready to shoot, and on his back was slung a small quiver. After him came a troop of other little people, all about the same size, and about forty in number.

Poor Gulliver felt, as you may guess, none too comfortable. He struggled to get loose, and at last broke the strings and pulled out the pegs that fastened his left leg down. Then he loosened the strings that fastened his hair to the ground and was thus able to move his head, but only for a few inches.

When the little people saw what he had done there was a great shout, and they ran away, one of them crying aloud in a shrill voice:

'Tolgo phonac!'

The next moment a hundred tiny arrows were shot into Gulliver's left hand, pricking him like needles. Then another volley came, but these were shot into the air, so that they fell on his face.

He was in such pain with these arrows that he groaned and cried aloud. Once more he struggled and tried to get free, but seeing this the little people tried to stick their spears into his side. However, they were not able to pierce the thick coat that he was wearing.

Then he thought that it would be better for him to keep quiet and wait until it was night, when it might be easy for him in the dark to set himself free. When they found that he was quiet the tiny people shot no more arrows at him.

For quite an hour after this Gulliver heard, close by his head, the sound of knocking, as if people were at work. Turning his head as far as the pegs and string would allow, he saw a stage being made, about a foot and a half from the ground, and large enough for four of the little people to stand upon.

When this was finished, one, who seemed to be the most

important person there, mounted the stage, followed by three others. He cried out three times, 'Langro dehul san,' and about fifty of the little people ran to Gulliver and cut the rest of the strips that bound him. This made it possible for him to turn his head and listen.

Then the chief spoke to him for some time, but of course, he could not understand a single word that was said. So far as Gulliver could guess, the speaker was promising that they would not harm him in any way if only he would do as they wished.

He felt hungry, and to make them understand this, he put his fingers to his mouth many times, hoping they would bring him some food, for he had eaten nothing for many long hours. The one who had been speaking seemed to be a great lord. He understood very well what his prisoner wanted, and he gave various orders to the others.

Some time passed, a long, long time it seemed to Gulliver, who was now growing very hungry indeed. At last several of the longest ladders were brought, and put against his side very carefully. Up these ladders very soon there climbed over a hundred of the little people, bearing baskets filled with meat and bread. The meat was legs, shoulders, and loins of mutton, no larger than the wings of a lark. The loaves of bread were very, very tiny, no larger than green gooseberries.

The little people were full of wonder when they saw how much Gulliver ate, while they could not guess that this seemed but a small meal to him. Two or three of their joints made only one good mouthful, while he popped three of their loaves in his mouth at a time.

When the little people had emptied their baskets they brought wine for Gulliver to drink. This was held in hogsheads, that is, in the largest kind of barrel they had, each of which held half a pint. He drank two of these, and thought it the nicest wine he had ever tasted in his life. When the two hogsheads were empty the small people shouted with joy and jumped and danced on Gulliver's breast.

Soon a messenger came from the Emperor, a tiny person dressed in rich clothing and seeming to be of high rank. He mounted on Gulliver's right leg and walked upwards towards his face. In his hand he held a long Royal Proclamation, which he read with care, holding it every now and then under Gulliver's eyes.

Having no wish to be kept prisoner, Gulliver made many signs that he would like to be set free. In reply, the Royal Messenger only shook his head, but tried to show that he would be well fed and treated with all kindness. Then the thought came to the prisoner that it would be easy for him to break the cords with which he was bound and then make his escape.

He looked round, however, and found that the number of Lilliputians, as the little people were called, had greatly increased, and, as his hands and face were still smarting from the pain of the arrows, he thought it would be better to do as the little people wished. So he made signs that he was ready to go where they pleased. Upon this they gave a most cheerful shout and seemed very glad. The Royal Messenger went away, and soon afterwards the little people brought sweet-smelling ointment which they rubbed over the prisoner's hands and face.

Gulliver then fell fast asleep, and did not awake for several hours. While he was sleeping, a carriage was brought which the Emperor had ordered to be made. Five hundred carpenters had been set to work so that it might be finished as quickly as possible. Nine hundred of the Lilliputians were needed to lift the sleeping body of Gulliver on to this carriage, while to draw it to the city one thousand and five hundred of the Emperor's largest horses were brought.

The carriage rested during the night with five hundred guards on each side. Half of these held torches and the other half held bows and arrows ready to shoot Gulliver should he try to escape. There was little chance, however, of his doing this, for they had tied him down to the carriage very firmly. The place in which they meant him to live was a temple that was no longer in use. This was by far the largest building in the country.

Great though it was to the Lilliputians, yet to the big man it looked hardly larger than a dog-kennel. The door was only about four feet high, and when Gulliver had crept in there would only be just enough room for him to lie down. He soon found that he was to be kept there as a prisoner, which really seemed a shame. All the smiths had been busy making a long, thick chain. One end of this they fixed very firmly to the door of the temple, and the other they fastened to their prisoner's left leg, with six and thirty padlocks. Then they cut the cords that bound him.

Poor Gulliver stood up, feeling as unhappy as ever he had been in his life. It was the first time for two days he had been allowed to stand. When the little people saw him stand up and begin to walk, they all began to shout as loudly as they could. The chain that held his leg was long enough to allow him to walk to and fro. It also allowed him to creep into the temple, and to lie down at full length, for it was fixed only about four inches from the door.

WHEN at last Gulliver found himself on his feet, the first thing he did was to look carefully around him. He was full of wonder at all that he saw. The country seemed to him like a large garden. The fields were as bright as beds of flowers. There were several woods in the distance, but the tallest trees that he could see were not much higher than his shoulders. While he stood gazing around, the natives watched him with great amusement, laughing all the time. They thought that he was the funniest sight that could be seen in all the world.

Now Gulliver was really very tired and sad, and wanted to be alone, so he crept into his house and tried to shut the door. This did not help him to get rid of the Lilliputians who swarmed in through the windows. As they would not go away he had to go out of his house again and walk backwards and forwards as far as his chain would allow.

The Emperor then came down from his tower and rode on his horse towards Gulliver. Getting down from his horse, he walked nearer, and then round him, taking good care, however, to keep a safe distance away, beyond the length of his prisoner's chain.

Near the Emperor stood the lords and ladies of his court. They were all so richly and so beautifully dressed that the ground on which they were standing seemed covered with a carpet of gold and silver.

The Emperor spoke many times to his prisoner, who replied as well as he could. As neither could understand the other this was of little use. However, it was easy to see that the Emperor was kind and meant to do him no harm. In about two hours the Emperor, with his court, went back to the palace, while a number of soldiers were left on guard to protect Gulliver.

By now the crowd of people around had become so eager to see the stranger that they pressed closer and closer. Then some of the more badly behaved began to shoot arrows at him as he sat on the ground by the side of his house. Six of these who had been first in the shooting were seized by the officer in charge, and pushed within the prisoner's reach. He took them all in his right hand, and put five into his pocket. The sixth he held in his hand, between his finger and thumb. Then, making a great grimace, he opened his mouth wide, pretending that he was going to eat alive the one he held in his hand.

The poor little fellow began to scream and cry out in fear, and those looking on were also much afraid: they did not at all want their friend to be eaten. But an end was soon put to their fright, for

Gulliver looked kindly at the little squealing man he was holding, and cut the cords with which he was bound. He put him on the ground, and the little fellow ran away in great haste. Then he took from his pocket, one by one, the other five, and set them free in the same way.

Those standing around were delighted to see how kind Gulliver was, and a messenger was sent at once to the Emperor's palace to tell him how the stranger had spared the lives of his six subjects. Gulliver afterwards found that his act of kindness had saved him from great danger.

At the time when the messenger reached the palace, the Emperor was sitting at a meeting of his nobles, trying to find out what would be the best thing to do with their prisoner. Most of them were afraid of Gulliver. Some of them did not like such a great giant, as he seemed to them, being in Lilliput, and said he might break loose and do great harm. Others thought there would not be enough food for the people of Lilliput if Gulliver were to be allowed to eat all that he wanted. Indeed, many of them thought it would be better for him to be put to death at once.

They said this could be done best with poisoned arrows. If they shot him in the hands and face with thousands of these they felt sure he would die. Others said it would be easier for them to starve him to death. Then, as they were making these cruel plans, the messenger came in to say how good Gulliver had been to the six little people who had shot at him. At this the Emperor said, 'We must do no harm to this giant. If he is so very kind it is quite sure that he will never hurt us. Some day, perhaps, he may be able to do some great work for us.' After this, for a time no one said any more against the big stranger.

As night came on Gulliver crept into his house and lay down. He had no bed, nor any covering, and as the floor was of stone it may be guessed that he did not sleep very well. In about two weeks, however, a bed was made for him, with sheets and blankets as well to cover him. These were not very good, though they might have been a great deal worse.

A royal order was sent out to all the villages round the city that every morning six oxen, forty sheep, and large quantities of good bread and wine, were to be sent in for Gulliver's food during the day. Six hundred persons were ordered to be his servants to wait upon him; three hundred tailors were told to make a suit of clothes for him like those worn in that country, and six of the most clever men in the kingdom were asked to give him lessons, so that he might learn to speak the language of the country.

The Emperor's horses and those of the nobles and of the guard were to be trotted back and forward before Gulliver every few days, so that they might get used to his immense size. For the first few weeks that the traveller lived in that country great crowds went daily to see him. To do this they left their proper work on the farms, in the fields, and in the workshops. This became so bad for the country that the Emperor had to send out a royal command that every one who had seen the stranger once was to go back to his work and not to go near him again.

Soon he began to speak the native language. The Emperor himself often went to see him and talked to him. Each time Gulliver did the same thing: he threw himself on his knees, and begged most earnestly that he might be set free. To this the Emperor had but one answer. He said that he could not set Gulliver free, until he had taken counsel with the great lords of his court. He promised, however, that they would always be kind to him and might some day let him go. At the same time, he told him that, if he wanted his freedom, the best thing for him to do was to behave so well that the people would look upon him as a friend. In the meantime he was to be patient.

A few days later the Emperor came to see him again, and told him that by the laws of the country he must allow himself to be searched. He promised that everything that was taken away would be given back when Gulliver was leaving that country, and that if anything was spoiled they would pay him all that he said it was worth.

Gulliver said at once that the Emperor's servants might search his pockets, and he promised to give them all the help in his power. Soon two officers were sent, both men of high rank. Gulliver took them both up and put them first into one of his coat pockets, and then into every other pocket about him, except two small fob pockets which were too tight for them to get into, and one secret pocket which they would be sure never to find by themselves.

In one of the fob pockets was a purse, in another watch, while in the secret pocket was a pair of spectacles and a small pocket compass that he did not mean to show them. He was afraid that if they took these away they might be broken or in some way injured.

The two officers who were searching made a list of the things they found. This is what they wrote:

'To His Majesty the Emperor of Lilliput.
'In the right-hand pocket of the great Man-Mountain we found one very large piece of cloth. This was quite big enough to cover the floor of the chief state-room in your Majesty's palace.'

(By this, of course, they meant Gulliver's pocket-handkerchief.)

'In the left pocket was a big silver box. The cover was shut down so tightly that we had to ask the great Man-Mountain to open it. He did so, and we found it full of a kind of dust.

'One of us stepped into it and some of this dust flew up into our faces, making us sneeze for a long time. The great Man-Mountain told us that this dust was called snuff.

'In the waistcoat pocket we found a very strange sort of engine. It was like a thick beam of some hard substance. From this there were sticking out in a row, twenty more beams much shorter, like the stakes of a fence. This engine, we believe, the Man-Mountain uses for combing his hair.

'In another pocket we found a pillar of iron, hollow and very thick, and about the length of a man. On one side of the iron pillar several other pieces of iron were sticking out, cut into strange figures. In the left pocket was another engine of the same kind.

'We did not know what to make of these. We asked the Man-Mountain their use, and he tried to tell us, but we could not understand his answer.'

(These, you must know, were Gulliver's pocket pistols.)

'In the smaller pocket on the right side we found several flat round pieces of white and red metal. Some of the white pieces, which seemed to be silver, were so heavy that we found it hard to lift them.

'In the left smaller pocket were two pillars of iron. Each of these had a sheet inside.

'The Man-Mountain told us that one of these was called a pocket-knife, and the other a razor. He said he used one to cut his meat with, and the other to shave his beard.

'Then there were two small tight pockets into which we could not get. These he said were called fobs. They were in his middle garment.

'Out of the right fob hung a great silver chain. At the end of this was a wonderful engine, such as your Majesty has surely never seen the like.

'We asked the Man-Mountain to draw out what was on the end of the chain, and he drew out this engine. It is a sort of flattened globe, half of silver and half of some substance through which we can see. Under this are certain strange figures placed round a circle. We tried to touch them, but our fingers were stopped by the clear, hard substance that was over them.

'The Man-Mountain put this engine to our ears, and we heard a noise like a great water-mill. We have never known such a strange engine. Indeed, we believe it must be some unknown animal or god that the Man-Mountain worships.

(You will guess at once that this was Gulliver's watch.)

'From his left fob he took out a great net, almost large enough for a fisherman. This could open and shut, and the Man-Mountain used it as a purse.

'In it were several very large round pieces of yellow metal, which, if they are of gold, must be of enormous value.

'We noticed a girdle round his waist after we had searched all his pockets. It was made of the hide of a very large animal. From it, on the left side, there was hanging a sword almost as long as five men; and, on the right, there was a bag or pouch with two large pockets in it.

'Each of the pockets was big enough to hold three of your Majesty's subjects. One of them was filled with balls of metal, about the same size as our heads; they were so heavy that they needed a strong man to lift them. The other had a great heap of black grains in it, but these were not the least bit heavy, for we could hold fifty of them in the palm of our hands with the greatest ease.

'This, your Majesty, is all that we found in the pockets, and about the person, of the Man-Mountain, who behaved with much civility and respect while we searched him.

'(Signed) CLEFRIN FRELOC.
'MARSI FRELOC.'

This list was read over to the Emperor, who told Gulliver very gently and quietly that he must give up these things. The first thing he asked for was the sword. Gulliver took it out, sheath and all. The emperor asked him to draw it from its sheath. He did so, and the troops gave a shout of terror and surprise; for, although there were spots of rust on it here and there, owing to the sea water, it was still bright. The sun was shining very clearly at the time, and as Gulliver waved the sword in the air, its brightness made every one's eyes smart.

His Majesty was not a coward by any means, and he did not seem so much afraid as his troops. Telling Gulliver to return the sword to its sheath, he next ordered him to throw it away from him as gently as he could. It landed about six feet from the end of his chain. Next, he asked for the pocket pistols. Gulliver drew these out and tried to show very clearly what was their use. Then he loaded one with gunpowder, and told the Emperor not to be afraid, for he was going to let it off in the air.

When he did so the astonishment was even greater than Gulliver had expected. Some hundreds of the little folk fell down flat on the ground, as if they were dead, so great seemed to them the shock and the noise. The Emperor stood his ground and did not fall down or run away, but he even could not speak for some time. When all was quiet again and the people were better from their fright, Gulliver gave up the pistols, and with them he gave up the pouch with gunpowder and bullets in it that he had hanging from his belt.

The next thing he gave up was his watch. The Emperor was most eager to see this, and two of his strongest men carried it to him, hanging from a pole on their shoulders. Then Gulliver gave up his silver and his copper money, his purse with nine coins of gold, his knife and his razor, his comb, his silver snuff-box, and his handkerchief. After a little time all these things were given back to him, except the pistols, which were kept for safety in the Emperor's largest store. As for the spectacles and the compass, which were in Gulliver's secret pocket, he took good care to say nothing of them.

HOPING that he might before long be set at liberty, Gulliver did his very best to please the people. He was so gentle and quiet that in time they lost all fear of him. Often he would lie down and let five or six of them dance on his hand. The tiny children, boys and girls, would even play hide-and-seek in his hair. He now could speak and understand the language of the country.

Now, the people of Lilliput had their country shows like any other nation. They were very clever at the tricks they played, and they had far prettier shows than any Gulliver had ever seen. One day the Emperor asked him to view the rope-dancers. This was the first of their games he had seen, and he enjoyed it very much. They performed on a slender white thread, which was just about twenty-four inches long, and raised from the ground about twelve inches.

Another thing Gulliver liked to see was the way in which the horses were managed. Every day the horses of the army, and those, too, from the royal stables, were led before him, as the Emperor had commanded.

At first they were full of terror at the sight, but soon they were able to be led up to his feet without starting. Often he would put his hand upon the ground for the best riders to leap their horses over. One of the Emperor's huntsmen, on a powerful horse, was able to jump over his foot, shoe and all. This leap was thought to be a most wonderful feat of horsemanship.

Gulliver was one day able to amuse the Emperor and his court in a strange manner. He asked if there might be brought for him several sticks, about two feet in length and the thickness of one of our walking sticks. The Emperor gave orders to his Master of the Woods, and in the morning the sticks were brought on six carriages, each one drawn by eight horses.

Taking these sticks, Gulliver planted them in a square of two and a half feet. Over these he spread his handkerchief, stretching it and tying it down until it was as tight as a drum. This being done, and all being made safe, he asked the Emperor to let a troop of his best horse, twenty-four in number, come and ride upon the plain which he had thus made.

The Emperor very readily allowed this, and Gulliver took up the twenty-four horses, mounted and armed, and put them on this handkerchief. There the officers on horseback made mimic war. They shot their arrows, drew their swords, and pretended to fight a battle.

The Emperor was so delighted with this sight that he had the same thing done over again for several days. He was never tired of watching Gulliver do something new and strange. One day he asked the Man-Mountain if he would stand with his legs as wide apart as possible. This being done, the General of the army drew up his troops and marched them under Gulliver, with drums beating, flags flying, and spears held out.

The day came at last when the Emperor felt obliged to give Gulliver his liberty. Before he did this, however, he had to call a council of his great nobles and ask them if they thought any harm could come to the people from setting the prisoner free. Every noble but one was in favour of granting Gulliver his wish. The one who wished to keep him a prisoner was the High Admiral, whose name was Skyresh Bolgolam. For some reason hard to understand, he was the captive's great enemy. Nevertheless, it was settled that the chain by which Gulliver was fastened should be unlocked. Before this was done, however, he had to make several promises.

First, he had to promise that he would not go into the large cities without leave. If he wished to go into one of them, the people who lived there were to have two hours warning, so that they could get safely into their houses and not be about the streets.

Secondly, he was to walk only on the high road, and not to read in, or lie down in, a meadow or field of corn.

Thirdly, when walking in the road he was to take the greatest care that he did not tread on the body of any person, or any horse or carriage. Neither was he to take up in his hand any of the people against their will.

Fourthly, if there were any need for great hurry he was to be ready to take a messenger in his pocket for a six days' journey. If it were needed he was also to bring back the messenger in the same way.

Fifthly, he was to be always ready to help the people against their enemies, who were even now getting ready a fleet of ships which they meant to send against Lilliput to destroy it.

Sixthly, he had to promise that he would never leave the country of Lilliput without first gaining leave from the Emperor.

Seventhly, he was always to be willing to help the Emperor's workmen in his spare time by lifting large stones for covering the park wall and the royal buildings.

Lastly, if he promised faithfully to do everything that was set down in the list, the Emperor, in his turn, would promise to give him every day a supply of food and drink, enough to serve one thousand seven hundred and twenty-eight of his own subjects for one day.

Gulliver was so glad to get his freedom that he promised to do all they wished. His chains were unlocked, and at last, to his great joy, he was set free. The Emperor stood by in state while this was being done. Gulliver knelt at his feet, but the Emperor, with much kindness, gently told him to rise. He said that he hoped Gulliver would prove a faithful and useful servant, and that he would do his best to deserve all that had been done for him and all that the people were going to do in the future.

When all this was over, and Gulliver had time to think, he began to wonder how the Emperor had guessed that he would eat as much in one day as one thousand seven hundred and twenty-eight of the little people. He found out afterwards, however, that without telling him anything about it, the Emperor had sent some very learned men to measure him and to count up how much he would eat. You will see from this that these little people never did anything without carefully thinking about it first. It seems quite a new idea to measure people in order to find out how much food they will need!

WHEN Gulliver was free and able to go where he liked, the first thing he did was to ask if he might walk round the chief city of Lilliput. The name of the city was Mildendo. The temple, which had been made into a house for Gulliver, was some little way outside. The Emperor at once agreed, but he gave a solemn warning also, that the Man-Mountain was to be very careful and do no harm either to the houses or to any of the inhabitants. A notice was sent to all the people of Mildendo, that Gulliver was going to visit their town. They were told that they must keep inside the houses, and were on no account to come out while he was about.

Around the city of Mildendo was a wall two and a half feet high and at least eleven inches broad. A coach could very well be driven along the top of this wall. There were strong towers at ten feet distance. Gulliver stepped very gently over the great western gate and walked sideways along the two chief streets. He walked with the greatest care for fear of hurting any stragglers who might have remained in the streets.

There were no people about, but the roofs of the houses and all the windows were crowded with the little folk looking on with curious eyes at the big man. Gulliver thought that in all his travels he had never seen a city with so many people as there were in Mildendo. Some of them were afraid for their homes, but they had no cause for fear. Gulliver stepped as carefully as he could, and did not harm even the leaf of a tree.

The Emperor's palace was in the middle of the city, where two great streets met. The wall around it was two feet high and twenty feet away from the building. Gulliver had been told that he might step over the wall. The rooms of the palace were the most splendid that he had ever seen. There he saw the Empress, herself, and the young princes and princesses with their chief servants all about them.

The Empress smiled very kindly at him out of the window, and presently she came out of the room and down into the court below to speak to him, and even gave him her hand to kiss, so that he went home very pleased with all that he had seen. He had often wondered who the enemy was that the people so greatly feared. Soon this was made clear to him. Late one night, about a fortnight after he had been set at liberty, one of the greatest of the lords at the Emperor's court came to visit him in great distress. This nobleman brought only one servant with him, and he ordered his coach to wait some little distance from the house. He sent his servant away, and then asked Gulliver eagerly if he could spare an hour to listen to some very important news.

Gulliver said he was most willing to do this, for he liked his visitor, whose name was Reldresal. He took him up tenderly in his hand and asked him to begin at once, for he was eager to hear all. The visitor began by saying how glad he was that the big man was at last free. 'I, myself, was one of those who begged the Emperor to give you your liberty,' he said.

When Gulliver had thanked him, this good-natured little person went on to say that there was much trouble in the country. 'We may seem to be getting on very well, but really, we are in great danger.'

'I am indeed sorry to hear that,' said Gulliver. 'Perhaps if you tell me what the trouble is, I may be able to help you.'

This kind offer delighted Reldresal. 'I am sure that you are the only one who can help us,' he cried, with tears of joy in his eyes.

Then he went on to tell what the trouble was. Close by the island of Lilliput, he said, there was another island called Blefuscu. This was ruled by another Emperor, and it was a kingdom nearly as large and powerful as Lilliput. Although the people of these two countries were much alike and lived so close to each other, yet they were not at all friendly. Indeed, there had been for some time a fierce war between the people of Lilliput and the people of Blefuscu.

The way in which the quarrel began was very strange, and somewhat silly. One day, when the grandfather of the present Emperor of Lilliput was going to eat an egg, he broke it in the usual manner at the large end, and in so doing he happened to cut one of his fingers. Because of this a law was passed that the people were ever after to break their eggs at the small end instead of at the large end.

For many years following there was a long and serious war because thousands of the people would not break their eggs at the small end. Although they were punished every time they were caught breaking an egg in the old way, there were many who would still go on doing so. Some fled to the court of the Emperor of Blefuscu. He was only too glad to give them all the help he could, and because of this a war sprang up between the state of Lilliput and the state of Blefuscu. In this war many ships were lost on both sides, and many brave soldiers and sailors were killed.

Gulliver was greatly surprised to hear the cause of this strange quarrel. He found it hard to believe that people who showed such good sense in many ways, could be ready to fight over such a small matter. It seemed to him that it did not matter in the least whether an egg was broken at the large end or at the small end.

Then the visitor said that he had been sent by the Emperor to ask Gulliver's help. He told him that the people of Blefuscu had for a long time been building a very strong fleet of ships, stronger than any that were in Lilliput, and these they meant to send against the people of Lilliput in a very short time. The danger was very great, and unless Gulliver would help there seemed every chance that they would be utterly beaten. In his trouble the Emperor had thought of Gulliver, knowing that if he chose to use his great strength their enemies would quickly be destroyed.

Gulliver said in reply that he was ready, at all costs, to defend the Lilliputians against their enemies; and the next day he sent to tell the Emperor that he had a plan in his mind by which Lilliput could be saved. He was, in fact, going to seize the whole fleet of Blefuscu.

UP to this time Gulliver had never seen Blefuscu, so he went round to the side of the island from which he could get a view of that country. He went very carefully, as he did not wish to be seen by the enemy, thinking that if they caught sight of him, they might guess he was making up some plan against them. He hid himself behind a hill, and from there he was able to see the great fleet of Blefuscu at anchor. He was able to count as many as fifty ships. They had a few others belonging to Blefuscu, but the ones he counted were the best.

Going back to the chief city he gave orders for a large quantity of the thickest rope, and for a number of the strongest bars of iron to be made. This was done, and when the rope was brought to him he found that it was about the thickness of packing thread. Each bar of iron was about the size and length of a knitting needle. Taking three lengths of the rope he twisted them together to make one long strand. In the same way he took three of the bars and twisted them together, bending the ends so as to form a hook. He made fifty hooks and fastened them very firmly to fifty of the ropes he had thus strengthened.

He then asked the seamen on that coast, what was the depth of the sea between Lilliput and Blefuscu, and they told him it was about seventy glumguffs in the middle at high tide. A glumguff, one of their measures, was about an inch, and so seventy glumguffs, were not quite six feet. Gulliver took off his coat, his shoes and stockings, and walked into the water. He was able to wade nearly all the way, but near the middle he had to swim for a few yards. This, of course, caused him no trouble, and he came up to the fleet of Blefuscu in less than half an hour.

When the sailors of Blefuscu saw him coming, they were so full of terror that those on the ships leaped off and swam to the shore. About thirty thousand of them did this, and they covered the surface of the water like so many flies. This was just what Gulliver wanted them to do. He had no wish to harm the people of Blefuscu, but only to capture their ships. So, taking the hooks he had made, he fastened one in each ship, and tied the cords together at one end.

While he was doing this, the enemy shot thousands of their arrows at him, many of which stuck in his hands and face. Gulliver was greatly afraid for the safety of his eyes, and it is certain that he would have lost his sight through these arrows but for a simple plan. He remembered the spectacles, which by great good luck he had kept in his pocket. To take these out and put them on was the work of a moment. Then he was able to continue his task in safety. The arrows kept striking against the glass of his spectacles, but this did him no harm.

Gulliver, who by now had fastened all the hooks to his ships, took the knot, into which he had tied the fifty cords, and began to pull. Up to this moment his enemies did not have the least idea of what he meant to do; but when they saw the whole fleet moving after him, they set up such a scream of grief and rage as he had never heard before.

The Emperor of Lilliput, with his court, was waiting upon the shore wondering what would happen next. Presently he saw the ships of Blefuscu moving towards them, but Gulliver, being up to his neck in water, could not be seen. The Emperor and his nobles made up their minds that he had been drowned, and that the fleet of Blefuscu was coming to destroy them.

It was a moment of great fear, and they were wondering what they should do, when suddenly, to their great joy, they saw Gulliver, who was now in shallower water, and fully in sight. Holding up the knotted ends of the ropes to show what he had done, he cried with a loud voice, 'Long live the Emperor of Lilliput!' The little folk began to cheer and clap their hands, and when Gulliver at last stepped ashore they greeted him with many words of praise.

NOW that he had taken the ships of his enemy, the Emperor began to think that Gulliver would help him to overthrow the Emperor of Blefuscu, and thus bring the whole kingdom under his own rule. Now Gulliver did not wish to bring into slavery a people so brave as his little foes had shown themselves to be, and he said so quite firmly. This greatly annoyed the Emperor, who, forgetting all that Gulliver had done for him, began to feel great anger and jealousy. Skyresh Bolgolam, who, as already has been said, was Gulliver's bitter enemy, did all he could to make the Emperor more angry still. However, at the time, no harm was done to the big man.

About three weeks after the ships had been taken, some messengers came from Blefuscu to beg for peace. There were six nobles with servants and followers, to the number of five hundred, and they all seemed very rich and grand. They did not speak the same language as the people of Lilliput, for, although the two countries were so near one another, each had its own tongue. But as soon as rich men's sons in Lilliput grew up, they were sent to Blefuscu to finish their education, and to see a bit of the world;

while the sons of wealthy people in Blefuscu were sent to Lilliput. So it came about that a great many men in both countries knew both languages. Moreover, nearly all the sailors living on the coast were able to speak in both languages.

Knowing this, the Emperor of Lilliput said that the messengers from Blefuscu must make their speech in the language of his people. Of course, he felt that he had a perfect right to make them do whatever he liked, as he had seized their fleet. Thus it came about that the nobles from Blefuscu had to give their message to the Emperor of Lilliput in his language, very much against their will. They, however, felt that they must agree with the Emperor, and peace was soon made. Having heard from some one that Gulliver had been their very good friend and spoken up for them very firmly, they came to visit him and gave him many thanks. They also asked him to pay a visit to the Emperor of Blefuscu, and he promised to do so as soon as he was allowed.

So when he was speaking to the Emperor of Lilliput, he asked for leave to pay a visit to Blefuscu. The Emperor gave his consent, but Gulliver could see that he was not pleased. He did not pay the visit at once but some weeks later, and many strange things had happened to him before that time came. Besides the trouble between the people of Lilliput and the people of Blefuscu, another great quarrel was going on in the former country. This had to do, chiefly, with the people of the court, and many angry words were used during the course of the dispute.

The reason for the quarrel was that they could not settle if it were right to wear high heels or low heels on their boots. Gulliver could not help laughing, when he saw so many people get into such an angry state about such a small matter. Those who wore high heels hated those who wore low heels, and those wearing low ones would neither eat, drink, nor speak with the others. All this was of course very sad, and also very stupid.

The people who wore high heels were called the Tramecksan. Those who wore low heels were called Slamecksan. Just at the time when Gulliver was in Lilliput the people who wore low heels had the most power. All the Emperor's chief servants, for instance, had low heels. It was feared, though, that the eldest prince, the heir to the throne, was in favour of high heels; at least, it was certain that he wore one high heel and one low heel. This, of course, made him walk in a curious hobbling manner, and no one knew really on which side he was.

The Tramecksan, or high-heeled people, declared that he was on their side, because of his one high heel, while the Slamecksan said that he was surely on their side. How absurd it was of them to think that it mattered whether their heels were high or low! And, yet the two parties were so very fierce and bitter against each other, that the quarrel almost led to civil war!

PERHAPS you would now like to hear something about the appearance and the customs of the little people Gulliver had come amongst. Most of them were no more than six inches high, and all the animals in the country were smaller still. The tallest horses were between four and five inches in height, while the sheep were only an inch and a half. The geese were about the same size as our sparrows, and the smallest animals were so small that Gulliver could not see them. However, the people of Lilliput could see them, for they had very good sight. In fact, Gulliver was often amused at watching them do work and at not being able to see their tools.

The children in Lilliput were all sent to boarding-schools or nurseries when they were mere babies. Their fathers and mothers came to see them twice a year, but they were only allowed to talk to them for an hour each time. There was a rule, too, that they were not to bring any toys or sweets to their children, and they were not to kiss them. One of the teachers stood in the room all the time.

The children did not have much time for breakfast and dinner at these schools, and they had to begin lessons just as soon as a meal was finished. However, they were allowed out for two hours every day to do drill and to play games. In the schools for little girls, the teachers were not allowed to tell any silly stories that were likely to frighten children.

All the children were told that they must dress themselves as soon as they had reached the age of four. This must have seemed to Gulliver a very hard rule. If the children in England were left to dress themselves at the age of four, many of them would cry all day, and perhaps want to stay in bed for a year! Children whose parents earned their living by tilling the soil did not go to school at all. Their fathers and mothers set them to weed and dig and hoe as soon as they were old enough. They said that they did not need to learn reading and writing and counting; they could weed just as well without knowing anything about these things.

When Gulliver looked into the law-courts in Lilliput to see what they were like, he was surprised at the strange image that he saw there. It was an image of Justice. She had six eyes, two of which were in her face, two at the back of her head, and one on each side of her head. In her right hand she was holding a bag of gold, which was open, and in her left she had a sword in its sheath. These things showed that she liked rather to reward people than to punish them.

Altogether, Gulliver was surprised and amused at many of the things he saw in the land of little people, but the people themselves were also very much surprised and amused at Gulliver. Nothing seemed to astonish them more than the quantity of food that he ate. He had two hundred cooks to prepare his meals. Every day each one had to prepare for him two dishes.

One day the Emperor sent to ask if he might see him dine. Gulliver, of course, was only too pleased, and so the Emperor with the Empress and the young princes and princesses came. Gulliver had cut down some of the trees in the royal forest and had made for himself a good chair and a strong table. His visitors sat on chairs of state, placed on the table, and watched while he had his dinner. It was a very pleasant visit, but Gulliver afterwards heard that the Emperor had taken notice of the large amount he ate, and had begun to wonder if it were right that so much good food should be taken from the people of Lilliput.

He had many other visitors who went from time to time to see him and to talk with him. Sometimes he had as many as four coaches on his table at once. It had a rim round it five inches high. While he was talking with one party the others would be driving round the table. Many delightful afternoons were spent in this way, but at last some trouble came of these visits. One lady, who was a relative of Gulliver's great enemy, came very often to see him, and some people began to think there was a plot between them that might be a great danger to the country. Of course this was not true, but it made many of the great lords think badly of Gulliver. In fact, some of them were beginning to hate him, though he did not find this out until afterwards.

Some time after this a very strange adventure happened to Gulliver; one that later on had a great deal to do with making him leave the country of Lilliput. One midnight he was sleeping quietly, when he was suddenly awakened by a loud knocking and the cries of many people at his door. They made so much noise, indeed, that at first he was in terror and almost afraid to open to them. When, after a few seconds, he did do so, several gentlemen of the Emperor's court quickly made their way to him through the crowd, and begged him to go with them at once to the Emperor's palace, which was on fire, and in the greatest danger of being burnt down.

One of the maids of honour had fallen asleep while she had been reading, and the candle had set fire to the room, which was next to that of the Empress. In a moment Gulliver had put on his clothes and made ready to start. Orders were given for every one to keep out of the way, and as it was a fine moonlight night he reached the palace without treading on any one. He found that the longest ladders had been put against the walls and that the people had brought all the buckets in the city, but that the ladders were some way from the room in which the fire was.

As the buckets were only about the size of fairly large thimbles, they were of little use to Gulliver.

Suddenly Gulliver thought of a splendid plan. He rushed to the lake and dipped out with his hat as much water as it would hold. He emptied his hat right over the flames and succeeded in putting out the fire; but then he found to his horror that he had nearly drowned the Empress and the royal children.

The room to which they had fled for safety had been filled with water. Gulliver had the greatest difficulty in getting them out, and quite a long time passed before they came to their senses. This was a great misfortune, as he afterwards found; in fact, nothing worse could have happened to him. It was, in that country, a great crime for any person even to touch the Empress or the royal children. Whoever did so, even by accident, had to suffer death. The flames had been put out and the beautiful palace saved, but he guessed that he would get no thanks and much blame for what he had done.

Some hours later a message came to him from the Emperor, saying that he had given orders that he should receive a free pardon for touching the Empress.

AS the Emperor of Lilliput had promised that Gulliver might pay a visit to the Emperor of Blefuscu, he began about two weeks after the fire at the palace to get ready to go. But one night a visitor came to see him secretly; and brought with him the worst of news. He was a lord from the Emperor's court; one whom Gulliver had helped in a time of great trouble. He came without any servants, and did not even send in his name. Gulliver saw at once that there was something wrong, so he locked the door, placed his visitor on the table, and sat by him as usual to hear what he had to say.

The friendly little fellow looked as if he were very sad at heart, and this was not to be wondered at as he had brought bad news to his big friend. After asking how Gulliver was, he begged him to pay the greatest attention to what he had to say. 'For I have something to tell you that is a matter of life and death,' he said, speaking in a tone of great sorrow. Then he went on to say that there were many cruel and envious persons in the Emperor's court, who were trying to bring about the death of the big stranger who had come to live among them. First among these was Skyresh Bolgolam. This bad man had been Gulliver's enemy, for no reason whatever, from the time he had first come into that country.

'I must tell you,' said the visitor, 'that the Emperor has called together his lords many times in order to decide what is to become of you. At last, two days ago, it was settled that it would be much better for the country if you were either put to death, or if something were done to take away your great power, which, they say, is a great danger to the country.'

'What can it mean?' cried Gulliver. 'I have done nothing wrong. I have done all I could to help the Emperor and the people of Lilliput. How is it that they wish to destroy me?'

His visitor went on to say that at the last meeting of the Emperor and his council four charges had been brought against him. Skyresh Bolgolam had helped to draw these up. The first charge was that Gulliver had broken the law of the country by touching the Empress and the royal children. Certainly the Emperor had promised to pardon Gulliver, but the nobles said this could not be done without their consent, which they would never give upon any condition. The second charge was that he had refused to take all the ships that the people of Blefuscu had left, and bring the Emperor of that country, with his nobles, prisoner to Lilliput.

'No one but a traitor,' one man had said, 'would have pleaded for an enemy in the way Gulliver did. He knew that the two states had been at war for thirty-six moons, for the Emperor's messenger had told him. Then why should he refuse to help the people of Lilliput to get rid of their enemy?

'It was nonsense for him to say that he did not want to destroy an innocent people. They were not innocent so long as they broke the big end of their eggs, and he ought to have known that.'

The third charge was that he had shown friendship towards the messengers from Blefuscu. Still more foolish was the last charge. It made them very angry to hear that Gulliver was going to pay a visit to Blefuscu. This, they thought, was quite wrong.

'He will do much harm,' they said. 'When he is in Blefuscu there is no end to the mischief that may be done.'

For a long, long time the Emperor and his lords had talked over these four charges. Some of them had made up their minds that Gulliver must be put to death, but the Emperor himself did not agree with them. He told the lords that Gulliver had helped him in many ways, and because of this his life must be spared. Bolgolam was full of rage when he heard this. He had even gone so far as to plan the way in which Gulliver was to die. He said that the best way was for his house to be set on fire at night, and while it was burning, twenty thousand men with poisoned arrows were to shoot him in the face and hands.

Other cruel lords had a different plan. It seemed certain that Gulliver would lose his life, when at last the Emperor asked Reldresal, who had always been a friend of the 'Man-Mountain', what he thought had best be done with him. There was only one thing to be done, said Reldresal, and that was to put out Gulliver's eyes. It would be quite enough for the big man to see with the eyes of the Emperor and his chief ministers.

Hearing this Bolgolam at once flew into the greatest of furies. He said Reldresal was quite wrong. The only safe plan was to put Gulliver to death. Another lord then got up to speak. He had a further reason why Gulliver should not be allowed to live any longer. This was that the large amount of food that the big man ate every day would soon make everybody quite poor. Nay, it might even happen that some poor people might die of hunger.

The Emperor listened very carefully to all these speeches. When everybody had finished, he said quite calmly that he though Reldresal was right. Gulliver's eyes, he said, should be put out to begin with. If that did not satisfy the lords of Lilliput, some other punishment could be given afterwards. As for his food costing so much, they need not worry about that. It would be easy to give him each day a little less, so that he would grow faint, and in time die.

By the time the Emperor had finished speaking, all the lords were of the same mind as His Majesty. That is to say, all but one. Only Gulliver's great enemy, Bolgolam, wished him to die. It was settled that in three days Reldresal was to go to read the sentence. The plan of starving him, little by little, was to be kept a secret for the present. He was only to be told, in the meantime, that he was to lose his eyes. All of this his visitor told Gulliver, who, as you may be sure, did not feel very happy.

WHEN the friend had gone away and he was left alone, he sat and wondered what he should do. His enemies would have no chance if once he made up his mind to fight them. However, being far from cruel himself, he felt that if he could escape without harming any one it would be much better. Besides, the thought came into his mind that, as he had given his word to the Emperor not to harm any of the people, it would be very mean of him to break his promise now.

Then a really splendid idea came into his mind. He would go to Blefuscu. He knew he would be treated with kindness, and even if the tiny people of that island wished to give him up, they would not be strong enough to do it. Anyhow, he must get away at once from these fierce little enemies. No sooner had Gulliver made this plan than he began to get ready for the journey. He wrote to his so-called friend Reldresal and told him that he was going to Blefuscu. Then, before any answer could be sent, he went off quietly to that side of Lilliput where the fleet lay at anchor.

Boldly seizing a large man-of-war, he tied a cable to it and then stripped himself. Into this vessel he put, not only his clothes, but also his coverlet, which he had carried to the shore under his arm to take with him, thinking it might be cold at night. Wading half the way and swimming the rest, and drawing the vessel after him the whole time, he at least reached the royal port of Blefuscu. The people there had been expecting him for a long time and they greeted him with joy.

296

He had, of course, to go at once to the capital city to see the Emperor of Blefuscu, and, as he did not know his way, two of the small people of Blefuscu kindly offered to be his guides. It would not have been possible for them to walk as quickly as Gulliver, so he took them in his hands, and went along with them while they pointed out the way he had to go.

When they had come to about two hundred yards from the great gates of the chief city he put down his two tiny guides, and they went on before him to tell the Emperor of Blefuscu that he had arrived. When they were gone Gulliver sat down and thought of his life in Lilliput. For some things he was sorry that he had been obliged to leave that country. He had grown fond of some of the little people.

In about an hour an answer came that His Majesty the Emperor, together with the royal family and the great officers of his court, were starting out to meet the visitor. Gulliver then went forward. The Emperor and his lords, when they saw him, got down from their horses, and the Empress and her ladies from their coaches. Nobody seemed in the least bit frightened, although they certainly had never seen anything or any one of Gulliver's size before.

He lay on the ground to kiss their hands, saying that he had come as he had promised, by permission of the Emperor of Lilliput, to have the honour of seeing so mighty a monarch and to do any service that might be asked, but he took good care to say nothing of the great trouble he was in.

He was taken into the city and treated with all honour. This, however, hardly made up for the loss of a house and bed. Truth to say, Gulliver had to sleep in the open air all night, wrapped in his coverlet. Although he was so far out of danger, yet he was not happy and by no means comfortable. Many times did he wish with all his heart that he was safely back in his own country, and away from all the little people.

For two or three days after his arrival in Blefuscu, he waited for a message to arrive from the Emperor of Lilliput, or from Reldresal to whom he had written the letter. No message came, and he began to wonder if they had made up their minds to leave him alone.

THREE days after he had arrived in Blefuscu, Gulliver was walking on the shore when he saw in the sea some distance away a strange-looking object. He watched and watched, and at last it seemed to him that it was an empty boat, one that must have floated away from some wreck.

He was full of joy. Not once had he thought that such good fortune would come his way. The tide brought the boat nearer and nearer to him, but not near enough for him to touch. The best thing for him to do now, he thought, was to go back to the chief city and get help. This he did. He sent to ask the Emperor of Blefuscu to lend him twenty of the best vessels that had been left when the rest of the fleet had been taken. The Emperor of Blefuscu was glad to help him, and not only lent him the ships, but also three thousand seamen to sail them.

Then Gulliver returned to the boat by the shortest way, across land, while the twenty vessels sailed round the coast. He found that the tide had driven the boat still nearer to the shore. The seamen had ropes with them, which Gulliver had made stronger by twisting three together. When the ships came up, he stripped himself and waded until he was within one hundred yards of the boat. Then he swam to it. The sailors threw to him the rope. He fastened one end of it to the front part of the boat, and the other end to a man-of-war, the largest left in Blefuscu.

He soon found that his work was far more difficult than he had thought at first. The only way in which he could move the boat was by swimming behind and pushing the boat along with his hand. He managed very well in this way, and at last got to water which was not so deep. He put his feet to the ground and found that he was able to hold his chin above the surface. Having taken a short rest at this place he began to push the boat again, and found that he was getting on faster. Then he took another rest, and so on until he reached water that was not deep and only reached his arm-pits.

The hardest part of the work was over now. Going to one of the ships, he brought out all the ropes that were left, and tied them first to his boat, and then to the nine vessels that had come out with him. When the boat was at last fastened firmly to the ships, they all pulled while Gulliver pushed, until it was brought ashore. Now the great trouble was to turn the boat over. However, two thousand men with ropes and engines gave all the help they could and at last this was done also. Gulliver found that the boat was not nearly so much damaged as he had feared, and he set about mending it at once.

THE Emperor of Blefuscu, of course, came to look. He was greatly amazed, and wanted to know all about it. Gulliver told him the story. The boat would carry him, he said, to some place from which he could get back to his own native country. The Emperor of Blefuscu very kindly said that he did not wish his visitor to leave that country. He begged Gulliver to stay there as long as he could. However, the big man asked the Emperor to let him go.

Now, as to Lilliput, the Emperor of that country never guessed that Gulliver had gone to Blefuscu for any other reason than to pay a friendly visit. He did not know that Gulliver had heard of his cruel plans. A week or two passed, and at last, when they found that the big man did not return, the Emperor of Lilliput and his lords began to be somewhat afraid. They wondered what had best be done. After talking the matter over they made up their minds to send a messenger to Blefuscu. He was to say that Gulliver had done wrong and had to be punished, and therefore must be sent back at once bound hand and foot.

However, the messenger was not to forget to say that the
Emperor of Lilliput had made up his mind to be kind to the Man-
Mountain, and not to punish him too severely. All he intended to
do was to put out his eyes, which, he felt sure, was not very cruel.
When the Emperor of Blefuscu heard this message he saw that he
was in a great difficulty. He did not make up his mind at once, but
took three days to think out what he should do. At the end of this
time he sent a message back full of excuses. Then he told Gulliver
what had happened. He promised his big visitor that if he cared to
stay there, he would give him all the help possible, and protect
him from his enemies.

Gulliver thought this a most kind offer, and he thanked the
Emperor with all his heart, but told him that it would be much
better for him to leave Blefuscu. If he stayed, there might be a war
between the two countries because of him. This would be but a
poor reward to the Emperor of Blefuscu for his kindness, and he
declared that he would sooner be lost in the ocean than cause such
trouble.

Upon hearing this the Emperor of Blefuscu certainly seemed
rather glad, and Gulliver afterwards found out why this was. His
lords had been telling him that if the dangerous visitor remained
he might be the cause of endless trouble to the country. When he
learned this, Gulliver made all the more haste to be gone, and the
court of Blefuscu gave him all the help that he needed, but because
of his haste he was not able to do all to the boat that he wished.

He had five hundred workmen to help him make the two sails, and he showed them all that he wished done. For the sails, he gave orders that thirteen folds of their strongest linen should be quilted together, hoping this would be strong enough. No wonder it took Gulliver a long time to make ready for the journey! Just think of two sails for a big boat being made of linen which was only three inches wide, and not strong enough without being folded over thirteen times! The five hundred little workmen must have done a great deal of sewing by the time they had finished the two sails.

Ten, twenty, and thirty of their thickest and strongest ropes and cables he twisted together to make cordage for his vessel. After searching for many long and weary hours by the seashore, he found a stone large enough to serve him for an anchor. The tallow of three hundred sheep and oxen was given him to grease the boat and to use in other ways. He cut down the largest timber trees in Blefuscu, to make for himself oars and masts.

It was quite a month before he was ready to go. When all was finished, he sent word to the palace that he was about to start. The Emperor and the royal family came out to see the last of their big visitor, and to wish him goodbye. Gulliver lay down on his face to kiss the Emperor's hand which was held out to him. The Empress and the young princesses also gave him their hands. The Emperor of Blefuscu was really a kind man, and to show his friendship towards Gulliver, he gave him fifty purses with two hundred sprugs in each. A sprug was the largest gold coin of that country, so the gift meant a great deal to the Emperor, although it was of no use to Gulliver, except as a curiosity.

Besides this gift of money the Emperor gave his picture, taken at full length. This the big man at once slipped into his glove to keep it from being scratched or spoiled.

Now, Gulliver was wise enough to remember that he might be out on the ocean for many days, and perhaps for weeks, before he would be seen by a passing ship and picked up. So he told the men who were helping him to kill a hundred oxen and three hundred sheep, which he stored in the boat, with plenty of bread and drink and as much ready cooked meat as four hundred cooks could prepare in the time.

Of live animals he took six cows and two bulls and as many sheep and lambs, meaning to carry them home to his own country to live there. To feed them on board he had a good bundle of hay and a bag of corn.

Had he been allowed, he would very much have like to take with him a dozen or more of the little people. However, the Emperor would not allow this, even though the small people themselves wished to go. He made Gulliver give a solemn promise that he would not take even one of the inhabitants of that country. To set the Emperor's mind at ease Gulliver said that his pockets might be searched before he went, and when this was done all minds were set at rest.

It was at six o'clock in the morning that Gulliver left the island of Blefuscu. Feasts had been held all the day before. Flags were flying from every high tower and steeple, while many thousands of people stood on the shore watching the visitor depart. It was to them a most wondrous sight. They watched and watched until they could see the boat no longer, and they knew that Gulliver had gone from them for ever.

ALL day, from six o'clock in the morning, Gulliver sailed to the northward. He found that he was able to steer pretty well with the help of his little pocket compass. In fact, he would not have known in which direction he was going, if it had not been for this useful friend. About the same hour in the evening, that is to say, about six o'clock, he reached a small island upon which no one seemed to be living. There he cast anchor, and after having something to eat, went to sleep.

It was a clear night and he slept soundly, but he woke just at daybreak, and had finished his breakfast before the sun was up. Then lifting his anchor, he steered his boat in the same direction as he had sailed during the day before. He hoped that he would soon find land, but he saw nothing all that day. Terrible fears came upon him, and he began to wonder if he had left the land of the tiny people, only to perish in the sea. The sun beat down upon his head, and he felt sick and sad.

Another night passed, a long, weary night, and on the third day Gulliver thought that he could see a sail. How full of joy he was! Eagerly he put out all the sail he could, and waved his handkerchief, making frantic signs for help. In about half an hour he was seen. The strange ship hung out her flag, and fired a gun. She slackened her sails, and Gulliver came up to her between five and six in the evening of September the twenty-sixth. He put into his coat pocket all the live cows and sheep that he had, and went on board, taking with him his little store of provisions.

The ship was returning to England from Japan, and the captain, Mr. John Biddle, was a good sailor and a very kind man. There were, Gulliver found, fifty men on the ship, and, strange to say, one of them, whose name was Peter Williams, had known him before. This sailor was able to speak well of him to the captain, and to say that he was an honest man.

The captain treated his new passenger with much kindness. Gulliver told him his whole story as plainly and simply as he could, but it was clear that the captain did not believe him. Indeed the honest seaman fancied that Gulliver had been driven mad by the dangers and hardships through which he had passed. To show the captain that his words were true, Gulliver put his hand into his pocket, drew out the tiny black cattle and sheep and put them on the table of the cabin where he was sitting. The captain was full of surprise. He had never seen tiny oxen and sheep, such as these were, and he was much delighted with them.

Then Gulliver took out his full-length picture of the Emperor of Blefuscu, and the purses of gold that His Majesty had given him, besides other tiny things. At last the ship reached England, and Gulliver hurried to London to see his wife and children. When he reached his home, his family could hardly believe it was he, for they had long given him up as dead. When they heard of his strange life, they were full of wonder, and begged that he would never go on the sea again, lest worse things should happen to him.

The Horse & the Stag

A HORSE was pastured upon a wide meadow, which he had all to himself until a stag broke in and trod down the grass. This greatly annoyed the horse, which appealed to a man for help in punishing the intruder.

'Yes,' said the man. 'I will help you to be revenged upon the stag; but first you must let me put a bit in your mouth and mount upon your back. I will provide weapons and we will soon overpower the silly beast.'

The horse readily agreed, and together they chased and overcame the stag. Very pleased with his revenge, the horse began to thank the man for his aid, but he received the answer:

'No, do not thank me. I did not know until now how useful you could be to me. I should thank you, for in future I will keep you for my servant.' Thus from that time the horse has been the slave of man.

Revenge is dearly bought at the price of liberty.

The Ass & the Frogs

O NE day an ass, with a burden of wood upon his back, had the ill-luck to sink into a bog among hoards of frogs. 'Woe is me!' he groaned and sighed as though his heart would break.

'Friend,' said one of the frogs to the unhappy ass, 'if you make such a noise about a bog you have just entered, what would you do if you had been here as long as we have?'

Custom makes things familiar and easy to us.

DAVID
FRANKLAND.

The Cat & the Fox

A CAT and a fox were exchanging views upon the difficulties of living in peace and safety from those who were always ready to take their lives.

'I do not care a bit for any of them,' said the fox at last. 'Things may be very bad, as you say, but I have a thousand tricks to show my enemies before they can do me harm.'

'You are fortunate,' replied the cat. 'For my part, I have only one way of evading my enemies, only one method of escape and if that fails all is lost.'

'I am sorry for you with all my heart,' said Reynard. 'If one could tell a friend from a foe in these difficult times, I would show you one or two of my tricks.'

Hardly had he finished speaking when a pack of hounds burst suddenly upon them.

The cat, resorting to her single trick, ran up a tree, and from the security of the topmost branches witnessed the downfall of the braggart.

Unable to make up his mind which of the thousand tricks he would adopt the fox was quickly caught before he could put even one of them into operation.

Pride goes before a fall.

The Arab & the Camel

A N Arab, having loaded his camel, asked him whether he preferred to go uphill or downhill.

'Why do you ask, master?' said the camel dryly. 'Is the level way across the plain shut up?'

What use is it to pretend there is a choice when there is none?

Pinocchio

NCE upon a time there was . . .
'A king!' my eager readers will exclaim. No, young children, you are mistaken. Once upon a time there was a piece of wood.

It was not the best wood, but just an ordinary piece, such as we use in stoves and fireplaces to kindle a fire and warm our rooms in winter.

I can't say how it happened, but the fact is that one fine day this piece of wood happened to be in the shop of an old carpenter whose name was Mr Antonio, but every one called him Mr Cherry, because the end of his nose was always red and shiny like a ripe cherry.

As soon as Mr Cherry saw this piece of wood, he was very pleased; he rubbed his hands together joyfully, and said:

'This has come in the nick of time; it is just what I want to make a leg for my little table.'

Without losing a moment he took his sharp hatchet, and was going to strip off the bark and trim it into shape. But just as he raised the hatchet to strike the first blow, he paused with his hand in the air, for he heard a tiny, tiny voice which said:

'Don't strike me too hard!'

Imagine Mr. Cherry's surprise!

He glanced around the shop in a fright to see where that little voice could have come from, but he saw no one. He looked under his bench. No one. He looked in a cupboard which he always kept locked; but there was no one. He looked in his basket of chips and sawdust. No one. He opened the shop door and looked out into the street, and no one! What then?

'I see,' he said at last, laughing and scratching his wig, 'I must have imagined that little voice. Let us get to work.'

He took up his hatchet again, and down it came on the piece of wood.

'Oh, you hurt me!' whimpered that same little voice.

This time Mr Cherry was thunderstruck. His eyes stood out of his head with fear; his mouth was wide open, and his tongue hung down over his chin.

As soon as he could speak he said, trembling and stammering with fright:

'But where did that little voice come from that cried "Oh"? There's not a living soul here. Can it be that this piece of wood has learned to cry and complain like a baby? I can't believe it. This piece of wood – look at it! It's just a piece of firewood, like all the others; when you put it on the fire it will help to boil a kettle.

Well, then? Is someone hidden inside it? If there is, so much the worse for him. I'll attend to his case!'

With these words he grasped that poor piece of wood with both hands, and began to beat it against the wall without mercy.

Then he stopped and listened to see if any little voice was complaining this time. He waited two minutes – nothing; five minutes – nothing; ten minutes – and still nothing!

'Now I understand,' he exclaimed, laughing and rumpling his wig. 'I must have imagined that little voice that said "Oh!" Let us get to work!'

And because he felt very much afraid, he began to sing to give himself courage.

Meanwhile he put the hatchet down and taking up his plane he began to plane and shape the piece of wood. But while the plane went back and forth, he heard again that little voice which said, laughing:

'Stop! you're tickling me!'

This time poor Mr Cherry fainted as if struck by lightning. When he opened his eyes he was sitting on the floor.

He was so changed you would hardly have recognised him. Even the end of his nose, which was always crimson, had turned blue with fright.

At that moment someone rapped on the door.

'Come in,' said the carpenter, but he did not have strength enough to get up.

A little, lively old man walked into the shop. His name was Geppetto, but when the boys in the neighbourhood wanted to tease him, they called him by his nickname of Polendina, on account of his yellow wig which looked very much like a dish of *polenta*, which is like porridge.

Geppetto was very quick-tempered. Woe to him who called him Polendina! He simply went wild, and no one could do anything with him.

'Good morning, Mr Antonio,' said Geppetto, 'what are you doing down there?'

'I am teaching the ants the alphabet.'

'Much good may it do you!'

'What brought you here, Mr Geppetto?'

'My legs. Do you know, Mr Antonio, I have come to ask a favour.'

'Here I am, ready to serve you,' replied the carpenter, getting to his knees.

'I had an idea this morning.'

'Let us hear it.'

'I thought I would make a lovely, wooden puppet, a really wonderful one, that could dance, and fence, and turn somersaults in the air. And then, with this puppet, I would travel round the world, and earn my bit of bread and my glass of wine. What do you think of that?'

'Bravo, Polendina!' cried that same little, mysterious voice.

When he heard himself called Polendina, Mr Geppetto became so angry that he turned as red as a ripe pepper-pod. He whirled on the carpenter, and said in a rage:

'Why do you offend me?'

'Who is offending you?'

'You called me Polendina!'

'No, indeed I didn't!'

'Oh! perhaps *I* said it! But I say that it was you.'

'No!'

'Yes!'

'No!'

'Yes!'

And getting more and more excited, from words they came to blows. They snatched at one another's wigs, and even slapped and bit and scratched each other.

At the end of the combat Mr Antonio found Geppetto's yellow wig in his hands, and Geppetto had the carpenter's grey wig between his teeth.

'Give me my wig,' said Mr Antonio.

'And you give me mine, and let us make a treaty of peace.'

So the two little old men, after each had put on his own wig,

shook hands, and vowed to be good friends as long as they both should live.

'Now, neighbour Geppetto,' said the carpenter, to show that they were friends again, 'what is it that I can do for you?'

'I would like a little piece of wood to make my puppet man. Will you give it to me?'

Mr Antonio, well pleased, went quickly to his bench, and took the piece of wood which had given him such a fright. But just as he was giving it to his friend it shook so hard that it slipped out of his hands, and struck poor Geppetto violently on the shin.

'Ah! this is a fine way to make me a present, Mr Antonio! You have almost lamed me.'

'Upon my honour, I didn't do it!'

'Oh! so *I* did it then!'

'It's all the fault of this piece of wood . . .'

'Yes, I know the wood struck me, but you threw it at my legs!'

'I did not throw it at you!'

'That's a lie!'

'Geppetto, don't insult me; if you do I will call you Polendina!'

'Blockhead!'

'Polendina!'

'Donkey!'

'Polendina!'

'Ugly monkey!'

'Polendina!'

When he heard himself called Polendina for the third time, Geppetto, blind with rage, rushed at the carpenter, and the second battle was worse than the first.

When it was over, Mr Antonio had two more scratches on his nose, and the other two buttons less on his jacket. Their accounts thus being even they shook hands again, and vowed to be good friends as long as they both should live. Then Geppetto took his piece of wood, and after thanking Mr Antonio, went limping home.

Geppetto lived in a little room on the ground floor that was lighted by a window under the stairs. His furniture could not have

been simpler. A rickety chair, a shaky bed, and a broken-down table. At the back of the room a fireplace could be seen, with the fire lighted; but the fire was painted, and over the fire was a painted kettle which was boiling merrily, and sending forth a cloud of steam that was just like real steam.

As soon as he came home, Geppetto took his tools and began to carve his puppet.

'What shall I call him?' he said to himself. 'I think I will call him Pinocchio. This name will bring good luck. I once knew a whole family of Pinocchios: there was Pinocchio the father, and Pinocchia the mother, and Pinocchii the children, and they all got along splendidly. The richest of them was a beggar.'

When he had thought of a name for his puppet, he set to work with a will. He made his hair, and his forehead, and his eyes in a very short time.

As soon as the eyes were finished, imagine his amazement when he saw them move, and look at him intently.

When Geppetto saw those two wooden eyes watching him, he didn't like it at all, and he said crossly:

'Naughty wooden eyes, why are you looking at me?'

But no one answered.

After the eyes he made the nose; but as soon as it was finished, it began to grow. It grew, and it grew, until in a few minutes it was so long that it seemed as if there was no end to it.

Poor Geppetto worked fast to shorten it, but the more he pared it down and cut it off, the longer that impertinent nose became.

After the nose he made the mouth; but before he had finished with it, it began to laugh and make fun of him.

'Stop laughing!' said Geppetto irritably, but he might as well have spoken to the wall.

'Stop laughing, I say!' he shouted in a menacing voice.

The mouth stopped laughing, and stuck out its tongue.

However, since old Geppetto did not want to spoil the puppet, he pretended not to see it, and went on with his work.

After the mouth he made the chin, then the neck, the shoulders, the stomach, the arms and the hands.

The moment the hands were finished, Geppetto's wig was snatched from his head. He glanced upward, and what did he see? There was his yellow wig in the puppet's hands.

'Pinocchio! Give me back my wig this minute!'

But Pinocchio, instead of returning the wig, put it on his own head, and was almost hidden under it.

This insolent, mocking behaviour made Geppetto feel sadder than ever before in all his life. He turned to Pinocchio, and said:

'You rogue of a son! You are not yet finished, and you begin to disobey your father! That's bad, my boy, very bad!'

And he wiped away a tear.

There were still the legs and feet to make.

When Geppetto had finished the feet, a kick landed on his nose.

'It serves me right,' he said to himself, 'I should have thought of that before! Now it is too late.'

He took up the puppet in his hands and placed him on the floor to see if he could walk; but Pinocchio's legs were stiff, and he didn't know how to move them. So Geppetto took him by the hand, and showed him how to put one foot before the other.

When the stiffness was out of his legs, Pinocchio began to walk alone, and run around the room; and finally he slipped out of the door into the street and ran away.

Aladdin & his Wonderful Lamp

N one of the large cities of the East there once lived a tailor, whose name was Mustapha. Mustapha was very poor, and he found it hard to provide food for himself, his wife, and his only child, Aladdin.

Aladdin was a very naughty and lazy boy. He would never do what his parents wished him to do, but played in the streets from noon till night with other naughty boys.

When Aladdin was old enough to learn a trade his father took him into his own shop and began to show him how he should use the needle. It was of no use. Aladdin had had his own way so long that now he could not settle down to work. His father tried him over and over again, and was at last so vexed at his son's idle habits that he became ill and soon died.

The poor widow thought that surely now her son would earn a little money. But no. Aladdin was as idle as ever. In despair, the good woman sold all the things that were in the shop, and with the money and a little she could earn by spinning cotton she got on fairly well.

One day when Aladdin was playing in the street with some more boys, a stranger saw him and stopped to look at him.

This stranger was a magician, and as he looked at Aladdin he said to himself, 'This is just the kind of boy I want. He is daring and bold, and will just suit me.' Going up to Aladdin, he drew him aside from his friends.

'Is your father called Mustapha?' the magician asked quietly. 'And is he not a tailor?'

'Yes,' replied Aladdin, 'but he is now dead.'

Hearing this, the stranger threw his arms around the boy and kissed him, while tears seemed to flow down his cheeks.

Aladdin asked him why he wept. 'Alas!' replied the stranger, 'how can I help it? I am your uncle. Your father was my brother. I have tried to find him all over the world, and now I have come too late.'

The stranger then asked Aladdin about his mother, and, putting some money into his hand, bade him go home and say he would call to see her next day.

Aladdin ran off home with glee.

'Mother,' said he, 'my uncle found me in the street to-day, and he bade me tell you he is coming here to-morrow.'

'Your uncle found you?' asked the good woman. 'Nonsense; you have no uncle.'

'At any rate, a stranger hugged and kissed me, and gave me this gold,' replied Aladdin. 'He surely *must* be my uncle.'

Aladdin's mother did not know what to think. She had never heard of this uncle before; but, as Aladdin then went out, nothing more was said.

Next day the stranger again saw Aladdin playing in the street. 'Here is some more money, boy,' said he, kissing him again; 'take it to your mother, and tell her to buy some things for to-night's supper. I shall call on you then.'

Aladdin took the money home, and, though his mother could hardly believe her senses, she spent the money in buying good food for supper. As for Aladdin, so eager was he to see his uncle once more that he went out into the street to show him the way to the house.

The stranger came. He brought some bottles of wine and some nice fruit. When these had been set on the supper table he said to the widow, 'Pray, show me the place where my poor brother used to sit.'

She showed him the corner of the sofa.

At once the stranger fell down before the place and began to kiss the sofa. 'My poor, poor brother,' he said. 'How I should like to see you! But I am too late! Too late!'

After a while the three sat down to supper and had a good meal. Then they talked, and the stranger said what joy it would give him to set Aladdin up in a shop, so that he might earn a fair living by the sale of goods.

In the course of the next few days the stranger brought Aladdin some new clothes and took him into the rich parts of the city. Aladdin was proud to be seen in fine clothes, and thought his uncle a very kind man. 'Tomorrow,' said the uncle to Aladdin, 'I will show you some finer sights than these. Be ready for me early.'

Morning came, and the two set out through the city gate. Their way led them past some large palaces with beautiful gardens round them, through which they walked. Each one was more handsome than the other, and Aladdin was full of joy on seeing them.

At last both were tired. 'Let us sit down here,' said the uncle to Aladdin. 'I want to offer you some good advice, before I let you have the shop.'

'How much farther are we going?' asked Aladdin. 'I'm afraid I cannot walk back unless we turn soon.'

'Take courage, my dear boy,' said the uncle. 'I wish to show you one garden more, which is better than all the others we have seen. You are rested now. Let us go on.'

Soon they came to a narrow valley where all was quiet. 'This is the place I wished to reach,' said the uncle. 'There are wonders here which you have never yet dreamt of. I am now going to strike a light, and you fetch for me some dry sticks in order to make a fire.'

There were plenty of sticks near at hand, and soon Aladdin had a large heap of them. The uncle then set them on fire, and, as the blaze got big, he threw perfume into it, and spoke some strange words.

Aladdin began to feel afraid, and thought of taking to his heels. Just at that moment, however, the ground beneath them shook, and there came into sight a square stone about a half a metre across, with a brass ring fixed right in the centre for the purpose of lifting it up.

'You have seen my power,' said the uncle to Aladdin. 'I want you now to do something for me.'

Aladdin, though he shook with fear, said he was quite ready to do all that was wanted of him.

'Then pull that stone up by the ring,' said the uncle. 'It will come up easily enough if you repeat the names of your father and grandfather.'

Aladdin took hold of the ring, and, strange to say, was able to lift the stone without the least effort.

'The next thing to do,' went on the uncle, 'is to go down that well. When you come to the bottom, go through the door into a large hall; then through many halls one after the other, keeping a straight course, till you come to where you will find a lamp burning in a niche in the wall. Bring the lamp to me.'

As he spoke these words he put a ring on Aladdin's finger, saying, as he did so, that it would keep him from all harm.

Then Aladdin went down the well, and found all things as the uncle had said. There were the halls, and there were gardens, too, with trees in them which bore strange-looking fruit of all colours – red, white, blue and so on. They were, in truth, precious stones of great value.

When Aladdin came to the lamp he took it down from the wall, and, having put out the flame, carried it in his bosom. He took also some fruit from the trees, and at last came to the bottom of the well.

Up the steps he went, and saw the stranger outside waiting for him. 'Give me the lamp,' said the uncle; 'you will be able to get out more easily.'

'No, no,' said Aladdin. 'Help me out first, and then I will give you the lamp.'

Now, I must tell you that it was the lamp the stranger wanted. He was not the real uncle of Aladdin, but had taken these means of getting it, for he alone knew where it was. He had come all the way from Africa for it, and was very much annoyed when Aladdin would not give it to him.

The stranger tried all the means he could, but Aladdin had sense enough not to part with the lamp. Seeing this, the stranger added a little more perfume to the fire, which he had all the time kept up. Then he said two magic words, and lo! the stone which had covered up the well, and kept it from view, flew back to its place of its own accord. Then he made off as fast as he could to Africa.

Aladdin, of course, did not know what to do. He shouted many times that if his uncle would take away the stone the lamp should surely be his. But the stranger was now a long distance off, and all Aladdin's cries were in vain.

For two full days Aladdin lay helpless in the well, without either eating or drinking. On the third day, when he had quite given up all hopes of ever seeing daylight again, he joined his hands together as he would have done had he been saying his prayers.

As he did so he chanced to rub the ring which the stranger had put on his finger.

The next instant a genie, an Eastern goblin, tall and strong, stood before him. 'What do you wish?' said the genie. 'I am ready to obey you as your slave, as the slave of him who has the ring on his finger, both I and the other slaves of the ring.'

'Pray, then, take me out of this place,' said Aladdin, hardly knowing what was going on.

In a moment Aladdin found himself on the spot where the fire had been made. He felt the fresh breeze blow upon him, and, losing no time ran as fast as he could home. How he ran, to be sure!

His mother was glad to see him, and, as she set him something to eat, he told her all about the strange cave and the lamp. He also showed her the precious stones which he had picked from the trees. Then he went to bed.

Next day he rose and asked for breakfast. Alas! there was no food in the house, for he had eaten it all the night before at supper. 'If you will wait a little, my son,' said his mother, 'I will sell a little of my cotton and then I can buy some food.'

'No,' said Aladdin, 'keep your cotton, mother, and I will sell the lamp instead.'

'It will fetch a better price if I clean it,' said his mother, and with that she began to rub the lamp.

Before she could turn round, a genie stood before her. 'What do you wish?' he roared with a voice like thunder. 'I am ready to obey you as your slave, and the slave of those who have the lamp in their hands, both I and the other slaves of the lamp.'

The mother could not speak, she was so full of fear. Aladdin, however, who had seen a genie before, and had good cause to be thankful, took the lamp from his mother's hands, and said in a firm voice, 'I am hungry. Bring me something to eat.'

In a moment the table was spread with all sorts of good things in dishes of gold and silver.

'What is the meaning of this?' said the good woman. 'Has the sultan taken pity on us and sent them?'

It took some time for Aladdin to explain to his mother all that he knew of the ring and the lamp. Being very afraid, she would have nothing to do with such evil spirits, as she was sure they must

be. 'Ah, child,' said she, 'put the lamp away. I would rather you threw it away or sold it, than I would run the risk of ever touching it again.'

'And I,' said Aladdin, 'will take care what I do with the things which have been so useful to me in times of trouble.'

Enough food was left from breakfast to last for two days. When this was gone Aladdin went to sell one of the silver plates. He soon found a buyer, but he was given little for it. With the money some more food was bought. This went on for some time. As often as food was wanted a plate was sold, until there was only one large dish left.

Aladdin sold this at a better price, and with the money lived for a long time. He also bought fine clothes and rings to wear. In fact, he became quite a gentleman.

It chanced, one day, that Aladdin saw the princess, the daughter of the sultan. Now, Aladdin had never seen a lady's face before, except his mother's, for in that land all ladies go about with their faces hidden under a veil. This time the princess's face was unveiled.

'How I should like to marry the princess!' said Aladdin, almost aloud. 'She is so pretty.'

That same night Aladdin told his mother whom he had seen, and what had passed in his mind the moment he saw her. His mother told him not to be foolish. 'Who can ask such a thing of the sultan?' said she.

'You must yourself ask,' replied Aladdin in a moment.

'I?' cried his mother, with surprise. 'I go to the sultan? Not I, indeed. I will take care I do not go on any such errand.'

'But indeed you must, mother; and, what is more, you shall,' said Aladdin, sulking. 'You must not refuse me, or I shall die.'

Thus Aladdin begged hard, but his mother would not change her mind. 'Think,' said she, 'who you are. What have you ever done for your prince? You can ask for no favour, I am sure. And, besides, those who ask favours always give presents. Tell me, what have you to give?'

For a moment or two Aladdin could make no reply. Then he thought of the fruit which he had brought from the cave, which, he had found out, was of great value.

'The jewels, mother,' said he, 'will make a nice present for the sultan.'

Fetching the precious stones, he put them in rows and groups on the table. They shone so brightly that both mother and son were nearly blinded. 'Here is a rich present for the sultan,' said Aladdin. 'Take them to him, and I am sure you will get whatever you ask for.'

'I cannot, my son,' said his mother. 'The sultan will order us both to be put to death.'

'Now, do not distress yourself, dear mother,' said Aladdin. 'Has not the lamp been a friend to us for these years past? and now I do not think it will desert us. At all events, try; do, mother dear.'

The good woman had now not a word to say, and in a day or two was ready to try her luck at the palace.

She took a dish with the jewels in, and folded it up in a fine linen cloth. She then took another less fine, and tied the four corners of it, that she might carry it with ease. Then she set off for the palace.

The grand vizier and all the rest of the court had gone in when she came to the gate. There was a large crowd outside, but at last the gate was opened, and she went into the salon with the others. She then placed herself right in front of the sultan.

When the court was over the sultan went out, and the vizier and the rest went after. The people then had to go away. For several days this sort of thing took place, and each time Aladdin was very annoyed.

One day, when the court was over and the sultan had gone to his own room, he said to his vizier, 'For some time past I have seen a woman, who has come every day I hold my court, and who carries something in her hand tied up in a linen cloth. She puts herself in front of me. Do you know what she wants?'

The vizier did not wish the sultan to think he had not seen her. So he said, 'Oh, she seems to have come on a small errand. Some one has been selling her some bad meat or rotten vegetables or has been short-changing her.'

This did not please the sultan, for he did not think that could be the reason for a woman coming to him every day as this one had done. 'The very next day the court sits,' said he to the vizier, 'if this woman comes, do not fail to call her, that I may hear what she has to say.'

The vizier then kissed the sultan's hand, and placed it on his head to show that he would sooner die than not do his duty.

It had now become no trouble for Aladdin's mother to go to the court, as she was quite used to it. The next time the court met there she was, right in front of the sultan.

The vizier pointed to her, which was the order for her to go to the throne and make known her wants.

Aladdin's mother bowed and took up her place. The sultan then spoke to her in these words: 'My good woman, for a long time past I have seen you at the court, but no one has spoken to you. What is your request?'

'I dare not tell you in the open court, in front of all these people,' said the woman.

'Then have the court cleared,' said the sultan to the vizier. 'This woman shall tell us what she wants in secret.'

'Now, my good woman,' said the sultan, when all had gone out, 'what do you want?'

'I am afraid even now to make it known, for you may put me to death for my pains,' said Aladdin's mother.

'Whatever it may be,' said the sultan, 'I pardon you from this moment; not the least harm shall come to you from anything you may say. Be brave, and speak out.'

Aladdin's mother then told the sultan how her son had seen the princess, and wished to make her his wife. He was not in the least angry, for he had given the woman permission to say all she wished. Before he made any reply, he pointed to her bundle and said, 'what have you there, tied up so well?'

At once the woman opened her bundle and gave the jewels to the sultan. 'They are a present for your highness,' said she. 'They come from my son.'

328

The sultan could not speak for a moment; the jewels were so rich and rare he had never before seen any so fine. Then he looked at them one by one. 'How grand!' said he. 'What say you, vizier, to such a present?'

'They are, in truth, of great value,' said the vizier.

'Yes indeed,' said the sultan. 'Must not he who sends such a present be worthy of the princess my daughter, and must I not give her to him who comes and asks for her at such a price?'

Now, some time before this took place, the sultan had told the vizier that he would bestow the hand of the princess on his son. The vizier was afraid, therefore, that the promise would be overlooked, and that after all his son would never be the sultan's son-in-law, a thing upon which he had set his heart.

So the vizier stepped up to the sultan and spoke something softly in his ear.

The sultan started. Then, turning towards Aladdin's mother, he said to her, 'go, my good woman, return to your home, and tell your son that I cannot give my daughter to him for three months. At the end of that time return here.'

Aladdin's mother went from the court with all speed and made quick steps for home. There she met her son, who had been awaiting her return. 'What news, mother?' he asked.

Now, Aladdin saw quite clearly that his mother's visit to the sultan had not been in vain this time, for she looked very pleased. He thought it would give his mother joy, however, to ask her what had occurred.

When she had taken off her veil, and had sat down on the sofa by his side, she said: 'My son, I will tell you first that you need not give up all hope of being the sultan's son-in-law. I gave the sultan your present, and, though he was quite taken by surprise at the request I made to him, he was not displeased. At the end of three months I am to go to the court again, when the sultan will tell me what he has made up his mind to do.'

Aladdin thought himself the most happy of men. He jumped and danced about for joy, and kissed his mother over and over again. He called her a good woman, and told her what a grand lady he would make her when he should be wedded to the princess.

The three months went by very slowly indeed. To Aladdin they seemed to be an age, but at last they were over. Aladdin did not fail to send his mother to the palace on the very next morning, to remind the sultan of his promise.

She went, therefore, to the palace, as her son wished, and took up her place near the sultan. The sultan no sooner cast his eyes that way than he knew her face, and called to mind the strange request she had made and the exact time to which he had put it off.

The sultan called his vizier. 'I see there,' said he, 'that good woman who brought me the jewels three months ago. Bid her come forward, and we will hear what she has to say.'

The vizier, doing as he was told, called the woman, who threw herself on the ground at the foot of the throne.

After she had risen the sultan asked what she wished. 'Sire,' said she, 'I have come to remind you of your promise to my son. The three months have gone by. What may I tell him when I return home?'

Now, when the sultan put the woman off for three months, he thought he should never see or hear from her again, since he knew how foolish the request was. Turning to his vizier, he asked him what he should now do.

'Sire,' said the vizier, 'it seems to be a very strange request, but it can be refused in an easy way without giving offence to any one. Set a very high price upon the princess your daughter, so that all his riches, however great they may be, cannot reach the value. That will be the way to put a stop to his requests.'

The sultan agreed, and in a few moments said to Aladdin's mother: 'Sultans, my good woman, ought always to keep their words, and I am ready to hold to mine; but, as I cannot give my daughter to any one unless I know him to be a rich man, tell your son I will keep my word as soon as he shall send me forty large basins of pure gold quite full of the same sort of things which you have already given to me. The basins must be brought each by a black slave, led by a white slave, young, well made, and richly dressed. These are the terms. Go, tell them to your son.'

Aladdin's mother once more fell at the sultan's feet, and then withdrew from the court. On her way home she smiled within herself at the foolish thoughts of her son. 'Where, indeed,' said she, 'is he to find so many gold basins and such a lot of jewels to fill them? Will he go back to the cave, the entrance to which is shut up, in order to gather them from the trees? And where can he get all those handsome slaves whom the sultan demands?'

As she went into the house her mind was full of these thoughts, and, meeting her son, she said: 'All hope is lost, my son; think no more of the princess. The sultan did, indeed, treat me with kindness, but I do not suppose for a moment that you will be able to meet his demands.'

She then told him all that the sultan had said, adding, 'he is even now waiting for your reply; but, between ourselves, he may wait a long time.'

'Not so long as you may think, my dear mother,' said Aladdin. 'I will give the sultan a great surprise. While I am thinking what to do, you go and get dinner and leave me to myself.'

As soon as his mother had gone out to buy the dinner, Aladdin took the lamp, and, having rubbed it, the genie stood before him.

In a gentle voice – for this time Aladdin had rubbed the lamp more gently than before – the genie asked the same question: 'What do you wish? I am ready to obey you as your slave, and the slave of those who have the lamp in their hands, both I and the other slaves of the lamp.'

Aladdin lost no time in telling the genie what he wanted. 'The sultan,' said he, 'agrees to give me the hand of the princess his daughter in marriage, but he first demands forty large basins of gold filled to the very top with that fruit of the garden from which I took the lamp that you are the slave of. He asks also that these forty basins shall be carried by as many black slaves, each led by a young and handsome white slave in rich attire. Go, get me his present as soon as you can, that I may send it to the sultan before the court is over.'

The genie said that it should be done at once.

In a very short time he came back, bringing with him the slaves and the basins full of jewels. Each basin was covered with a cloth of silver, and the slaves were richly dressed. There were so many of them that they filled the house, as well as the court in front and the garden behind.

The genie asked Aladdin if there were any further orders for him, and on being told no, went quickly out of sight.

Aladdin's mother, now coming back from the market, was in the greatest surprise to see so many persons and so much riches. Having set down the food she was about to take off her veil, but Aladdin put his hand on her shoulder and stopped her.

'My dear mother,' he cried, 'there is no time to lose. Go with these to the court at once, and tell the sultan they are for him.'

Without waiting for her reply, Aladdin opened the door that led into the street, and told all the slaves to go out one after the other. He then put a white slave in front of each of the black ones, who carried the golden basins on their heads.

When his mother, who went with the last black slave, had gone
out, he shut the door, and waited quietly in his room, thinking
that now the sultan would be sure to give him his daughter for a
wife.

Every one in the street stopped to see the long line of eighty
slaves. The dress of each slave was made of a rich stuff, and so
covered with precious stones that those who were good judges
thought each of them worth more than a kingdom.

The graceful manner of each slave caused those who saw them
not to take their eyes from them, so that each person stood stock
still in the street.

As the way was long it took some time to get to the palace
gates, but at last they were reached.

When the first of the eighty slaves was about to pass through,
the porters took him to be a king, so richly was he dressed. They
were about to kiss the hem of his robe when the slave, who had
had his orders from the genie, stopped them, saying, 'Our
master will come when the time is right.'

Through the gates the slaves all went one after the other, and
soon found their way into the court. Their dresses were far
more splendid than those of the sultan's officers, or even the
sultan's. The slaves made two rows and stood on two sides in
front of the throne.

The mother of Aladdin then threw herself at the sultan's feet,
and when she had been told to rise, said, 'This, sire, is what my
son sends in answer to your demands. He awaits your reply.'

The sultan hardly heard the good woman speak, for he could
not take his eyes away from the slaves and the golden basins of
jewels which they had brought.

At length he turned to the vizier, and, in a loud voice, so that all
might hear, said: 'Well, vizier, what think you of the person,
whoever he may be, who has now sent me so rich and fine a

present, a person whom neither of us knows or has heard of before? Do you not think he is worthy of the princess?'

It was the duty of the vizier to make a reply that would please the sultan, so he answered, 'far be it from me, sire, to say no to a person who can send a present like this.'

Then all the people in the court clapped their hands in glee, and the sultan rose from his throne. 'Go, my good woman,' said he, 'and tell your son that I am waiting with open arms to embrace him. The sooner he comes to claim the hand of the princess my daughter, the more pleased I shall be.'

Aladdin's mother bowed and retired. The sultan then sent everybody away but the vizier. He told the slaves to carry the golden basins and the jewels into the palace, that he might show them to the sultana and his daughter.

In the meantime, Aladdin's mother, reaching home, showed by her manner how she had got on with the sultan. Nor did she lose a moment in telling her son what had taken place. 'The sultan awaits you,' she added, 'and I advise you to make yourself fit to appear before him.'

Aladdin went to his own room and took down the lamp which had been so true a friend to him. No sooner had he rubbed it than the genie again appeared to do his bidding.

'Genie,' said Aladdin, 'I want you to take me to the bath, and when I have bathed, to have a rich and handsome dress ready for me.'

Aladdin had no sooner given his orders than he was lifted up and carried through the air without being seen. Then he was put into a bath of the finest marble, where he was washed and rubbed with sweet perfumes. His skin became white and fresh, and his body felt lighter and more active.

He then went to the dressing-room, where, in place of his old robe, he found one more rich and handsome than a sultan's. By the help of the genie, who waited on him, he put on each part until he was quite dressed.

Then the genie took him home in the same way as he had carried him to the bath. 'Have you any further demands?' he asked.

'Yes,' said Aladdin. 'Bring me a horse as soon as you can, which shall be more beautiful than any horse in the sultan's stables, and let the saddle and bridle and the wrappings be worth more than a million pounds. Let them flash with jewels of all kinds.

'I order you also at the same time to get me twenty slaves as well and richly dressed as those who carried the basins of gold, to walk on each side and behind me, and twenty more to walk in two ranks before me. You must also get six female slaves to wait on my mother. These must be dressed more richly than the princess. I also want ten thousand pieces of gold in ten purses. These are all my commands at present. Go, and make all haste.'

All in a moment the genie went and came back. He brought the horse, the slaves, ten of whom had each a purse with ten thousand pieces of gold in every one, and the six female slaves each with a fine dress for Aladdin's mother wrapped in a piece of silver cloth. These he gave to Aladdin.

Aladdin took only four of the ten purses, and gave them to his mother, as he said she might want them. He left the other six in the hands of the slaves, and told them that as they went along the streets they were to throw the coins in heaps to the people.

He then gave the six female slaves to his mother, telling her that they were for her, and that the dresses which they had in the silver cloths were for her use.

And now a start was made for the palace. Aladdin mounted his horse and began the march in the order we have told. Though he had never been on horseback in his life he rode quite well, and everybody praised the grace he showed in the saddle.

The streets were thronged with people, who shouted and cheered as the slaves threw the gold pieces among them. Aladdin was so changed in looks and dress that no one knew him, not even those with whom he had played in the streets. This all came from the power of the wonderful lamp.

338

At length the palace was reached. The sultan was overjoyed to see so handsome a man as Aladdin, and so gay and rich a dress as he wore. He himself had not one so thickly covered with jewels. He came down from his throne two or three steps so as to prevent Aladdin from falling down at his feet, and holding out his hand, put Aladdin to sit between himself and the vizier.

Aladdin then rose and spoke to the sultan in these words: 'O sire, I beg you not to think me rash in asking for the hand of the princess your daughter, but I should die if I did not have her for my wife.'

The sultan was charmed with Aladdin, and made a sign. At once the air was filled with the sounds of trumpets and cymbals, and Aladdin was led by the sultan into a saloon where a great feast was served up. The sultan and Aladdin sat at a table together, and the vizier and the chief guards waited on them.

The sultan talked as a friend with Aladdin, and was more and more pleased with him each moment. Then he gave orders for the marriage papers to be made ready.

Aladdin, however, did not wish the wedding to take place at once. He told the sultan that first of all he wanted to prepare a house, good and large, fit for a princess.

'That is well,' said the sultan. 'There is a large open space before my palace. Take that, and build a house upon it fit for my daughter the princess.'

Then Aladdin, going home, called the genie, to whom he gave orders to build him a house on the space of ground in front of the palace. It was to be built of precious stones and to contain a room full of gold for his use.

Knowing the house would be built to his orders, Aladdin sent his mother, richly dressed and attended by her slaves, to tell the princess it was ready. She set out at once.

That same night the house was built. It rose in the air with its rooms one above another. Its walls shone and its furniture was of pure gold and pearls.

In the morning the porters opened the gates of the palace, and were not able to believe their eyes, for, till that moment, they had never seen so large and so handsome a building as that which they now saw. The sultan saw it, and called his vizier, who put it down to magic. 'We shall see,' he said, 'what is to come of all this finery of Aladdin's.'

And now the marriage took place. There had been nothing seen like it in all the world before. There were gold and silver dishes and cups, wines of the rarest sorts, and cakes of the best.

For some time Aladdin and the princess lived in happiness. They loved each other dearly, and were a joy to the sultan and the sultana. Sad to say, an event took place which put an end to it all.

The powerful magician had been away, but now he began to think of the lamp and what had become of it. By his magic he found out it was still Aladdin's, and that he had become a rich man and a prince. The magician once more went to the city. There he saw the fine house which Aladdin had built, and felt pretty sure that the lamp was somewhere inside. Oh, if he could only tell where!

He thought of a plan. He went to the shop of a man who made and sold lamps. 'I want,' said he to the man, 'a dozen copper lamps. Can you make them for me?'

'To be sure!' replied the man. 'You may have them to-morrow.'

Next day the magician had the lamps sent to his inn, and he thereupon took them round the city in a basket, crying out, 'Who will change old lamps for new?'

Everybody thought the magician was mad, and laughed at him. 'That man,' said they, 'has surely lost his senses to offer new lamps for old ones.' And the children hooted at him.

By and by he came to the street which led to Aladdin's house and the sultan's palace. Aladdin had gone to the hunt, but his princess sat at an open window at her spinning with her maidens. All of them heard the cry, 'Who will change old lamps for new ones?'

One of the maidens laughed at the idea of changing old lamps for new, and said that the man must be joking. Then it was agreed to try him with Aladdin's lamp. 'Take it down,' said the princess, 'we shall then see if he is a madman or not.'

The slave went down to the street with the lamp, which the magician saw and knew in a moment. 'A new lamp for an old one?' said he. 'Certainly,' said the slave; 'the princess desires it.' The slave then chose out a pretty new lamp, leaving the old one with the magician, and ran off to her mistress.

No sooner did the magician get the lamp in his hands than he went back towards his inn. On the way he passed along a very quiet street, where he put down his basket of new lamps and left them. Then, instead of going to his inn, he turned through the gate of the city and got out into the country.

When night came on he drew the lamp from his bosom and rubbed it. 'What do you wish?' cried the genie, who had come in an instant.

'I command you to take up the house, which you and the other slaves of the lamp have built, near the sultan's palace, and carry it with me and all that is in it, dead and alive, to Africa,' said the magician.

At once he and the whole palace was lifted up and carried by the genie right to the spot where the magician desired.

Next day, as soon as it was light, the sultan cast his eyes towards the palace of Aladdin. Alas! there was nothing left but the open space of land on which it had been built. He thought his eyes were grown dim, and that he could not see; so he rubbed them. Still there was no Aladdin's palace. Then he called his vizier. 'Look there,' cried he. 'The new palace is gone. It has not fallen, or the ruins would be left. Alas! my poor daughter is gone. Where is the wretch who asked her for a wife? I will strike off his head.'

The sultan was told that Aladdin had been gone on the hunt for over two days.

'Then send my horsemen to drag him before me in chains.'

The horsemen were at once sent into the forest where Aladdin had gone, and there they found him. 'Prince Aladdin,' said the chief of the horsemen, 'I am sorry to have to tell you that you must come to the sultan. I hope you will pardon me, but I must do my duty.'

He then took hold of Aladdin, bound him hand and foot, and carried him to the sultan.

The moment the sultan saw him he ordered his head to be struck off.

'Not so fast, sire,' put in the vizier. 'Do you not see the people making their way into the palace? Aladdin has been kind to them, and they are now going to shield him from your wrath and save him.'

The sultan looked, and saw a huge crowd of people, with swords drawn, coming with all speed to the palace. His face showed that he was in great fear. 'Put up your sword,' said he to the headsman, 'and you, vizier, tell the people that Aladdin is safe from harm. I pardon him.'

When all was quiet the sultan called Aladdin to him. 'What have I done, sire, to vex you?' asked Aladdin, who had not yet been told what had taken place.

'Don't talk to me,' said the sultan. 'Where is my dear daughter? Where is the house you built for her on the open space in front of my palace?'

Aladdin looked through the window of the room he was in, and lo! he, too, was struck dumb for a moment. 'Sire,' said he, 'the palace is surely gone, but I have had no hand in it. Pray give me forty days in which to search for your daughter, my wife; and if I do not find her, kill me.'

This was granted, and Aladdin left the sultan to mourn alone. Going through the city, he asked all he met if they had seen anything done to his palace, whereupon they thought he had gone mad. Then he made up his mind to leave the city and make his search beyond it.

Towards night he found himself near a river, and the idea came to him that he would drown himself. But, as he stepped down the steep bank he slipped, and in doing so rubbed the ring he was wearing on the rock.

'What do you wish?' cried the genie, who had come in an instant. 'I am ready to obey you as your slave, and the slave of him who has the ring upon his finger, both I and the other slaves of the ring.'

'Welcome, dear genie,' cried he. 'You have saved my life before. Save it again by giving me back my palace and my dear wife, the princess.'

'What you ask,' said the genie, 'is not in my power. I am only the slave of the ring; you must address yourself to the slave of the lamp.'

'In that case, then,' said Aladdin, 'at least take me to the spot where my palace is, and place me under the window of the

princess.' He had barely said this before the genie, lifting him up, bore him through the air to Africa, near a large city, and in the midst of a meadow, in which the palace stood. Setting him down under one of the windows of the princess's room, he there left him.

It was night, and Aladdin slept soundly beneath a tree. Next morning he was roused by the princess opening the window. He looked up and saw her there. She saw him too, and bade him come to her through a secret door.

Soon they embraced each other with tears of joy, and then Aladdin asked her what had become of the lamp. The poor princess told him all, and begged him to forgive her, which he did, saying it must be got again by some means. He felt sure that the taking away of the palace was the work of the magician.

Then Aladdin formed his plans. He went into the city and bought a drug, which he gave to the princess later in the day, asking her to put it in the magician's wine at supper that evening.

The princess hardly liked to do such a thing, even though the magician had treated her so badly; but she did it, and no sooner had he drunk his wine than he sank, a corpse, on the floor.

Aladdin lay in hiding near the palace, and at a signal went to the princess. All the slaves and servants were sent to their own rooms while Aladdin searched for the lamp. He found it in the magician's bosom, and at once rubbed it hard.

In less time than it takes to tell the story the genie came, to whom Aladdin gave orders for the palace to be carried home.

The sultan, who, in the meantime, had hardly had a wink of sleep, looked once more through his window and beheld the palace in its place. Aladdin, who had risen early, thought the sultan would lose no time in coming to see his daughter, so he went out to meet him. The sultan came, and he and Aladdin were friends once more. Great was the joy of every one of them, and all trouble was cast aside.

Now it chanced that the magician had a brother from whom he had been parted many years. This brother found out that the magician had been put to death by poison, and that it had been done by a princess who was wedded to a rich man of low birth. He looked for this princess in all parts of the world, and at last came to the city where Aladdin lived.

In the city there also lived a holy woman whose name was Fatima. The magician's brother made his way to her, and bade her, under pain of death, to change her clothes for his. When this was done the brother, whom we will now call Fatima and speak of as a woman, went to the palace of Aladdin and began to talk with the princess.

So pleased was the princess with the holy woman that she asked her to stay with her in the palace.

That was just what Fatima wanted, so she said she would. 'Rise, then,' said the princess, 'follow me, and we will choose your room.'

346

Fatima did so with feeble steps, and soon the holy woman was lodged in the palace. Every day she saw the princess, and the two became close friends.

One day, when walking through the rooms, they came to the saloon which was the best room in the palace. Fatima said she liked it very much, but there was one thing missing – the egg of a roc hung from the centre dome.

When Aladdin came home, having been absent for some days, the princess was sad. 'What is the matter, my dear?' he asked. 'Have you not all you wish for to make you happy?'

'I thought we had the most beautiful palace in the world,' said the princess, 'but now I find out that there is one thing wanting to make it complete – the egg of a roc hung from the centre dome of the saloon.'

'As for that,' said Aladdin, 'it shall be done at once.' Then going to the saloon he rubbed the lamp, which he now always kept in his bosom. The genie came, and, on hearing what Aladdin wished, he gave such a wild and loud shriek that all the walls of the palace shook.

'Wretch,' cried the genie, 'you want me to hang my master from the dome; but it is a good thing for you that the request is not your own. It comes from the magician's brother, who is now in this palace, dressed as a holy woman. Find him, and slay him at once.'

Then Aladdin went back to the princess, and the holy woman was sent for. She came, and Aladdin asked her to cure a pain which he had in his head.

Now was the holy woman's chance to slay Aladdin and secure the lamp.

He bent his head for Fatima to place her hand upon it, when lo! all at once Aladdin rose, seized a dagger which Fatima had already grasped from under her cloak, and thrust it into her heart.

'What have you done?' cried the princess.

'This is not a holy woman at all,' said Aladdin, 'but the brother of that cruel magician who has done us both so much harm. He has come to his fate. Now we shall indeed be happy.'

These words were spoken in truth, for Aladdin and his dear princess lived for many years in each other's love; and, when the sultan died, Aladdin took his place and ruled his land in peace.

The Lazy Tortoise

WHEN the great god Jupiter was married he gave a huge feast to which all living creatures were invited. They all arrived early except the tortoise, who came dawdling along at the end of the feast.

Jupiter was very angry. 'Why are you so late?' he demanded.

'I did not want to leave my home,' said the tortoise. 'I was quite content and happy there.'

Jupiter was angrier than ever to think that his guest preferred a ditch to a splendid palace. 'Very well,' said he, 'if you are so fond of your home, you will never again move around without carrying it on your back.'

And to this day, the tortoise still carries its house on its back.

Laziness finds its own punishment.

The Miser's Gold

A VERY mean man once sold all his estate and melted the money he received for it into one solid mass of gold. This he buried in the ground in his garden, and visited his hoard night and morning to gloat over it.

One night a robber spied on him and when the miser had gone back home dug up the treasure and went off with it. Next day the miser missed it and went nearly out of his mind at the loss of his gold. 'Why are you making such a noise?' said a neighbour. 'You might as well have a stone in the ground instead of your gold, for it was no use to you when you had it.'

Riches are meant to be used.

The Miller, his Son & the Ass

A MILLER and his son were driving their ass to a neighbouring fair to sell him.

They had not gone far when they met a troop of girls returning from the town, talking and laughing.

'Look there!' cried one of them; 'did you ever see such fools, to be trudging along the road on foot, when they might be riding!'

The old man, hearing this, quietly bade his son get on the ass, and walked along merrily by the side of him. Presently they came to a group of old men, who were talking together.

'There!' said one of them, 'it proves what I was saying. What respect is shown to old age in these days? Do you see that idle young rogue riding while his old father has to walk?'

'Get down, you good-for-nothing, and let the old man rest his weary limbs!' cried another.

Upon this the father made his son dismount and got up himself; but they had not proceeded far when they met a company of women and children.

'Why, you lazy old fellow!' cried several people at once, 'how can you ride upon the beast while this poor little lad can hardly keep pace by the side of you?'

The good-natured miller immediately took up his son behind him, and they rode in this manner until they had almost reached the town.

'Pray, honest friend,' said a townsman, 'is that ass your own?'

'Yes,' replied the old man.

'By the way you load him, one would not have thought so,' said the other. 'Why, you two fellows are better able to carry the poor beast than he you!'

'If you think it the right thing to do,' said the old man, 'we can but try.'

So, alighting with his son, they tied the ass's legs to a stout pole, which they shouldered, and so got ready to carry him over a bridge that led to the town.

This was so entertaining a sight that the people ran out in crowds to laugh at it, until the ass, not liking the noise nor the

situation, broke from the cords that bound him and tumbled off the pole into the river below.

Annoyed and ashamed, the old man made his way home again, convinced that by endeavouring to please everybody he had pleased nobody, and lost his ass into the bargain.

He who tries to please everybody pleases nobody.

The Fairy Cobbler

THIS is the story that granny told me, sitting in her garden one summer evening, when I was sure I had just seen a fairy among the beans. Do I believe in fairies? Why, of course I do. Haven't I seen one with my own eyes. Seeing is believing, you know, and although this was many, many years ago, I can still tell you what the little fellow was like.

One day, I was sitting in the garden here, with my knitting in my hand. It was a fine, sunny day, about the middle of June. The bees were humming among the flowers; the birds were chirping and hopping on the bushes, and everything smelt fresh.

All of a sudden I heard among the rows of beans a noise that went tick-tack, tick-tack; it was just like a cobbler putting on the heel of a shoe.

'What can that be?' I said to myself.

So I laid down my knitting and went quietly over to the beans, and what do you think I saw? A little old man no bigger than my thumb, with such a funny little hat on his head! He had a little red coat on his back, and silver buckles on his shoes. Of course, I knew at once the little man was a fairy cobbler. You didn't think that the fairies needed shoemakers?

Oh, but they do, for the little people are so fond of dancing that they soon wear out their shoes. The fairy cobbler is the only fairy who works really hard. All the others do nothing but dance and play tricks.

The cobbler always carries a purse with a bright piece of silver in it. It is a great find to get your hands on a fairy purse.

Well, I kept as still as a cat when she is watching a mouse-hole. I could hear the tip-tap of the little fellow's hammer.

The fairy was laughing, too, all the time, as happy as a lark on an April morning. He had his back turned towards me, and was bending over the tiniest shoe I had ever seen.

Here was my chance to get a real fairy purse, I thought.

'That's hard work you're doing on this hot day,' I said to him.

The fairy turned swiftly round, and looked up at my face with a frightened look. I thought he was going to run away, so I caught hold of him.

'Where is your purse of money?' I asked.

'Money?' cried he; 'Money, indeed! And where would a poor little man like me get money?'

'Come, come,' I said, 'none of your tricks. Every one knows that the fairy cobblers always have money.'

I gave him a bit of a shake, and the little man looked so frightened that I almost pitied him.

'Come with me to the meadow,' said he, 'and I will show you where I keep my money.'

So I went to the meadow, still holding him in my hand, and keeping my eyes fixed upon him. If you take your eyes off a fairy for one moment, the little fellow can run away. All of a sudden I heard a loud *buzz* behind me.

'There! there!' cried the little man, 'your bees are all swarming and going off by themselves.'

Without thinking, I turned my head, but could see nothing. Then I looked angrily at the fairy, but, would you believe it? there was nothing in my hand. The moment I had looked round, he had slipped away, and he never came near my garden again.

Little Harry Twiggs' Picnic

This short story by Mary Howitt (1799–1888) reminds us that at one time – and not so very long ago – young people were expected to go out to work from a very early age. Harry Twiggs was only a child, but his job on a farm kept him busy every day of the week.

ONE Sunday it was excessively hot; so hot that the children did not know what to do. The heat and their coughs together made them very fretful; if they sat in the house they were hot; if they went out they were almost melted. In the evening they sat at tea with the windows open, flowers on the table, and the butter almost like oil though it was in water. Nobody ate or drank much, indeed to drink hot tea was out of the question. Herbert was almost cross and so was Meggy; they wished they had ice to put in their tea; they said that the Chinese were a deal wiser than the English, because they drank their tea cold; and that they did not believe any body in all the world was as hot as they had been all day.

Their father said what would they think if they were little Harry Twiggs?

They had never heard of little Harry Twiggs, and they asked who he was. Their papa said that at five o'clock that very morning, little Harry Twigs went out with a wooden clapper in his hand to frighten away the birds from Farmer Broadbent's corn. This corn grew in a thirty-acre field – a monstrous field; the whole parish called it 'the big field', and it was full of corn, beautiful corn, just getting ripe; and the birds, great and small, came from far and near to peck it. Farmer Broadbent meant that that one field should pay the rent of his whole farm. He was very particular about having the birds kept out, so he hired little Harry

Twiggs, who was one of the poorest boys in all the parish, at threepence a day, to walk round and round the corn field, and down the footroad that went across it from end to end, to make a noise with his little wooden clapper, and to shout with his weak voice, and thus to frighten away the birds. For the last six days, from Monday till Saturday, little Harry had done so; he went at five o'clock in the morning, and came away at eight o'clock at night, and all day long he saw nobody except by chance any body went along the footroad when he was on it, for otherwise he was so little, and the corn was so tall, that he could not have seen them; and in all that long week he had only seen a beggar, and he was deaf and dumb, and so could not talk to him, and the parish constable, of whom he was always afraid, because when he saw him he thought of the round-house which was the parish prison.

All round the field there were tall hedges full of wild roses and honey suckles, and meadow-sweet, and pretty purple vetches, which made them very delightful, only that poor Harry soon grew tired of looking at them by himself. In the hedges there also grew, here and there, tall old oak trees, which cast, one or other of them, all day long, a pleasant shade; and Harry used to think that if he could but lie down under the shady trees it would be pleasant, but then he was so afraid of Farmer Broadbent coming into the field when he should be lying there, and perhaps fast asleep, for the hot sun and weariness often made him sleepy. He therefore never dared to indulge himself; and all day long he went round and round and up and down that great, wide, corn field, on which the sun shone without any shadow, unless it might be a passing cloud. Poor Harry often was so tired that he did not know what to do, and he was always glad when, by the height of the sun, he thought it was noon, and then he might sit down and eat his dinner, his little dinner of bread and cheese and buttermilk. Sometimes he made a mistake and ate it an hour too soon – he never took it an hour too late – and then the afternoon seemed so long that he thought it never would end; and he often, besides that, was ready to cry because he was so hot and tired, and had nobody to speak to – not even a dog.

Harry lived with his old grandmother: they lived by themselves in a little mud cottage, one story high, beside the common, and Harry used to play with all the neighbours' children, for they were none of them too grand to play with a poor little lad like him. There was Dick Tattersall – he was Harry's favourite playfellow, and the son of the blacksmith, a stout lad, who would have made two of such little fellows as Harry Twiggs, though he was not quite half a year older; and then there were all Dick's brothers and sisters – such a flock of them! who always came trooping at his heels, because he was such a funny, good-natured fellow, and was always so kind to them, and there was Peggy Ford, Widow Ford's little daughter, who lived in the least house in all the parish – less even than the Twiggs's, for the Fords, like them, were very poor – and she used to play with Dick Tattersall's sisters, and that made her very friendly also with Harry and Dick.

Poor little Harry often told his friends in the evening, when he got home and found them all playing, and he was too tired to play, how solitary and forlorn he felt in 'the big field' all by himself from morning till night. One evening when Harry had been talking in this way, Dick said, 'As sure as he was alive he would go and keep him company in the big field all next Sunday'; and Peggy Ford said, 'So would she, if Nancy Tattersall would'; and Nancy said, 'She would, if little Joshua might go,' and every body said little Joshua might, and so it was all agreed and settled, and Harry wished it was Sunday.

On Sunday morning – this very Sunday morning, said the children's papa – while you were fast asleep in bed, up got little Harry as usual, put on his clean shirt, stockings he had none, and his good pair of trousers – his common ones were very old indeed – and his Sunday jacket, which was but an old one after all, and off he set as soon as he had swallowed his breakfast, with his dinner in an oldish grey-looking basket. It was a capital dinner that he had that day: a little bit of cold mutton, a huge hunch of bread, some treacle in an old teacup with a teapot lid that fitted it, and this with bread was to be the grand second course. Besides this, he had a little can of buttermilk. It was a particularly good dinner, and Harry meant to divide it amongst his friends if it were better than what they brought.

He hoped as he passed the blacksmith's to see some of the family about, perhaps even Dick himself. But no! it was all shut up, shop and all; for they were taking their rest an hour or two later, as it was Sunday morning. He then turned down the lane towards the little house where Widow Ford lived; but the door was shut, and the white cotton curtain drawn in the window, and no signs of life were visible about the place, excepting the old greyish tortoise-shell cat which had been shut out all night. As soon as the cat saw Harry, she heaved up her back and tail, and rubbed in a sidling way against the door-post, and mewed with a long whining mew.

'Poor pussy!' said Harry, and stroked her, and wished he could only leave a message with her; but it was no use wishing that, so he stroked her again, and called her 'poor pussy!' in rather a louder voice, that they might hear him if they were awake, for he knew where their bed stood. But they must have been fast asleep, for though he waited five minutes, and talked a great deal to the cat, they never heard him; and as the curtains did not move, he thought it could be no use staying, so he went slowly, looking back every now and then to see if anybody by chance peeped out, but nobody did. There was nothing then to be done but to trudge off to the field as fast as he could, for he now heard the church clock strike a quarter to six, and he was frightened lest Farmer Broadbent should take a walk into the field, as he often did before breakfast, and not find him there. He was frightened of Farmer Broadbent, partly because he was such a large man, and had such a large voice, and walked with such a large stick; and partly because he was overseer of the poor, and often sent poor folks to the union workhouse, the bastille as they called it, and that was enough to make him afraid. So whenever he saw the farmer in the field, he contrived to be a good way off, always clapping industriously and shouting to the birds; and the farmer who was very fat, and not at all nimble, could not follow after him, and thus Harry contrived to keep quite out of his way.

The first thing Harry did when he got into the field was to walk all round it, clapping as he went, though he never once thought about the birds, because he was thinking of the party he was going to have, and he wanted now to find out which was the pleasantest place in all the field. To be sure he had fixed that in his mind some days ago, even before he knew that his friends would come to visit him, but he now wanted to be quite sure about it. The nicest place in all the field was that on which he had before decided, and he now felt sure that it was the sweetest spot in all the parish.

It was in an old overgrown marl pit which separated this field from the next, and where there was no regular fence, but a great many oaks and ashes, and plenty of hazel bushes, which formed a close and cool thicket, where at any time of the day they were sure of shade. There were something like regular seats in the broken sides of the hollow, so he trampled down the long grass and tall plants, and broke off hazel boughs, or twisted them in one with another, till he formed a little open cove in the bushes, just like a little parlour in a wood, or a sweet little nest, just big enough to hold five or six children. He gathered beautiful green moss which was now wet with dew, and laid it in the sun to dry, and this he meant for cushions for the seats. There never was a prettier little spot than that; it was a regular bower, and though it was midsummer, the blackbirds and thrushes sang with all their might, and so did the larks up in the clear bright sunshine.

'It's a regular Sunday morning,' said Harry joyfully to himself, 'everything, dumb creatures, as well as Christians, know when it is Sunday morning!'

His heart was full of joy; he had but one fear, and that was, lest they should come before he was ready for them.

But he need not have feared that! He was ready hours before they came. The church bells began ringing for morning service. Harry never thought they would be so late, never! He expected they would come by eight o'clock, by nine at farthest, and now it wanted only a quarter to eleven.

All at once a thought came into his mind. Suppose they did not come at all! It was a miserable thought. He climbed upon a low bough of an oak, and looked out over the whole extent of the 'big field'. The sun shone burning hot; there was not a single shadow upon the whole extent of yellow corn. It quite dazzled his eyes. He could see the heads and shoulders of people who were walking along the footpath on their way to church, for the church lay half a mile from the village, and those who liked the fields best must go that way. He saw them moving onwards at little intervals above the level of the yellow corn; they were in their Sunday best, and seemed to be so happy. He jumped down from the tree, and ran to the end of the footpath; for some of these people must have passed Dick Tattersall's, and could tell him if he seemed to be coming. At the end of the road he met old Nelly Wardle, and her daughter Jenny, and they lived next door to the blacksmith's.

'Did you see any thing of Dick Tattersall?' asked he from them.

'Oh yes,' old Nelly said, 'Dick was sitting among the children, as usual, on the shady side of the house, making dandelion chains for them, poor things!'

'Then he does not mean to come!' said Harry to himself, with a great pang at his heart. He did not speak a word aloud, but walked on without looking any body in the face lest they should see that he was crying.

At the end of the footpath was a gate, which opened into a shady lane, down which Dick and his young party ought to have come. Harry climbed on the bottom bar; and as the gate was a tall one, his chin just rested on the top bar, and there he stood with great blinding tears in his eyes staring up the empty lane. The church bells had left off ringing, every body was in church, not a soul was now coming from the village. Every thing looked silent and solitary; and as Harry thought of all the long morning he had spent in getting things ready, and in waiting, and all the long rest of the day that he should now have to spend by himself in disappointment, he felt quite miserable and forsaken. He thought that Dick and all the children who had promised to come and see him, were sitting on the shady side of the house, making dandelion chains, as happy as could be. They had forgotten him; they had forgotten their promise; they cared for nothing but amusing themselves! He shut his eyes to keep back the tears for a while, and then, fairly overcome, slipped down from the gate, threw himself on the grass, and cried bitterly.

If he had not been crying, and if he had not been so miserable, and if he had only stayed a little longer looking over the gate, he would soon have seen a very pleasant sight! He would have seen Dick Tattersall carrying the sturdy little Joshua on his back, with Nancy with a sheaf of Timothy-grass in one hand, on every bent of which were at least four-and-twenty wild strawberries like great coral beads, and in the other, a little basket as full as ever it would hold, and covered with a cloth; and Peggy Ford, with something in her hand, that looked very like a big basin tied up in a buff handkerchief. And down the lane they were trudging as fast as they could come, chattering as they came along.

Poor Harry, who lay crying in the grass, heard something just before they reached the gate, which made him jump up all at once and rush forward. He heard their voices, and there they were all four of them! They saw that he had been crying and he did not pretend to deny it, for he said he thought that they would not come; he thought they would stay at home and make dandelion chains instead.

'Not come!' Dick exclaimed, why he had been out ever so early that very morning to get strawberres out of Smith's spinny! and they would have been there two hours earlier, only Mrs. Ford's cat was lost, and they had to find her. She had been shut out all night, and Mrs. Ford was quite miserable till she was found, and they all went to hunt her. And then Peggy had such a deal to tell about their trouble on her account; and Harry had to tell how he had seen her mewing at the door, and little Joshua had to tell that he it was who saw her first, and nobody would believe it was she; and she was in Martin's old pig sty, and nobody could tell how she got there. And then Nancy wanted Harry to look at the strawberries all strung on the tall Timothy-grass; and then they had to tell that they were doing this, and not making dandelion chains when Mrs. Wardle saw them, and there was such a clatter of merry voices all talking together as never was heard before.

Harry gave little Joshua the clapper, and he strutted on clapping with all his might, and the others ran on down to the little parlour among the hazel-bushes, and there they examined what they all had for dinner. Nancy Tattersall opened her basket, and there was such a plenty of cold beans and bacon, and bread, and a lustre-mug, that looked like silver, to drink out of, and a great three-cornered piece of cold batter pudding, at the bottom of which was a layer of currants an inch thick; and there was a cold rice pudding in Peggy Ford's basin, which her mother had baked the night before, and all the strawberries beside! Now, was not it a famous dinner? They all thought it was as good as a Lord Mayor's feast.

The visitors said that Harry had made a beautiful little parlour for them, and they admired the seats and the moss cushions, and every thing. Harry felt very happy, and so did they all; and as they were hungry, they agreed to eat Peggy Ford's rice pudding now, by way of luncheon. Little Joshua did nothing all the morning but strut about and clap, and not a single bird came near the corn.

Of course, they supposed that old Farmer Broadbent was gone
to church; but instead of that he was walking down to his big corn
field, and reached the other side of the old marl-pit just as they had
finished eating the cold pudding. They did not see him because he
stood behind the hazel bushes, but *he* saw *them*; and presently,
crash! he came through the hedge just below, and stood before
them, with his face all red with heat, and with his hat in one hand,
and his stick and a great red pocket-handkerchief with which he
was going to wipe his face, in the other. He was dressed in his
Sunday clothes; his brown coat, yellow and black and white
striped waistcoat, which was all unbuttoned, and drab kerseymere
breeches, and grey stockings, for today he was without his gaiters
because it was so hot. He was dressed just as he was when he sat as
overseer of the poor; and Harry was quite frightened, for his face
looked very red, and when he lifted up his red pocket-
handkerchief to wipe his face, he lifted also his great stick, because,
as we said, he held them both in the same hand.

‘You children seem to be very merry thear!’ said he, ‘you’ve
gotten a famous feast, and a nice shady corner to eat it in! But you

364

would na be worser for a nice bottle o' my best fizzing beer; so if one on you will go wi' me, I'll gie you one!"

'Thank you, sir!' said Dick, jumping up at once, ready to go with him.

'Thank ye, mester!' said Harry, surprised, and looking as pleased as Punch.

'And th' little one does a' th' work today, I reckon!' said the farmer, smiling at little Joshua, who was making noise enough to deafen any body.

Dick went with the farmer for the bottle of 'fizzing beer', and he heard him laughing in the best kitchen, where Mrs. Broadbent, who had just come in from church, was sitting, and he told her all about 'a parcel o' children that were having a feast wi' little Harry Twiggs, all among the hazzle bushes,' and how he had promised them a bottle of 'fizzing beer'; and then Mrs. Broadbent was heard laughing too, and she said that one of 'those gooseberry pies' would not come in amiss among them; and then out she came with a great big gooseberry pie, baked in a brown dish, with all sorts of zigzags on the crust, and a bottle in her hand; and Mr. Broadbent came after her, and neither of them could help laughing still, and he said, and so did she, that they hoped the pie would be to their liking, and the beer too; only one thing they must remember, not to break either bottle or dish, for if they did they should both of them make a pretty row!

Away went Dick as fast as he could with the great big pie in the brown dish, and the bottle of fizzing beer. Now, only think what a surprise to every body! Nancy, when she saw the pie exclaimed, 'My goodness!' and Peggy, 'Oh my!' Little Joshua's eyes opened twice as wide as common, and he clapped louder than ever, while Harry capered about like a wild Indian, singing with all his might —

'Oh my!
Here's a gooseberry pie
With a zigzag crust for dinner.'

When they had set out their dinner, they sat down to it; and, would any body believe it? there they sat eating their dinner among those pleasant shady 'hazzle bushes', as old Farmer Broadbent called them, from half-past twelve o'clock till a quarter to three, when the bells began ringing again for afternoon service.

There never was such a dinner as that! And all the time it lasted little Joshua kept strutting about clapping as loud as he could, so that the birds heard him all over the big field; and so did Farmer Broadbent as he sat under the sycamore tree, before his kitchen door, smoking a pipe after dinner.

About an hour after this, up rose the farmer from the bench under the tree where he had been having a comfortable nap after his pipe and smiled to himself as he thought of the children in the cornfield. And what did he do then? Why, without saying a word to any body, he walked down to see what they were after, saying all the time to himself, what a foolish old fellow he was to find so much amusement in 'a parcel of poor children'. And though he knew that it was not right to be a listener yet he went and stood close behind the hazel-bushes again, just on purpose to hear what they were talking about; and if the children had not been so much taken up with their own talk, they must have heard him laughing.

They had drunk all the 'fizzing beer', every drop of it; and now Dick Tattersall was lying on his back, among the grass and flowers before the little wood-parlour door, and kicking up his legs, and thumping down his great heels again in a very ecstasy of delight, and all the time his tongue was rattling away like a mill-clapper. The afternoon service at the church was just over, and Dick was pretending that he could see all the folks come out, and was talking for them; now, very solemnly for the clergyman; now, very pompously for the schoolmaster; and now, very savagely for the constable, who was so hard and pitiless to the poor, and whom every body disliked so much. And then he told them a long story of how, the very Sunday after the constable had seized on poor old Nelly Wardle's bed for rent, he stuck a pin into a long stick, and sat in the pew behind the constable, and poked the stick through the bottom of the broken pew, and pricked the great calves of his legs. The constable fancied it was horse-flies that were biting him so keenly, and kept slapping his calves, till they could hear him half over the church; and then the pin pricked him again, and then he slapped; and then another prick, and another great slap, until at last up he jumped in a great rage and went out. When church was over he gave the clerk a great scolding for not opening the church doors and windows on week days, that the flies might not so be famished on Sundays, till they were ready to eat folks' flesh off their bones! That was what Dick was saying, while Farmer Broadbent was listening.

How the children laughed! and Dick kicked up his legs and banged them down again, just as if it was a great steam-engine at work. The farmer behind the bushes laughed quite as much as they did; and then he walked away, thinking how pleased he was that poor little Harry Twiggs had such a merry company, and feeling sorry only for one thing, and that was, that he could not give Dick Tattersal sixpence for pricking the constable who had so sorely distressed a poor widow, without betraying himself as a listener. That was the only thing that troubled him; nothing at all troubled the children, they were as merry as fairies.

'And there they are at this moment,' said Herbert's and Meggy's father, 'and are you not as much pleased as the farmer, that they have had a merry day of it, and such a good dinner?'

'What a long day tomorrow will seem to poor little Harry all by himself!' said Meggy.

'Not at all so!' returned her father, 'Harry will do nothing all day but think of the fun he had the day before; one day like that would last him a week. And besides that they promised to come and see him again on Sunday. The farmer heard them; and so he told his wife, hardly an hour ago, as they were sitting in the arbour at tea, and she said in a minute that she would take care that they should have another gooseberry pie, and another bottle of fizzing beer to make merry with.'

The Selfish Giant

EVERY afternoon, as they were coming from school, the children used to go and play in the giant's garden.

It was a large lovely garden, with soft green grass. Here and there over the grass stood beautiful flowers like stars, and there were twelve peach-trees that in the spring-time broke out into delicate blossoms of pink and pearl, and in the autumn bore rich fruit. The birds sat on the trees and sang so sweetly that the children used to stop their games in order to listen to them. 'How happy we are!' they cried to each other.

One day the giant came back. He had been to visit his friend the Cornish ogre, and had stayed with him for seven years. After the seven years were over he had said all that he had to say, for his conversation was limited, and he determined to return to his own castle. When he arrived he saw the children playing in the garden.

'What are you doing here?' he cried in a very gruff voice, and the children ran away.

'My own garden is my own garden,' said the giant; 'any one can understand that, and I will allow nobody to play in it but myself.' So he built a high wall all round it, and put up a notice-board

TRESPASSERS
WILL BE
PROSECUTED

He was a very selfish giant.

The poor children had now nowhere to play. They tried to play on the road, but the road was very dusty and full of hard stones, and they did not like it. They used to wander round the high walls when their lessons were over, and talk about the beautiful garden inside. 'How happy we were there!' they said to each other.

Then the spring came, and all over the country there were little blossoms and little birds. Only in the garden of the selfish giant it was still winter. The birds did not care to sing in it as there were no children, and the trees forgot to blossom. Once a beautiful flower put its head out from the grass, but when it saw the notice-board it was so sorry for the children that it slipped back into the ground again, and went off to sleep. The only people who were pleased were the snow and the frost. 'Spring has forgotten this garden,' they cried, 'so we will live here all the year round.' The snow covered up the grass with her great white cloak, and the frost painted all the trees silver. Then they invited the north wind

to stay with them, and he came. He was wrapped in furs, and he roared all day about the garden, and blew the chimney-pots down. 'This is a delightful spot,' he said, 'we must ask the hail to visit.' So the hail came. Every day for three hours he rattled on the roof of the castle till he broke most of the slates, and then he ran round and round the garden as fast as he could go. He was dressed in gray, and his breath was like ice.

370

'I cannot understand why the spring is so late in coming,' said the selfish giant, as he sat at the window and looked out at his cold, white garden; 'I hope there will be a change in the weather.'

But the spring never came, nor the summer. The autumn gave golden fruit to every garden, but to the giant's garden she gave none. 'He is too selfish,' she said. So it was always winter there, and the north wind and the hail and the frost and the snow danced about through the trees.

One morning the giant was lying awake in bed when he heard some lovely music. It sounded so sweet to his ears that he thought it must be the king's musicians passing by. It was really only a little linnet singing outside his window, but it was so long since he had heard a bird sing in his garden that it seemed to him to be the most beautiful music in the world. Then the hail stopped dancing over his head, and the north wind ceased roaring and a delicious perfume came to him through the open casement. 'I believe the spring has come at last,' said the giant; and he jumped out of bed and looked out.

What did he see?

He saw a most wonderful sight. Through a little hole in the wall the children had crept in, and they were sitting in the branches of the trees. In every tree that he could see there was a little child. And the trees were so glad to have the children back again that they had covered themselves with blossoms, and were waving their arms gently above the children's heads. The birds were flying about and twittering with delight, and the flowers were looking up through the green grass and laughing. It was a lovely scene, only in one corner it was still winter. It was the farthest corner of the garden, and in it was standing a little boy. He was so small that he could not reach up to the branches of the tree, and he was wandering all round it, crying bitterly. The poor tree was still covered with frost and snow, and the north wind was blowing and roaring above it. 'Climb up! little boy,' said the tree, and it bent its branches down as low as it could; but the boy was too tiny.

And the giant's heart melted as he looked out. 'How selfish I have been!' he said; 'now I know why the spring would not come here. I will put that poor little boy on the top of the tree, and then I will knock down the wall, and my garden shall be the children's playground for ever and ever.' He was really very sorry for what he had done.

So he crept downstairs and opened the front door quite softly, and went out into the garden. But when the children saw him they were so frightened that they all ran away, and the garden became winter again. Only the little boy did not run for his eyes were so full of tears that he did not see the giant coming. And the giant stole up behind him and took him gently in his hand, and put him up into the tree. And the tree broke at once into blossom, and the birds came and sang on it, and the little boy stretched out his two arms and flung them round the giant's neck, and kissed him. And the other children, when they saw that the giant was not wicked any longer, came running back, and with them came the spring. 'It is your garden now, little children,' said the giant, and he took a great axe and knocked down the wall. And when the people were going to market at twelve o'clock they found the giant playing with the children in the most beautiful garden they had ever seen.

All day long they played, and in the evening they came to the giant to say good-bye.

'But where is your little companion?' he said: 'the boy I put into the tree.' The giant loved him the best because he had kissed him, and had not been afraid.

'We don't know,' answered the children; 'he has gone away.'

'You must tell him to be sure and come tomorrow,' said the giant. But the children said that they did not know where he lived, and had never seen him before; and the giant felt very sad.

Every afternoon, when school was over, the children came and played with the giant. But the little boy whom the giant loved was never seen again. The giant was very kind to all the children, yet he longed for his first little friend. 'How I would like to see him!' he used to say.

Years went by, and the giant grew very old and feeble. He could not play about any more, so he sat in a huge arm-chair, and watched the children at their games, and admired his garden. 'I have many beautiful flowers,' he said, 'but the children are the most beautiful flowers of all.'

One winter morning he looked out of his window as he was dressing. He did not hate the winter now, for he knew that it was merely the spring asleep, and that the flowers were resting.

Suddenly he rubbed his eyes in wonder and looked and looked. In the farthest corner of the garden was a tree quite covered with lovely white blossoms. Its branches were golden, and silver fruit hung down from them, and underneath it stood the little boy he had loved.

Downstairs ran the giant in great joy, and out into the garden. He hastened across the grass, and came near to the child. And when he came quite close his face grew red with anger, and he said, 'Who has dared to wound you?' For on the palms of the child's hands were the prints of two nails, and the prints of two nails were on the little feet.

'Who has dared to wound you?' cried the giant; 'tell me, that I may take my big sword and kill him.'

'No,' answered the child; 'for these are the wounds of love.'

'Who are you?' said the giant, and a strange awe fell on him, and he knelt before the little child.

And the child smiled on the giant, and said to him, 'You let me play once in your garden, today you shall come with me to my garden, which is paradise.'

And when the children ran in that afternoon, they found the giant lying dead under the tree, all covered with white blossoms.

The Wild Swans

FAR away, in a country where the swallows fly in our winter-time, there lived a king who had eleven sons, and one daughter, the beautiful Elise. The eleven brothers went to school with stars on their breasts, and swords by their sides; they wrote on golden pads with diamond pens, and could read either with a book, or without one; in fact, it was easy to see that they were princes. Their sister Elise used to sit upon a little glass stool, and had a picture-book which had cost half a kingdom. Oh, the children were so happy! But they were not to remain so for long.

Their father, the king, married a very wicked queen, who was not at all kind to the poor children. They found this out on the first day after the marriage, when there was a grand ball at the palace; for when the children played at receiving company, instead of giving them as many cakes and sweets as they liked, the queen gave them only some sand in a little dish.

The week after, she sent little Elise to be brought up by some peasants in the country, and it was not long before she told the king so many lies about the poor princes, that he would have nothing more to do with them.

'Away out into the world, and take care of yourselves,' said the wicked queen. 'Fly away in the form of great speechless birds.' But she could not make their transformation as disagreeable as she wished – the princes were changed into eleven white swans. Sending forth a strange cry, they flew out of the palace windows, over the park and over the wood.

It was still early in the morning when they passed by the place where Elise lay sleeping in the peasant's cottage; they flew several times round the roof, stretched their long necks, and flapped their wings, but no one either heard or saw them; they were forced to fly away, up to the clouds, and into the wide world; so on they went to the forest, which extended as far as the seashore.

Poor little Elise stood in the peasant's cottage amusing herself with a green leaf, for she had no other plaything. She pricked a hole in the leaf and peeped through it at the sun, and then she fancied she saw her brothers' bright eyes, and whenever the warm sunbeams shone down upon her cheeks, she thought of her brothers' kisses.

One day passed exactly like another. When the wind blew through the thick hedge of rose-trees, in front of the house, she would whisper to the roses 'Who is more beautiful than you?' but the roses would shake their heads and say, 'Elise.' And when the peasant's wife sat on Sundays at the door of her cottage reading her hymn-book, the wind would rustle in the leaves and say to the book, 'Who is more pious than you?' 'Elise,' replied the hymn-book. And what the roses and the hymn-book said, was no more than the truth.

Elise, who was now fifteen years old, was sent for to return home; but when the queen saw how beautiful she was, she hated her even more, and would willingly have transformed her like her brothers into a wild swan, but she dared not do so, because the king wished to see his daughter.

So the next morning the queen went into a bath which was made of marble, and fitted up with soft pillows and the gayest carpets; she took three toads, kissed them, and said to one, 'settle yourself upon Elise's head, that she may become dull and sleepy like you.' 'Settle yourself upon her forehead,' said she to another, 'and let her become ugly like you so that her father may not know her again.' And 'place yourself upon her bosom,' whispered she to the third, 'that her heart may become corrupt and evil, a torment to herself.'

She then put the toads into the clear water, which was immediately tinted with a green colour, and having called Elise, took off her clothes and made her get into the bath – one toad settled among her hair, another on her forehead and the third upon her bosom; but Elise seemed not at all aware of it. She rose up, and three poppies were seen swimming on the water.

Had not the animals been poisonous and kissed by a witch, they would have been changed into roses while they remained on Elise's head and heart – she was too good for magic to have any power over her. When the queen realised this, she rubbed walnut juice all over the girl's skin, so that it became quite swarthy, smeared a nasty ointment over her lovely face, and entangled her long thick hair. It was impossible to recognise the beautiful Elise after this.

When her father saw her, he was shocked, and said she could not be his daughter; no-one would have anything to do with her but the mastiff and the swallows; but they, poor things, could not say anything in her favour.

Poor Elise wept, and thought of her eleven brothers, not one of whom she saw at the palace. In great distress she stole away and wandered the whole day over fields and moors, till she reached the forest. She knew not where to go, but she was so sad, and longed so much to see her brothers, who had been driven out into the world, that she determined to seek and find them.

She had not been long in the forest when night came on, and she lost her way amid the darkness. So she lay down on the soft moss, said her evening prayer, and leaned her head against the trunk of a tree. It was still in the forest, the air was mild, and from the grass and mould around gleamed the green light of many hundred glow-worms and when Elise lightly touched one of the branches hanging over her, bright insects fell down upon her like falling stars.

All night long she dreamed of her brothers. They were all children again, playing together, writing with diamond pens upon golden pads, and looking at the pictures in the beautiful book which had cost half a kingdom.

But they did not, as formerly, make straight strokes and question marks upon the pads; no they wrote of the bold actions they had performed, and the strange adventures they had encountered, and in the picture-book everything seemed alive. The birds sang, men and women stepped from the book and talked to Elise and her brothers. However, when she turned over the pages, they jumped back into their places, so that the pictures did not get confused together.

When Elise awoke the sun was already high in the sky. She could not see it clearly, for the tall trees of the forest entwined their thick-leaved branches closely together, and, as the sunbeams played upon them, they looked like a golden veil waving to and fro. The air was fragrant, and the birds perched upon Elise's shoulders. She heard the noise of water; there were several springs forming a pool, with the prettiest pebbles at the bottom; bushes were growing thickly round. But the deer had trodden a broad path through them, and by this path Elise went down to the water's edge. The water was so clear that, had not the boughs and bushes around been moved by the wind, you might have fancied they were painted upon the smooth surface, so distinctly was each little leaf mirrored upon it.

As soon as Elise saw her face reflected in the water, she was quite startled, so brown and ugly did it look; however, when she wetted her little hand, and rubbed her brow and eyes, the white skin again appeared. So Elise took off her clothes, stepped into the fresh water, and in the whole world there was not a king's daughter more beautiful than she then appeared.

After she dressed herself, and plaited her long hair, she went to the bubbling spring, drank out of the hollow of her hand, and then wandered farther into the forest. She did not know where she was going, but she thought of her brothers, and of the good God who, she felt, would never forsake her. It was He who made the wild crab-trees grow in order to feed the hungry, and who showed her a tree whose boughs bent under the weight of their fruit. She made her noonday meal under its shade, propped against the boughs, and then walked on amid the dark twilight of the forest.

It was so still that she could hear her own footsteps, and the rustling of each little withered leaf that was crushed beneath her feet. Not a bird was to be seen; not a single sunbeam penetrated through the thick foliage; and the tall stems of the trees stood so close together, that when she looked straight before her, she seemed encircled by trellis-work. Oh! there was a loneliness in this forest such as Elise had never known before.

And the night was so dark! Not a single glow-worm sent forth its light. Depressed, she lay down to sleep and then it seemed to her as if the boughs above her opened, and she saw an angel looking down with a gentle face, and a thousand little cherubs all around him. When she awoke in the morning she could not tell whether this was a dream, or whether she had really been so watched.

She walked on and met an old woman with a basket full of berries; the old woman gave her some of them, and Elise asked if she had seen eleven princes ride through the wood.

'No,' said the old woman, 'but yesterday I saw eleven swans with golden crowns on their heads swim down the brook near this place.'

And she led Elise to a precipice, the base of which was washed by a brook; the trees on each side stretched their long leafy branches towards each other, and where they could not unite, the roots had disengaged themselves from the earth and hung over the water.

Elise bade the old woman farewell, and wandered by the side of the stream till she came to the place where it reached the open sea.

The beautiful sea lay stretched out before the girl's eyes, but not a ship, not a boat was to be seen; how was she to go on?

She observed the little stones on the shore, all of which the waves had washed into a round form; glass, iron, stone, everything that lay scattered there, had been moulded into shape, and yet the water which had done this was much softer than Elise's delicate little hand. 'It rolls on tirelessly,' she said, 'and softens what is so hard; I will be just as strong! Thank you for the lesson you have given me, bright rolling waves; some day, my heart tells me, you shall carry me to my dear brothers!'

There lay upon the wet seaweeds eleven white swan-feathers; Elise collected them together; drops of water hung about them, whether dew or tears she could not tell. She was quite alone on the seashore, but she did not mind that for the sea presented an eternal variety to her, more indeed in a few hours than the gentle inland waters would have offered in a whole year.

When a black cloud passed over the sky, it seemed as if the sea was saying, 'I too can look dark;' and then the wind would blow and the waves fling out their white foam. But when the clouds shone with a bright red tint, and the winds were asleep, the sea also became like a rose-leaf in hue. It was now green, now white; but as it rested peacefully, a slight breeze on the shore caused the water to heave gently like the bosom of a sleeping child.

At sunset Elise saw eleven wild swans with golden crowns on their heads flying towards the land; they flew one behind another, looking like a streaming white ribbon. Elise climbed the precipice, and concealed herself behind a bush; the swans settled close to her, and flapped their long white wings.

As the sun sank beneath the water, the swans also vanished, and in their place stood eleven handsome princes, the brothers of

Elise. She uttered a loud cry, for although they were very much altered, Elise knew them to be her brothers. She ran into their arms, called them by their names – and how happy *they* were to see and recognise their sister, who was now grown so tall and so beautiful! They laughed and wept, and soon told each other how wickedly their step-mother had treated them.

'We,' said the eldest of the brothers, 'fly or swim as long as the sun is above the horizon, but, when it sinks below, we appear again in our human form. We are therefore obliged to look out for a safe resting-place, for, if at sunset we were flying among the clouds, we should fall down as soon as we resumed our own form. We do not live here. A land quite as beautiful as this lies on the opposite side of the sea, but it is far off. To reach it, we have to cross the deep waters, and there is no island midway on which we may rest at night; one little solitary rock rises from the waves, and upon it we find only just room enough to stand side by side.

'There we spend the night in our human form, and when the sea is rough, we are sprinkled by its foam; but we are thankful for this resting-place, for without it we should never be able to visit our dear native country. Only once in the year is this visit to the home of our fathers permitted. We require two of the longest days for our flight, and can remain here only eleven days, during which time we fly over the large forest from where we can see the palace in which we were born, where our father lives, and the tower of the church in which our mother was buried.

'Here even the trees and bushes seem related to us; here the wild horses still race over the plains, as in the days of our childhood; here the charcoal burner still sings the same old tunes to which we used to dance in our youth; here we are still drawn, and here we have found you, dear little sister! We have two more days staying here; then we must fly over the sea to a land beautiful indeed, but not our fatherland. How shall we take you with us? We have neither ship nor boat!'

'How shall I be able to let you go?' said the sister. And so they went on talking almost the whole of the night. They slept for only a few hours.

Elise was awakened by the rustling of swans' wings which were fluttering above her. Her brothers were again transformed, and for some time flew around in large circles. At last they flew far, far away; one of them remained behind; it was the youngest, and he laid his head in her lap and she stroked his white wings. They remained the whole day together. Towards evening the others came back, and when the sun set, they stood again on the firm ground in their natural form.

'Tomorrow we shall fly away, and may not return for a year, but we cannot leave you; have you the courage to come with us? My arm is strong enough to bear you through the forest; shall we not have strength enough in our wings to carry you over the sea?'

'Yes, take me with you,' said Elise. They spent the whole night in weaving a mat of the pliant willow bark and the tough rushes, and their mat was thick and strong. Elise lay down upon it, and when the sun rose, and the brothers were again transformed into wild swans, they seized the mat with their beaks and flew up high among the clouds with their dear sister, who was still sleeping. The sunbeams shone full·upon her face, so one of the swans flew over her head, and shaded her with his broad wings.

They were already far from land when Elise woke; she thought she was still dreaming, so strange did it appear to her to be travelling through the air, and over the sea. By her side lay a cluster of pretty berries, and a handful of delicious roots. Her youngest brother had laid them there; and she thanked him with a smile, for she knew him as the swan who flew over her head and shaded her with his wings.

They flew so high that the first ship they saw beneath them seemed like a white seagull hovering over the water. Elise saw behind her a large cloud, which looked like a mountain, and on it she saw the shadows of herself and the eleven swans. It formed a picture more splendid than any she had ever seen. But soon, however, the sun rose higher, the cloud remained far behind, and then the floating shadowy picture disappeared.

The whole day they continued to fly with a whizzing noise, like an arrow; but yet they went slower than usual – they had their sister to carry. A heavy tempest gathered as the evening approached; Elise anxiously watched the sun. It was setting; still the solitary rock could not be seen; it appeared to her that the swans flapped their wings with increasing vigour.

Alas! it would be her fault if her brothers did not arrive at the place in time! they would become human beings when the sun set, and if this happened before they reached the rocks, they would fall into the sea and be drowned. She prayed to God most fervently; still no rock was to be seen; the black clouds drew nearer, violent gusts of wind announced the approach of a storm, the clouds rested upon a huge wave which rolled quickly forwards, and one flash of lightning rapidly succeeded another.

The sun was now on the rim of the sea. Elise's heart beat violently; the swans shot downwards so swiftly that she thought she must fall. But again they began to hover; the sun was half sunk beneath the water, and at that moment she saw the little rock below her; it looked like a seal's head when he raises it just above the water. And the sun was sinking fast – it seemed scarcely larger than a star – her foot touched the hard ground, and the sun vanished like the last spark on a burnt piece of paper.

Arm in arm stood her brothers around her; there was only just room for her and them – the sea beat tempestuously against the rock, flinging over them a shower of foam. The sky seemed in a blaze, with the fast succeeding flashes of fire that lightened it, and peal after peal of thunder rolled on, but sister and brothers kept firm hold of each other's hands. They sang a hymn, and their hymn gave them comfort and courage.

By daybreak the air was pure and still, and, as soon as the sun rose, the swans flew away with Elise from the rock. The waves rose higher and higher, and when they looked from the clouds down upon the blackish-green sea, covered with white foam, they might have fancied that millions of swans were swimming on its surface.

As day advanced, Elise saw floating in the air before her a land of mountains with glaciers, and in the centre, a palace kilometres in length, with splendid colonnades, surrounded by palm-trees and gorgeous-looking flowers as large as mill-wheels. She asked if this was the country to which they were flying, but the swans shook their heads, for what she saw was the beautiful airy castle of the fairy Morgana, where no human being was admitted. Whilst Elise still bent her eyes upon it, mountains, trees, and castle all disappeared, and in their place stood twelve churches with high towers and pointed windows – she fancied she heard the organ play, but it was only the murmur of the sea. She was now close to these churches, but behold! they changed into a large fleet sailing under them; she looked down and saw it was only a sea-mist passing rapidly over the water. An endless variety floated before her eyes, till at last the land to which she was going appeared in sight. Beautiful blue mountains, cedar woods, towns and castles rose to view. Long before sunset Elise sat down among the mountains, in front of a large càvern; delicate young creepers grew thickly around, so that it appeared covered with gay embroidered carpets.

'Now we shall see what you will dream of tonight!' said her youngest brother, as he showed her the sleeping chamber destined for her.

'Oh, that I could dream how you might be freed from the spell!' she said; and this thought filled her mind. She prayed for God's help; even in her dreams she continued praying, and it appeared to her that she was flying up high in the air towards the castle of the fairy Morgana. The fairy came forward to meet her, radiant and beautiful, and yet she fancied she resembled the old woman who had given her berries in the forest, and told her of the swans with golden crowns.

'You can free your brothers,' said she; 'but have you courage and patience enough? The water is indeed softer than your delicate hands, and yet can mould the hard stones to its will, but then it cannot feel the pain which your tender fingers will feel; it has no heart and cannot suffer the anxiety and grief which you must suffer. Do you see these stinging-nettles which I have in my hand? There are many of the same kind growing round the cave where you are sleeping; only those that grow there or on the graves in the churchyard are of use, remember that!

'You must pluck them although they will sting your hand; you must trample on the nettles with your feet, and get yarn from them, and with this yarn you must weave eleven shirts with long sleeves; throw them over the eleven wild swans and the spell is broken. But remember this: from the moment you begin your work till it is completed, even should it take you years, you must not speak a word; the first syllable that escapes your lips will fall like a dagger into the hearts of your brothers; on your tongue depends their lives.'

And at the same moment the fairy touched Elise's hands with a nettle, which made them burn like fire, and Elise awoke. It was broad daylight, and close to her lay a nettle like the one she had seen in her dream. She fell upon her knees, thanked God, and then went out of the cave in order to begin her work. She plucked with her own delicate hands the stinging-nettles; they burned large blisters on her hands and arms, but she bore the pain willingly in the hope of releasing her dear brothers. She trampled on the nettles with her naked feet, and spun the green yarn.

At sunset her brothers came. Elise's silence quite frightened them; they thought it must be the effect of some fresh spell of their wicked stepmother. But when they saw her blistered hands, they realised what their sister was doing for their sakes. The youngest brother wept, and, when his tears fell upon her hands, Elise felt no more pain, and the blisters disappeared.

The whole night she spent in her work, for she could not rest till she had released her brothers. All the following day she sat in her solitude, for the swans had flown away, but never had time passed so quickly. One shirt was ready; she now began the second.

Suddenly a hunting horn resounded among the mountains. Elise was frightened. The noise came nearer; she heard the hounds barking; in great terror she fled into the cave, bound up the nettles which she had gathered and combed into a bundle, and sat down upon it.

In the same moment a large dog sprang out from the bushes. Two others immediately followed; they barked loudly, ran away, and then returned. It was not long before the hunters stood in front of the cave; the handsomest among them was the king of that country; he stepped up to Elise. Never had he seen a lovelier maiden.

'How did you come here, you beautiful girl?' he said.

Elise shook her head; she dared not speak, for a word might

have cost her the life of her brothers, and she hid her hands under
her apron in case the king should see how she was suffering.

'Come with me,' said he, 'you must not stay here! If you are as
good as you are beautiful, I will dress you in velvet and silk, I
will put a gold crown upon your head, and you shall live in
my palace!' So he lifted her upon his horse, while she wept and
wrung her hands; but the king said, 'I only desire your happiness!
you shall thank me for this some day!' and away he rode over
mountains and valleys, holding her on his horse in front, while the
other hunters followed.

When the sun set, the king's magnificent capital with its churches and domes lay before them, and the king led Elise into the palace, where, in a marble hall, fountains were playing, and the walls and ceilings displayed the most beautiful paintings. But Elise did not care for this splendour; she wept and mourned in silence, even while some female attendants dressed her in royal robes, wove costly pearls in her hair, and drew soft gloves over her blistered hands.

And now she was fully dressed, and, as she stood in her splendid attire, her beauty was so dazzling that the courtiers all bowed low before her, and the king chose her for his bride, although the archbishop shook his head, and whispered that the 'beautiful lady of the wood must certainly be a witch, who had blinded their eyes, and infatuated the king's heart.'

But the king did not listen; he ordered that music should be played. A sumptuous banquet was served up, and the loveliest maidens danced round the bride; she was led through fragrant gardens into magnificent halls, but not a smile was seen to play upon her lips, or beam from her eyes. The king then opened a small room next to her sleeping apartment; it was adorned with costly green tapestry, and exactly resembled the cave in which she had been found; upon the ground lay the bundle of yarn which she had spun from the nettles, and on the wall hung the shirt she had completed. One of the hunters had brought all this, thinking there must be something wonderful in it.

'Here you may dream of your former home,' said the king; 'here is the work which employed you; amidst all your present splendour it may sometimes give you pleasure to fancy yourself there again.'

When Elise saw what was so dear to her heart, she smiled, and the blood returned to her cheeks; she thought her brothers might still be freed, and she kissed the king's hand. He embraced her and ordered the bells of all the churches in the city to be rung, to announce the celebration of their wedding. The beautiful dumb maiden of the wood was to become queen of the land.

The archbishop whispered evil words in the king's ear, but they made no impression upon him; the marriage was solemnised, and the archbishop himself was obliged to put the crown upon her head. In his rage he pressed the narrow rim so firmly on her forehead that it hurt her, but a heavier weight – sorrow for her brothers – lay upon her heart, and she did not feel bodily pain. She was still silent, a single word would have killed her brothers; her eyes, however, beamed with heartfelt love to the king, so good and handsome, who had done so much to make her happy.

She became more warmly attached to him every day. Oh! how much she wished she might confide to him all her sorrows. But she was forced to remain silent; she could not speak until her work was completed. To this end she stole away every night, and went into the little room that was fitted up in imitation of the cave; there she worked at her shirts, but by the time she had begun the seventh, all her yarn was used up.

She knew that the nettles she needed grew in the churchyard, but she must gather them herself; how was she to get them?

'Oh, what is the pain in my fingers compared to the anguish my heart suffers!' she thought. 'I must venture to the church-yard; the good God will protect me!'

Fearful, as though she were about to do something wrong, one moonlight night she crept down to the garden, and through the long avenues into the lonely road leading to the churchyard. She saw sitting on one of the broadest tombstones a number of ugly old witches.

Elise was obliged to pass close by them, and the witches fixed their wicked eyes upon her; but she repeated her prayer, gathered the stinging-nettles, and took them back with her into the palace.

One person only had seen her; it was the archbishop, who was awake when others slept. Now he was convinced that all was not right about the queen: she must be a witch, who had, through her enchantments, infatuated the king and all the people.

Privately, he told the handsome king what he had seen, and what he feared; and, when the words came from his lips, the images of the saints shook their heads as though they would say, 'It is untrue; Elise is innocent!' But the archbishop explained the omen otherwise; he thought it was a testimony against her that the holy images shook their heads at hearing of her sin.

Two large tears rolled down the king's cheeks; he returned home in doubt; he pretended to sleep at night, though sleep never came to him and he noticed that Elise rose from her bed every night, and every time he secretly followed her and saw her enter her little room.

His countenance became darker every day; Elise noticed it, though she knew not the cause. She was much pained, and besides, what did she not suffer in her heart for her brothers! Her bitter tears ran down on the royal velvet and purple; they looked like bright diamonds, and all who saw the magnificence that surrounded her, wished themselves in her place.

She had now nearly finished her work, only one shirt was to be done; unfortunately, she needed more yarn also; she had not a single nettle left. Once more, only this one time, she must go to the churchyard and gather a few handfuls. She shuddered when she thought of the solitary walk and of the horrid witches, but her resolution was as firm as her trust in God.

Elise went, the king and archbishop followed her; they saw her disappear at the churchyard door, and, when they came nearer, they saw the witches sitting on the tombstone as Elise had seen them, and the king turned away, for he believed her whose head had rested on his bosom that very evening to be amongst them. 'Let the people judge her!' said he. And the people condemned her to be burned.

She was now dragged from the king's apartments into a dark damp prison, where the wind whistled through the barred window. Instead of velvet and silk, they gave her the bundle of nettles she had gathered; on that she must lay her head, and the shirts she had woven must serve her as mattress and counterpane.

But they could not have given her anything she valued so much; and she continued her work, at the same time praying earnestly to her God. The boys sang scandalous songs about her in front of her prison; not a soul comforted her with one word of love.

Towards evening she heard the rustling of swans' wings at the grating. It was the youngest of her brothers who had at last found his sister, and she sobbed aloud for joy, although she knew that the coming night would probably be the last of her life; but then her work was almost finished, and her brother was near.

The archbishop came in order to spend the last hour with her; he had promised the king he would; but she shook her head, and entreated him with her eyes and gestures to go. This night she must finish her work, or all she had suffered – her pain, her anxiety, her sleepless nights – would be in vain. The archbishop went away with many angry words, but the unfortunate Elise knew herself to be innocent, and went on with her work.

Little mice ran busily about and dragged the nettles to her feet wishing to help her; and the thrush perched on the iron bars of the window, and sang all night as merrily as he could, that Elise might not lose courage.

It was still darkness, just one hour before sunrise, when the eleven brothers stood before the palace gates, requesting an audience with the king. But it could not be, they were told; it was still night, the king was asleep, and they dared not wake him. They entreated, they threatened; the guard came up, and the king himself at last stepped out to ask what was the matter. At that moment the sun rose, the brothers could be seen no longer, and eleven white swans flew away over the palace.

The people poured forth from the gates of the city; they wished to see the witch burned. One sad old horse drew the cart in which Elise was placed. A coarse frock of sackcloth had been put on her, her beautiful long hair hung loosely over her shoulders, her cheeks were of a deadly paleness, her lips moved gently, and her fingers wove the green yarn. Even on her way to her cruel death she did not give up her work; the ten shirts lay at her feet, and she was now labouring to complete the eleventh. The rabble insulted her.

'Look at the witch, how she mutters! She has not a hymn-book in her hand; no, there she sits with her accursed black magic. Tear it from her; tear it into a thousand pieces!'

And they all crowded about her, and were on the point of snatching away the shirts, when eleven white swans came flying towards the cart; they settled all round her, and flapped their wings. The crowd gave way in terror.

'It is a sign from heaven! She is certainly innocent!' whispered some; they dared not say so aloud.

The sheriff now seized her by the hand; in a moment she threw the eleven shirts over the swans, and eleven handsome princes appeared in their place. The youngest had, however, only one

arm, and a wing instead of the other, for one sleeve was missing
from his shirt – it had not been quite finished.

'Now I may speak,' said Elise: 'I am innocent!'

And the people who had seen what had happened bowed
before her as before a saint. She, however, sank lifeless in her
brothers' arms; suspense, fear and grief had quite exhausted her.

'Yes, she is innocent,' said her eldest brother, and he now related
their wonderful history. Whilst he spoke a fragrance as delicious
as though it came from millions of flowers spread itself around, for
every piece of wood in the funeral pile had taken root and sent

forth branches. A hedge of blooming red roses surrounded Elise, and above all the others blossomed a flower of dazzling white colour, bright as a star. The king plucked it and laid it on Elise's bosom, whereupon she awoke from her trance with peace and joy in her heart.

And all the church-bells began to ring of their own accord; and birds flew to the spot in swarms; and there was a festive procession back to the palace, such as no king has ever seen equalled.

Robin Hood and the Widow's Three Sons

THERE are twelve months in all the year,
  As I hear many men say,
But the merriest month in all the year
  Is the merry month of May.

Now Robin Hood is to Nottingham gone,
  With a link a down and a day,
And there he met a silly old woman,
  Was weeping on the way.

'What news? what news, thou silly old woman?
  What news has thou for me?'
Said she, 'There's three squires in Nottingham town
  Today is condemn'd to die.'

'O have they parishes burnt?' he said,
  'Or have they ministers slain?
Or have they robbed any virgin,
  Or other men's wives have ta'en?'

'They have no parishes burnt, good sir,
  Nor yet have ministers slain,
Nor have they robbed any virgin,
  Or other men's wives have ta'en.'

'O what have they done?' said bold Robin Hood,
    'I pray thee tell to me.' –
'It's for slaying of the King's fallow deer,
    Bearing their long bows with thee.' –

'Dost thou not mind, old woman,' he said,
    'Since thou made me sup and dine?
By the truth of my body,' quoth bold Robin Hood,
    'You could tell it in no better time.'

Now Robin Hood is to Nottingham gone,
    With a link a down and a day,
And there he met with a silly old palmer,
    Was walking along the highway.

'What news? what news, thou silly old man?
    What news, I do thee pray?' –
Said he, 'Three squires in Nottingham town
    Are condemned to die this day.' –

'Come change thy apparel with me, old man,
    Come change thy apparel for mine;
Here is forty shillings in good silver,
    Go drink it in beer or wine.' –

'O thine apparel is good,' he said,
    'And mine is ragged and torn;
Wherever you go, wherever you ride,
    Laugh never an old man to scorn.' –

'Come change thy apparel with me, old churl,
    Come change thy apparel with mine;
Here are twenty pieces of good broad gold,
    Go feast thy brethren with wine.'

Then he put on the old man's hat,
    It stood full high on the crown:
'The first bold bargain that I come at,
    It shall make thee come down.'

Then he put on the old man's cloak,
    Was patch'd black, blue, and red;
He thought no shame, all the day long,
    To wear the bags of bread.

Then he put on the old man's breeks,
    Was patch'd from side to side;
'By the truth of my body,' bold Robin did say,
    'This man lov'd little pride!'

Then he put on the old man's hose,
    Were patch'd from knee to wrist;
'By the truth of my body,' said bold Robin Hood,
    'I'd laugh if I had any list.'

Then he put on the old man's shoes,
    Were patch'd both beneath and aboon;
Then Robin Hood swore a solemn oath,
    'It's good habit that makes a man!'

Now Robin Hood is to Nottingham gone,
    With a link a down and a down,
And there he met with the proud Sheriff,
    Was walking along the town.

'O save, O save, O Sheriff,' he said,
    'O save, and you may see!
And what will you give to a silly old man
    Today will your hangman be?'

'Some suits, some suits,' the Sheriff he said,
    'Some suits, I'll give to thee;
Some suits, some suits, and pence thirteen
    Today's a hangman's fee.'

Then Robin he turns him round about,
    And jumps from stock to stone;
'By the truth of my body,' the Sheriff he said,
    'That's well jumped, thou nimble old man.'

'I was ne'er a hangman in all my life,
    Nor yet intends to trade;
But curst be he,' said bold Robin,
    'That first a hangman was made!

'I've a bag for meal, and a bag for malt,
    And a bag for barley and corn;
A bag for bread, and a bag for beef,
    And a bag for my little small horn.

'I have a horn in my pocket,
    I got it from Robin Hood,
And still when I set it to my mouth,
    For thee it blows little good.' –

'O wind thy horn, thou proud fellow,
    Of thee I have no doubt;
I wish that thou give such a blast
    Till both thy eyes fall out.'

The first loud blast that he did blow,
    He blew both loud and shrill;
A hundred and fifty of Robin Hood's men
    Came riding over the hill.

The next loud blast that he did give,
    He blew both loud and amain;
And quickly sixty of Robin Hood's men
    Came shining over the plain.

'O who are yon,' the Sheriff he said,
    'Come tripping over the lee?'
'They're my attendants,' brave Robin did say,
    'They'll pay a visit to thee.'

They took the gallows from the slack,
    They set it in the glen,
They hang'd the proud Sheriff on that,
    And releas'd their own three men.

Snow-White

IT was in the middle of winter, when the broad flakes of snow were falling around, that a certain queen sat working at a window, the frame of which was made of fine, black ebony, and as she was looking out upon the snow she pricked her finger and three drops of blood fell from it. Then she gazed thoughtfully upon the red drops which sprinkled the white snow, and said, 'Would that my little daughter may be as white as that snow, as red as the blood, and as black as the ebony window-frame.' And so the little girl grew up: her skin was as white as snow, her cheeks as rosy as the blood, and her hair as black as ebony, and she was called Snow-White.

But this queen died, and the king soon married another wife, who was very beautiful, but so proud that she could not bear to think that anyone could surpass her. She had a magical looking-glass, where she used to go and gaze upon herself and say:

> 'Tell me, glass, tell me true!
> Of all the ladies in the land,
> Who is the fairest? Tell me who?'

and the glass answered:

> 'Thou, Queen, art fairest in the land.'

But Snow-White grew more and more beautiful, and when she was seven years old she was as bright as the day and fairer

than the queen herself. Then the looking-glass one day answered
the proud queen, when she went to consult it as usual:

> 'Thou, Queen, may'st fair and beauteous be,
> But Snow-White is lovelier far then thee!'

When she heard this she turned pale with rage and envy, and
called to one of her servants and said: 'Take Snow-White away
into the wide wood that I may never see her again.' Then the
servant led her away, but his heart melted when she begged him
to spare her life, and he said, 'I will not hurt you, you pretty child.'
So he left her by herself, and though he thought it most likely that
the wild beasts would tear her to pieces, he felt as if a great weight
were taken off his heart when he had made up his mind not to kill
her but to leave her to her fate.

Then poor Snow-White wandered along through the wood in
great fear, and the wild beasts roared about her, but none did her
any harm. In the evening she came to a little cottage and went in
there to rest herself, for her little feet would carry her no farther.
Everything was spruce and neat in the cottage; on the table was
spread a white cloth, and there were seven little plates with seven
little loaves, and seven little glasses with wine in them, and
knives and forks laid in order; and by the wall stood seven little
beds. Then, as she was very hungry, she picked a little piece off

each loaf, and drank a very little wine out of each glass, and after that she thought she would lie down and rest. So she tried all the little beds, and one was too long, and another was too short, till at last the seventh suited her and there she laid herself down and went to sleep.

Presently in came the masters of the cottage, who were seven little dwarfs that lived among the mountains, and dug and searched about for gold. They lighted up their seven lamps and saw directly that all was not right. The first said, 'who has been sitting on my stool?' The second, 'who has been eating off my plate?' The third 'who has been picking my bread?' The fourth, 'who has been meddling with my spoon?' The fifth, 'who has been handling my fork?' The sixth, 'who has been cutting with my knife?' The seventh, 'who has been drinking my wine?' Then the first looked round and said, 'who has been lying on my bed?' And the rest came running to him, and everyone cried out that somebody had been upon his bed. But the seventh saw Snow-White, and called all his brothers to come and see her, and they cried out with wonder and astonishment and brought their lamps to look at her, and said: 'Good heavens, what a lovely child she is.' And they were delighted to see her and took care not to wake her, and the seventh dwarf slept an hour with each of the other dwarfs in turn, till the night was gone.

In the morning, Snow-White told them all her story and they pitied her and said if she would keep all things in order, and cook and wash, and knit and spin for them, she might stay where she was and they would take good care of her. Then they went out all day long to their work, seeking for gold and silver in the mountains, and Snow-White remained at home, and they warned her and said: 'The queen will soon find out where you are, so take care and let no one in.'

But the queen, now that she thought Snow-White was dead, believed that she was certainly the handsomest lady in the land and she went to her glass and said:

'Tell me, glass, tell me true!
Of all the ladies in the land,
Who is the fairest? Tell me who?'

And the glass answered:

'Thou, queen, art the fairest in all this land;
But over the hills, in the greenwood shade,
Where the seven dwarfs their dwelling have made,
There Snow-White is hiding her head, and she
Is lovelier far, O queen, than thee!'

Then the queen was very much alarmed, for she knew that the glass always spoke the truth, and was sure that the servant had betrayed her. And she could not bear to think that anyone lived who was more beautiful than she was, so she disguised herself as an old pedlar and went her way over the hills to the place where the dwarfs lived.

Then she knocked at the door and cried, 'fine wares to sell!'

Snow-White looked out of the window and said, 'Good day, good woman, what have you to sell?'

'Good wares, fine wares,' she said, 'silks and cottons of all colours.'

'I will let the old lady in, she seems to be a very good sort of person,' thought Snow-White, so she ran down and unbolted the door.

'Bless me,' said the old woman, 'your belt is undone. Let me do it up for you.' Snow-White did not dream of any mischief, so she stood up before the old woman, who set to work nimbly and pulled the belt so tight that Snow-White lost her breath and fell down as if she were dead. 'There's an end of all your beauty,' said the spiteful queen, and went away home.

In the evening the seven dwarfs returned, and were so grieved to see their faithful Snow-White stretched upon the ground motionless as if she were quite dead. However, they lifted her up and when they found what was the matter, they cut the belt and in a little time she began to breathe and soon came to life again. Then they said: 'The old woman was the queen herself, take care another time and let no one in when we are away.'

When the queen got home she went straight to her glass and spoke to it as usual, but to her surprise it still said:

'Thou, queen, art the fairest in all this land;
But over the hills, in the greenwood shade,
Where the seven dwarfs their dwelling have made,
There Snow-White is hiding her head, and she
Is lovelier far, O queen, than thee!'

Then the blood ran cold in her heart with spite and malice to see that Snow-White still lived, and she dressed herself up again in a disguise, but very different from the one she wore before, and took with her a poisoned comb. When she reached the dwarfs' cottage she knocked at the door and cried, 'fine wares to sell!' But Snow-White said, 'I dare not let anyone in.' Then the queen said, 'only look at my beautiful combs,' and gave her the poisoned one. And it looked so pretty that she took it up and put it into her hair to try it, but the moment it touched her head the poison was so powerful that she fell down senseless. 'There you may lie,' said the queen, and went her way. But by good luck the dwarfs returned very early that evening, and when they saw Snow-White lying on the ground they thought what had happened, and soon found the poisoned comb. And when they took it away, she recovered and told them all that had passed, and they warned her once more not to open the door to anyone.

Meantime the queen went home to her glass and trembled with rage when she received exactly the same answer as before, and she said, 'Snow-White shall die, if it costs me my life.' So she went secretly into a chamber and prepared a poisoned apple: the outside looked very rosy and tempting, but whoever tasted it was sure to die. Then she dressed herself up as a peasant's wife and travelled over the hills to the dwarfs' cottage and knocked at the door, but Snow-White put her head out of the window and said, 'I dare not let anyone in, for the dwarfs have told me not to.' 'Do as you please,' said the old woman, 'but at any rate take this pretty apple; I will make you a present of it.' 'No,' said Snow-White, 'I dare not take it.' 'You silly girl,' answered the other, 'what are you afraid of? Do you think it is poisoned? Come, you eat one part and I will eat the other.' Now the apple was so prepared that one side was good though the other side was poisoned. Then Snow-White was very much tempted to taste it for the apple looked extremely nice, and when she saw the old woman eat she could refrain no longer. But she had scarcely put the piece into her mouth when she fell down dead upon the ground. 'This time nothing will save you,' said the queen; and she went home to her glass, and at last it said:

'Thou, queen, art the fairest of all the fair.'

And then her envious heart was glad and as happy as such a heart could be.

When evening came and the dwarfs returned home they found Snow-White lying on the ground; no breath passed her lips and they were afraid that she was quite dead. They lifted her up and combed her hair and washed her face with wine and water, but all was in vain for the little girl seemed quite dead. So they laid her down upon a bier and all seven watched and bewailed her for three whole days, and then they proposed to bury her, but her cheeks were still rosy and her face looked just as it did while she was alive, so they said, 'We will never bury her in the cold ground.' And they made a coffin of glass so that they might still look at her, and wrote her name upon it in golden letters, and that she was a king's daughter. And the coffin was placed upon the hill and one of the dwarfs always sat by it and watched. And the birds of the air came too, and mourned Snow-White: first of all came a wise owl, and then a coal-black raven, but at last came a gentle dove.

And thus Snow-White lay for a long, long time, and still only looked as though she were asleep, for she was even now as white as snow, and as red as blood, and as black as ebony. At last a prince came and called at the dwarfs' house, and he saw Snow-White and read what was written in golden letters. Then he offered the dwarfs money and earnestly prayed them to let him take her away, but they said: 'We will not part with her for all the gold in the world.' At last, however, they had pity on him and gave him the coffin: but the moment he lifted it up to carry it home with him, the piece of apple fell from between her lips and Snow-White awoke and said, 'Where am I?' And the prince answered, 'You are safe with me.' Then he told her all that had happened and said, 'I love you better than all the world, come with me to my father's palace and you shall be my wife.' And Snow-White consented and went home with the prince, and everything was prepared with great pomp and splendour for their wedding.

To the feast was invited, among the rest, Snow-White's old
enemy, the queen; and as she was dressing herself in fine, rich
clothes, she looked in the glass and said:

> *'Tell me, glass, tell me true!*
> *Of all the ladies in the land,*
> *Who is the fairest? Tell me·who?'*

And the glass answered:

> *'Thou, lady, art loveliest here, I ween;*
> *But lovelier far is the new-made Queen.'*

When she heard this, she started with rage, but her envy and
curiosity were so great that she could not help setting out to see
the bride. And when she arrived and saw that it was none other
than Snow-White who, as she thought, had been dead a long
while, she choked with rage and fell ill and died. But Snow-
White and the prince lived and reigned happily over that land
for many, many years.

down upon a bier and all seven watched and bewailed her for three whole days, and then they proposed to bury her, but her cheeks were still rosy and her face looked just as it did while she was alive, so they said, 'We will never bury her in the cold ground.' And they made a coffin of glass so that they might still look at her, and wrote her name upon it in golden letters, and that she was a king's daughter. And the coffin was placed upon the hill and one of the dwarfs always sat by it and watched. And the birds of the air came too, and mourned Snow-White: first of all came a wise owl, and then a coal-black raven, but at last came a gentle dove.

And thus Snow-White lay for a long, long time, and still only looked as though she were asleep, for she was even now as white as snow, and as red as blood, and as black as ebony. At last a prince came and called at the dwarfs' house, and he saw Snow-White and read what was written in golden letters. Then he offered the dwarfs money and earnestly prayed them to let him take her away, but they said: 'We will not part with her for all the gold in the world.' At last, however, they had pity on him and gave him the coffin: but the moment he lifted it up to carry it home with him, the piece of apple fell from between her lips and Snow-White awoke and said, 'Where am I?' And the prince answered, 'You are safe with me.' Then he told her all that had happened and said, 'I love you better than all the world, come with me to my father's palace and you shall be my wife.' And Snow-White consented and went home with the prince, and everything was prepared with great pomp and splendour for their wedding.

To the feast was invited, among the rest, Snow-White's old enemy, the queen; and as she was dressing herself in fine, rich clothes, she looked in the glass and said:

> *'Tell me, glass, tell me true!*
> *Of all the ladies in the land,*
> *Who is the fairest? Tell me who?'*

And the glass answered:

> *'Thou, lady, art loveliest* here, I ween;
> *But lovelier far is the new-made Queen.'*

When she heard this, she started with rage, but her envy and curiosity were so great that she could not help setting out to see the bride. And when she arrived and saw that it was none other than Snow-White who, as she thought, had been dead a long while, she choked with rage and fell ill and died. But Snow-White and the prince lived and reigned happily over that land for many, many years.